Customer Orientation and Market Action

Customer Orientation and Market Action

Michael D. Johnson

National Quality Research Center
University of Michigan Business School

Prentice Hall, Upper Saddle River, New Jersey 07458

Acquisitions Editor: David Borkowsky
Assistant Editor: John Larkin
Editorial Assistant: Linda Albelli
Editor-in-Chief: James Boyd
Director of Development: Steve Deitmer
Marketing Manager: John Chillingworth
Production Editor: Aileen Mason
Production Coordinator: Renee Pelletier
Managing Editor: Valerie Q. Lentz
Manufacturing Buyer: Kenneth J. Clinton
Manufacturing Supervisor: Arnold Vila
Manufacturing Manager: Vincent Scelta
Design Director: Patricia Woszyk
Interior Design: Ann France
Cover Design: Bruce Kenselaar
Illustrator (Interior): University Graphics, Inc.
Composition: University Graphics, Inc.

Copyright © 1998 by Prentice-Hall, Inc.
A Simon & Schuster Company
Upper Saddle River, New Jersey 07458

Library of Congress Cataloging-in-Publication Data
Johnson, Michael D. (Michael David)
    Customer orientation and market action / Michael D. Johnson.
    p.   cm.
    Includes bibliographical references and index.
    ISBN 0-13-328667-3
    1. Consumer satisfaction. 2. Customer relations. 3. Customer
services. 4. Consumer behavior. I. Title.
HF5415.5.J639 1997
658.8'12—dc21   97-1581
                                              CIP

Prentice-Hall International (UK) Limited, London
Prentice-Hall of Australia Pty. Limited, Sydney
Prentice-Hall Canada, Inc., Toronto
Prentice-Hall Hispanoamericana, S.A., Mexico
Prentice-Hall of India Private Limited, New Delhi
Prentice-Hall of Japan, Inc., Tokyo
Simon & Schuster Asia Pte. Ltd., Singapore
Editora Prentice-Hall do Brasil, Ltda., Rio de Janeiro

Printed in the United States of America
10 9 8 7 6 5 4 3 2

To Jill Marie, Alexander, Andrew, and
our newest addition, Thomas

Brief Contents

Preface   xiii

PART I: CUSTOMER ORIENTATION AND MARKET ACTION   1

    Chapter 1   A Customer Orientation   1
    Chapter 2   Market Action   12
    Chapter 3   Understanding and Anticipating Customer Needs   26

PART II: THE PURCHASE AND CONSUMPTION EXPERIENCE   41

    Chapter 4   The Customer Experience Model   41
    Chapter 5   Customers in the Marketplace   52
    Chapter 6   Customer Information Processing   68
    Chapter 7   Customer Choice   86
    Chapter 8   Customer Satisfaction and Priority Setting   102
    Chapter 9   Macro Satisfaction and Firm Strategy   129

PART III: IMPLEMENTATION AND QUALITY IMPROVEMENT   143

    Chapter 10   Customer Orientation and the Design Function   143
    Chapter 11   From Customer Satisfaction to Quality Improvement   156

Index   173

Contents

Preface   xiii

PART I: CUSTOMER ORIENTATION AND MARKET ACTION   1

CHAPTER 1   A Customer Orientation   1

Taking a Customer Orientation   2
  The Three Goals of a Customer Orientation   2
Challenges   4
  Customer Orientation as a Shared Vision   5
  Customer Orientation as a Leadership Perspective   6
  Customer Orientation Myopia   6
  Organizational and Structural Barriers   6
  A Lack of Gestalt: Understanding the "Whole Picture"   7
An Integrated Approach 7
Customer Orientation, Market Orientation,
  and Total Quality Management   9
Summary   10
Discussion Questions   11

CHAPTER 2   Market Action   12

Managers' Information Needs   12
  Market Strategy Decisions   12
  Monitoring-Based Market Action Decisions   13
  Problem-Driven Market Action Decisions   14
The Four Phases of Customer Orientation   15
  Phase I: Customer Strategy and Focus   15
  Phase II: Customer Satisfaction Measurement   16
  Phase III: Analysis and Priority Setting   16
  Phase IV: Implementation   17
The Transformation of Sweden Post   18
  The Transformation Process   19
  The Measurement Process   20
Sweden Post: Lessons Learned   23
Summary   24
Discussion Questions   25

CHAPTER 3   Understanding and Anticipating Customer Needs   26

The Goal of Customer Research   26

Reactive Research   27

Proactive Research and the Information Pyramid   30
History and Cultural Factors   32
Unobtrusive or Nonreactive Measures   33
Value Segmentation   33
Laddering   36
Comparing Noncomparables   38
Projective Techniques   38

Summary   39

Discussion Questions   40

PART II: THE PURCHASE AND CONSUMPTION EXPERIENCE   41

CHAPTER 4   The Customer Experience Model   41

Customer Acquisition and Retention   41
Satisfaction, Retention, and Profits   43

The Customer Experience Model   46
Disney's Customer Orbit   48

Four Customer Types   49

Summary   51

Discussion Questions   51

CHAPTER 5   Customers in the Marketplace   52

Roots in Economic Theory   52
Normative and Predictive Models   53

From Caveat Emptor to the Federal Trade Commission: The Changing
Information Environment   56
Types of Market Information   57

Learning in the Marketplace: The Nature of Expectations   58
Expectation Models   58
The Nature of Expectations: Adaptation and Aggregation   60

Customer Satisfaction in the Marketplace: The Matching of
Supply and Demand   62

Customer Dissatisfaction in the Marketplace: Exit or Voice?   65

Summary   66

Discussion Questions   67

CHAPTER 6   Customer Information Processing   68

The Vehicle Purchase Process   69

The Information Processing Paradigm   71
Limited Resources   72
Attention and Involvement   73

Perception and Cognitive Representations   74
Information Acquisition and Memory   79
Categorization   83
Summary   85
Discussion Questions   85

CHAPTER 7   Customer Choice   86

Choice Strategies   86
Brand-Level Choice   86
Category-Level Choice   90
Noncomparable Choice   90
Price, Quality, and Value   91
Risky Choice: Heuristics and Framing Effects   92
The Howard Model   95
Extensive Problem Solving   95
Limited Problem Solving   96
Routinized Response Behavior   96
Management over the Life Cycle   97
Cascading Strategies   98
Summary   100
Discussion Questions   101

CHAPTER 8   Customer Satisfaction and Priority Setting   102

A Customer Satisfaction Framework   103
The Psychology of Customer Satisfaction   104
The Disconfirmation Model   105
The Performance Model   107
Which Model to Use?   109
When Are Expectations Important?   110
Building a Customer Satisfaction Measurement System   112
Elements of a Customer Satisfaction Model   114
The Consequences of Satisfaction   115
Price as a Satisfaction Driver   115
Estimating Importance Weights   116
Priority Setting   119
Bridging Internal and External Quality   120
Customer Satisfaction at Cathay Pacific   121
Customer Satisfaction at DrainCo   124
Summary   127
Discussion Questions   128

CHAPTER 9   Macro Satisfaction and Firm Strategy   129

The Development of National Satisfaction Indices   129
The ACSI Methodology   130
1994 Baseline Index Results and General Comparisons   132

Global Competition in the Automobile Industry   134
Time Trends in the SCSB   138
Summary   139
Challenges for the Auto Industry   139
Discussion Questions   141

PART III: IMPLEMENTATION AND QUALITY IMPROVEMENT   143

CHAPTER 10   Customer Orientation and the Design Function   143
Two Schools of Design   143
The Functionalist School of Design   144
Design as an Aesthetic Tool   145
Which School to Follow?   146
Evolutionary Product Design   148
Revolutionary Product Design   148
Laddering, Value Projection, and Reverse Laddering   149
Product Concepts   150
Service Design   151
Summary   154
Discussion Questions   155

CHAPTER 11   From Customer Satisfaction to Quality Improvement   156
Implementing the Four Phases of Customer Orientation   156
Phase I: Customer Strategy and Focus   157
Phase II: Customer Satisfaction Measurement   158
Phase III: Analysis and Priority Setting   158
Phase IV: Implementation   159
Quality Function Deployment   159
The House of Quality   161
Phases 2, 3, and 4   164
Bridging the Quality-Satisfaction Gap   164
Customer Needs as Benefits versus Attributes   166
Benefit and Attribute Importance   166
Benchmarking and Priority Setting   167
Method Myopia   168
Summary   169
Going Forward   170
Discussion Questions   171

Index   173

Preface

My purpose in writing this book is to provide a rigorous yet practical understanding of customers in the marketplace. Through an integration of research and application, the book helps both students and practitioners to focus on customers and use this orientation to improve business decisions. This represents an important departure from existing customer-related texts that typically follow two very different paths. The first is the path of the detailed consumer behavior text. Although these texts provide important details on a broad range of consumer research topics, the practical implications of this information are often forced. The second path includes texts targeted squarely at practitioners. These works hail the benefits of being customer oriented, satisfying customers, and delivering customer value while taking a skin-deep approach to understanding and operationalizing important concepts and models.

The main reason for taking one or the other of these paths has been the traditional distinction between theory and practice. This distinction is disappearing in business research. As competition intensifies in the marketplace, practitioners must understand the details of how customers make decisions and evaluate product and service performance. This is only possible by delving selectively into the wealth of models and knowledge available in psychology, economics, consumer research, and marketing.

ABOUT THE BOOK

As the title suggests, the overriding goals of the text are (1) to orient business decision makers on customers and (2) to use the information gained to improve business decisions. A major orienting theme is how to go about satisfying customers. Customer satisfaction has a long history in economics, consumer research, and marketing. An interdisciplinary approach to customer satisfaction is essential to gain an understanding of what satisfaction is, how to measure it, how to change it, and how to track its bottom-line impact on firm performance.

The book is divided into eleven chapters and three major parts. Part I provides an overview of a customer orientation and its role in taking market action. Chapter 1 introduces the three goals of a customer orientation: the attainment of customer information, the dissemination of this information throughout an organization, and the implementation of quality improvements. The chapter presents an integrated approach to understanding customers that balances a psychologist's view of the dynamics of customer behavior, an economist's view of the predictability of market behavior, and a manager's need to use this information to make business decisions.

Chapter 2 looks at these business decisions in more detail and integrates them into the four phases of customer orientation: customer strategy and focus (phase I), customer satisfaction measurement (phase II), analysis and priority setting (phase III), and implementation (phase IV). This framework identifies the major challenges in the customer orientation process. The case of Sweden Post, a former government service monopoly turned customer-oriented firm, is used to illustrate the framework. Chapter 3 provides an overview of the types of customer information used in management decisions and the variety of customer and market research methods used to obtain this information. A major emphasis in this chapter is the need to anticipate customer needs through the use of proactive research methods.

Part II takes a detailed look at customers as they purchase, experience, evaluate, and repurchase products and services in the market place. Chapter 4 details the economics of customer retention and introduces the customer experience model. This model describes four main components affecting a customer's purchase–consumption–repurchase cycle: (1) perception, judgment, and choice processes; (2) the consumption experience and its evaluation; (3) external market information; and (4) customers' internal knowledge base. Walt Disney World's customer "orbit" provides a concrete example of the model's components.

Chapters 5–8 detail the individual components of the customer experience model. Chapter 5 provides an economic view of customers in the marketplace and describes the nature and role of market place information in customer decisions. Chapters 6 and 7 describe the perception, judgment, and choice processing component of the model using an information processing perspective from psychology. The attention, perception, information acquisition, memory, and categorization processes that customers use to adapt to the marketplace are the focus of chapter 6. Chapter 7 examines the choice models and processes customers use to make product and service purchase and consumption decisions.

Customer satisfaction, a customer's evaluation of his or her purchase and consumption experience, is the topic of chapter 8. The chapter introduces a customer satisfaction framework that links a firm's internal quality improvements to satisfaction, customer loyalty, and subsequent retention. Competing approaches to measuring customer satisfaction are described and used to model this evaluation process. The chapter develops customer satisfaction models that enable managers to identify the drivers of satisfaction, evaluate product and service performance, and set priorities for quality improvement. Chapter 9 elevates customer satisfaction research to a macro level by introducing national satisfaction indices and illustrating their value through an analysis of customer satisfaction and competition in the automobile industry.

The two chapters in part III provide closure through their focus on implementing quality improvements. Chapter 10 describes the important role of the design function in following through on customer information to design revolutionary products and services. Chapter 11 first overviews the implementation of the four phases of customer orientation and then introduces quality function deployment as a method for translating customer priorities into their means of accomplishment.

The book is a flexible tool for use in a variety of teaching and research contexts. All eleven chapters serve as the basis for my own MBA-level consumer behavior course at the University of Michigan Business School. The references used throughout the text provide an excellent source of additional reading for use in class. The book is also designed to appeal to advanced practitioners interested in customer behavior, customer satisfaction, and quality improvement. In several week-long executive courses I typically cover most of the material in part I (chapters 1–3) and selected chapters thereafter. Chapters 4, 8, and 9, for example, work particularly well in a customer satisfaction course, while chapters 10 and 11 work equally well in a quality management course. Chapters 5, 6, and 7, meanwhile, enable students, managers, and researchers to explore selected topics on the psychology and economics of customer behavior.

I have relied primarily on two sources for material throughout the text: (1) my own research on customer psychology, customer behavior, customer satisfaction, and the implementation of quality tools; and (2) a body of both older and more modern business, marketing, design, psychology, and economic "classics" that have significantly influenced my thinking. My overriding goal is to provide a unified view of how customers learn and behave in a market environment and how managers can use this information to take market actions and improve firm performance. It is not to present the reader with an unbiased survey of customer behavior as a field of study. If I have forgotten, ignored, or otherwise overlooked the work of others in the process, I apologize. This was not my intent.

ACKNOWLEDGMENTS

I would like to thank those individuals who have both directly and indirectly contributed to the text. First are the wonderful people at Prentice Hall who made this project happen, especially Sandra Steiner, Eric Severson, and David Borkowsky. I also thank the hundreds of MBA students and executives who have taught me so much over the years. J. Edward Russo of Cornell University, my dissertation chairman at The University of Chicago's Graduate School of Business, helped to lay the foundation for the book through his outstanding research and teaching. Andreas Herrmann, Frank Huber, Tom Granzow, and four anonymous reviewers all provided thoughtful and greatly appreciated feedback.

Yet most of what is contained herein is a product of my affiliation with the University of Michigan Business School. In particular I thank the individuals with whom I have worked and from whom I have learned so much since coming to Ann Arbor, especially Claes Fornell, Gene Anderson, Jaesung Cha, and Barbara Everitt Bryant (my colleagues in the National Quality Research Center). Not forgotten are Don Lehmann and John Howard of Columbia University's Graduate School of Business. I thank Don for being such a valued coauthor and mentor and John Howard for both his encouragement over the years and his classic research.

But most of all I thank my wife, Jill Marie, and my boys, Alexander and Andrew, for seeing me through this project as well as the most difficult time in my life. Shortly after signing the contract for this book I suffered from a debilitating virus that required months of recovery to regain such basic skills as reading, writing, and walking. Their love and encouragement helped me to fully recover and return to the profession that I love.

Michael D. Johnson
Ann Arbor, Michigan
August, 1996

A Customer Orientation

CHAPTER 1

Success in the marketplace rests on a firm's ability to attract, satisfy, and retain its customers. Customer satisfaction is the primary determinant of customer loyalty and subsequent retention and the key to creating a valuable business organization. This is true for goods as well as services, durables as well as nondurables, and competitive firms as well as government agencies. Continued success rests on reinventing oneself in the eyes of one's customers and adapting to their evolving needs. Simply understanding which products or product attributes customers currently desire is insufficient. Firms must also anticipate where customer preferences are headed.

This all requires a thorough understanding of customers in the marketplace and ways to use this information to take market action. The purpose of this text is to develop these skills. This requires us to bridge the gap between academic theories and business practice. Although managers often complain that theories and research are divorced from the market decisions and action steps they are intended to improve, this need not be the case. There is a wealth of research findings, models, and theories available to help us better understand customers, their experiences, and their behavior, and they provide useful guidelines for market action.

This chapter overviews the general goals of a customer orientation and the challenges inherent in its application. Our purpose throughout the text is to be rigorous yet practical. Models of customer behavior, customer satisfaction, and decision making are introduced and used because of the pragmatic insight they provide. These models are also general in that they apply to business-to-business markets as well as consumer markets. The term *customer*, rather than *consumer*, is used to refer to buyers at multiple levels of the marketing and production process. Not only is the term more general, but it has also become difficult to distinguish between consumers and customers in the traditional sense. Any differences have become more a matter of degree than of kind. Therefore, the term *customer* is used here to include any individual, group, or organization that purchases and consumes a product and/or service offering.

A major orienting theme throughout the book is how to go about satisfying these customers. Customer satisfaction has a long history in economics, in which it is synonymous with consumption utility; consumer research, in which several psychological models have been developed; and marketing strategy, in which customer loyalty

1

and retention are the keys to long-term success. Therefore, an interdisciplinary approach to customer satisfaction is essential to gain an understanding of what satisfaction is, how to measure it, how to improve it, and how to track its impact on a firm's performance.

Taking a Customer Orientation

Most managers these days will agree that one of their primary organizational goals is to orient, or focus, on customers. Yet the number of firms that are truly customer oriented remains small. Taking a customer orientation is a central theme in marketing and strategic market planning. Marketers have long argued that business is a process of matching heterogeneous customer needs with market offerings.[1] This matching process falters and firms stop growing because they focus on their own products or services rather than the customer benefits that these products provide.[2] They become product oriented rather than customer oriented. When this happens, competitors find better ways to meet customer needs.

   Xerox provides a good example of a firm that has gone through this transition toward a customer orientation. For years the firm focused on its products, mostly copiers, and its differential advantage in providing outstanding support services. Meanwhile, foreign competitors were changing the playing field through the development of self-service personal and small-volume copiers that neutralized Xerox's traditional service strength. Xerox is now a "document processing" company whose leadership is committed to focusing on customer benefits and is not afraid to reinvent itself in order to remain so.[3] Similarly, Schlumberger viewed itself as a technology-focused producer of seismic recorders. In the 1980s it began viewing itself as an information provider to the petroleum industry to focus more closely on its customers and their needs. The result was a host of successful new products and double-digit growth.[4]

THE THREE GOALS OF A CUSTOMER ORIENTATION

There are a variety of perspectives and frameworks that managers use to improve product and service quality and customer satisfaction. From these two common themes emerge.[5] First is the need to obtain an accurate set of customer specifications for the target market segment(s) of interest. This involves understanding just what benefits,

---

[1]Wroe Alderson, "The Analytical Framework for Marketing," in ed. Delbert Duncan, *Proceedings: Conference of Marketing Teachers from Far Western States* (Berkeley, CA: University of California, 1958), 15–28.

[2]Theodore Levitt, "Marketing Myopia," *Harvard Business Review* (1960), Reprint No. 75507.

[3]Tim Smart, "Can Xerox Duplicate its Glory Days?" *Business Week* (October 4, 1993).

[4]J. Edward Russo and Paul J. H. Schoemaker, *Decision Traps: The Ten Barriers to Brilliant Decision-Making and How to Overcome Them* (New York: Simon & Schuster, 1989).

[5]See W. Edwards Deming, *Management of Statistical Techniques for Quality and Productivity* (New York: New York University, Graduate School of Business 1981). A. V. Feigenbaum, *Total Quality Control: Fortieth Anniversary Edition* (New York: McGraw-Hill, Inc. 1991). Joseph M. Juran and Frank M. Gryna, *Juran's Quality Control Handbook: Fourth Edition* (New York: McGraw-Hill, Inc., 1988). Ajay K. Kohli and Bernard J. Jaworski, "Market Orientation: The Construct, Research Propositions, and Managerial Implications," *Journal of Marketing*, 54 (April 1990), 1–18.

attributes, and features customers need and want from a product or service. Health-conscious consumers with limited free time have created a demand for expanded menus at fast-food restaurants, which include everything from applesauce and carrot sticks to tofu hot dogs. Even buyers of small cars have come to expect air bags and antilock brakes in their vehicles.

The second theme is to have a production and service or maintenance process that achieves conformance to these desired specifications. Customers want reliability in their products and services to minimize the number of "things gone wrong." Achieving conformance is, however, complex and better understood by considering two separate goals. Everyone in the organization must first understand, at some level of detail, the customers' target specifications. The organization must then follow through on this common knowledge, produce superior products and services, and learn from its actions. This discussion suggests that there are three conceptually distinct goals that provide a philosophical foundation for the development of a customer orientation. As depicted in figure 1.1, a customer orientation is a sequential process in which firms (1) attain customer information, (2) disseminate that information, and (3) implement product and service improvements.

One must first attain customer information to understand customers' root needs and values, how they are served by current products and services, and how they will likely be served by future products and services. This process should include both

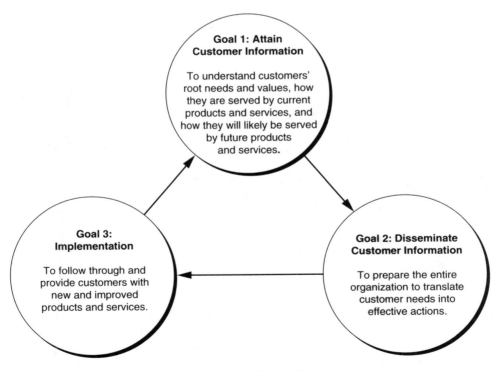

FIGURE 1.1 The Three Goals of a Customer Orientation

current target customers and desired future customers. It is often far more difficult to achieve this goal than it appears. One cannot simply go out and survey people as to what features they would like in their home entertainment systems in five years or whether they would purchase a particular technology. Chapter 3 outlines the different types of customer information required to make business decisions and the methods used to obtain this information.

The second goal is to disseminate this customer information to all the elements in an organization that are either directly or indirectly involved in satisfying customers. *The purpose is to prepare the entire organization to translate customer needs into effective actions.* When customer information is disseminated throughout an organization, everyone can both take actions and monitor their performance against a common benchmark. At the other extreme, information may be hoarded and used as a tool with which one department browbeats another into submission—in which case the entire effort is likely to fail.

The third goal is to act on this disseminated customer information through processes of implementation. *The purpose is to follow through and provide customers with new and improved products and services.* Firms must find ways to use the knowledge they have gained and implement the decisions they have made. If General Motors determines that a large portion of future car buyers want a factory-installed navigation system with certain features, then GM must find a way to coordinate marketing, design, and manufacturing to make this option available at a price that delivers significant customer value.

Throughout the entire customer orientation process an organization must learn from its actions. Which source or sources of customer information provided the best estimate of future demand? Why did marketing have such trouble communicating the product or service concept to the design staff? Which of the test clinics was most useful in fine-tuning the product? Why were we surprised when a given segment of customers opted for a competitor's product?

These types of questions are raised throughout this book. Some specific tools for implementing a customer orientation on both product and service dimensions are also described and illustrated. The output of the implementation process provides critically important information regarding the degree of customer orientation actually achieved. One learns how to do things in a more customer-oriented fashion the next time around—whether it is the next model year, the next visit of a patron, the next service call, or the next contract between supplier and manufacturer. In theory, and ideally in practice, the process depicted in figure 1.1 never stops. Being customer oriented is a continuous process of understanding, communicating, implementing, and learning.

Challenges

Unfortunately, a firm's tendency to focus on its products rather than its customers is not the only problem that inhibits a customer orientation. There are at least five categories of challenges: (1) having a shared, customer-oriented vision throughout an organization; (2) having a leadership perspective that drives this shared vision; (3) avoiding market and market research myopia; (4) overcoming organizational and structural barriers; and (5) understanding the whole picture.

CUSTOMER ORIENTATION AS A SHARED VISION

A customer orientation requires that an entire organization have a shared vision that focuses directly on its customers. This vision lies at the heart of the marketing concept, as is evident in Kotler's popular definition of marketing, which "holds that the key to achieving organizational goals consists in determining the needs and wants of target markets and delivering the desired satisfactions more effectively and efficiently than competitors."[6] It is a theme around which all parts of the organization should exert their efforts to varying degrees. A lack of shared vision creates competing interests and inefficiencies.

A good example here is the contrast between internal and external perspectives. Some argue that the key to satisfying customers is to develop competitive and efficient internal processes for such elements as design, manufacturing, and communication. This process improvement is accomplished by benchmarking on the internal processes of competitors or admired peers, which involves making visits to firms with quality reputations to gauge their practices, or reverse engineering their products to learn what others are doing, how they are doing it, and what is possible.[7] A problem arises when this internal quality focus becomes confused with an external focus on customers. Followers of Crosby, for example, believe that "quality is free."[8] Doing things correctly the first time, through an emphasis on internal process changes, should lower costs and increase customer satisfaction. The emphasis is clearly on improving a firm's ability to conform to a given set of customer specifications, or improve reliability, for a product or service.

This involves assuming that customer specifications are themselves accurate and unchanging. If not, then all the process improvement in the world will do little to improve customer satisfaction. When Ford Motor Company phased out the Tempo/Topaz car line in 1994, the car line had attained the company's highest marks for reliability while its sales and popularity continued to decline. An improved set of customer specifications for the Tempo/Topaz replacement, the much-heralded "world" car (Mondeo/Conquest/Mystique), has helped to improve the company's customer orientation. The lesson is that one cannot conform to specifications and improve satisfaction without first having an accurate set of specifications.

One implication is that even an important practice such as process benchmarking may do as much harm as good if used as an end in itself rather than a means to an end. This idea was recently supported in two studies in which process benchmarking was found to have negative consequences on a firm's performance. In one study, process benchmarking actually decreased the ability of business units to focus on customers when implementing a quality improvement method.[9] In the other, process benchmarking proved to be too much for smaller firms to handle. These firms

[6]Philip Kotler, *Marketing Management: Analysis, Planning, Implementation, and Control*, 9th Ed. (Upper Saddle River, NJ: Prentice Hall, Inc., 1997).

[7]Robert C. Camp, *Benchmarking* (Milwaukee: ASQC Quality Press, 1989).

[8]Philip B. Crosby, *Quality is Free* (New York: Penguin Books, 1979).

[9]John E. Ettlie and Michael D. Johnson, "Product Development Benchmarking versus Customer Focus in Applications of Quality Function Deployment," *Marketing Letters*, 5 (2, 1994), 107–16.

ended up trying to do too much too quickly and failed to improve the quality of either their internal processes or their products and services.[10]

CUSTOMER ORIENTATION AS A LEADERSHIP PERSPECTIVE

A shared vision of customer orientation requires a leadership perspective that believes in and acts upon this vision. A customer focus is likely to backfire or be weak at best in firms whose leaders either allow strong competing interests to coexist or are themselves advocates of an alternative vision. Many firms retain a corporate culture that directly conflicts with the attainment of a customer orientation by overemphasizing short-run financial objectives. They see only the cost side of long-term investments in improving quality and customer satisfaction. Luckily, this situation is changing as more business leaders understand the long-term benefits of their customer investments.

CUSTOMER ORIENTATION MYOPIA

Another general challenge that firms face when implementing a customer orientation is finding a way to keep the process going. We all, at times, become myopic in the way we view the world. The problem is that the adage "if it ain't broke, don't fix it" lies in direct contrast to the marketing concept. Relying on the status quo can manifest itself in two ways. As mentioned, it can lead to a focus on currently successful products rather than on customers. The reality is that customer preferences change while competitors constantly seek better ways to deliver customer value. Current success does not translate into future success unless a firm constantly adapts to these changing market conditions.

A firm that relies on the status quo may also be myopic in its use of traditional market research methods. Focus groups, interviews, and surveys have become the standard solutions to many market research problems even though they provide limited customer insight in certain contexts. As explored in chapter 3, it is important to augment traditional research methods with more proactive and creative approaches.

ORGANIZATIONAL AND STRUCTURAL BARRIERS

Inevitably in the course of implementing change, organizational structures impose barriers on the customer-orientation process. This problem relates to the lack of a shared vision. The goals captured in figure 1.1 may simply be at odds with certain functional specialists in a firm who are unwilling to change. An important trap to avoid is the tendency of some to view marketing as just another specialist function. Marketing is not simply a process of sales and advertising; *rather, marketing is a diagnostic way of thinking about your business and making decisions.* The long-run solution to organizational and structural barriers is, of course, to change the organization. Greater reliance on "horizontal" corporate structures and cross-functional teams—in which people from different parts of the organization, from marketing to design to manufacturing to finance, are all working toward the same goal—is a ma-

---

[10]Otis Port and Geoffrey Smith, "Beg, Borrow—and Benchmark," *Business Week* (November 30, 1992), 74–75.

jor step in this direction. In the short run, the solution is to accomplish what is possible within organizational or structural constraints.

A LACK OF GESTALT: UNDERSTANDING THE "WHOLE PICTURE"

Finally, attempts to be customer oriented falter because managers fail to see the whole picture. At the highest levels managers must balance a variety of perspectives, from customers' perspectives to the firm's financial perspective to an internal process perspective to a learning perspective, and understand how they interact. As described in chapter 2, approaches such as the "balanced scorecard" have been developed to provide upper managers with this broader view.[11] Because of its impact on customer retention, customer satisfaction commands a central position in one's scorecard. Without customers, there are no revenues! Moreover, the longer customers are retained the more profitable these revenues become as marketing and production costs decrease.[12]

Yet one must balance an emphasis on customer satisfaction and its relationship to owner satisfaction with other "voices," including the voice of employees, the voice of the community or communities in which a firm operates, and the voice of the environment. In the Sweden Post case in chapter 2, there is a tremendous effort being made to increase quality and customer satisfaction. The trade-off is that Sweden Post has laid off thousands of employees in the process. Not surprisingly, employee satisfaction has declined.

An Integrated Approach

The key to leveraging one's understanding of customers lies in the proper integration of three perspectives: the manager's perspective on business decisions; the economist's perspective on how buyers and sellers interact in the marketplace; and the psychologist's perspective on how customers perceive, store, and evaluate information. Figure 1.2 (page 8) illustrates the importance of all three perspectives within an overall customer orientation.

Too often these perspectives are seen as competing and contradictory. An integration illustrates how they complement each other rather than compete. It is not simply the case that one perspective or another is right or wrong. Rather, each brings something important to a customer orientation. Although the following discussion highlights differences among the perspectives, the reader should keep in mind that these differences are often a matter of degree rather than kind. Both economists and psychologists, for example, aim to understand and predict behavior at some level.

---

[11]Robert S. Kaplan and David P. Norton, "The Balanced Scorecard—Measures that Drive Performance," *Harvard Business Review* (January–February 1992), Reprint No. 92105.

[12]Frederick F. Reichheld, *The Loyalty Effect: The Hidden Force Behind Growth, Profits, and Lasting Value* (Boston: Harvard Business School Press, 1996).

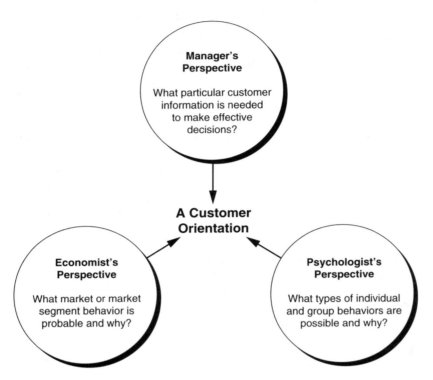

FIGURE 1.2 An Integration of Three Perspectives

Manager, as used here, refers to high-level business decision makers. What makes the manager's perspective different is its focus on decision making. Managers are routinely in the position of having to integrate a large amount of information from several sources. This highlights the need to provide managers with the most pertinent customer-related information as they bring together other equally complicated sources of information from other areas in order to make decisions. Senior managers, for example, must be able to integrate information about customers, competitors, investors, employees, corporate strategy, environmental conditions, political conditions, changes in technology, and so on. A good example comes from the banking industry of the early 1980s, which was marked by significant turbulence and change in the face of deregulation and increased competition. Senior managers of business units in this industry who were able to integrate diverse sources of information performed significantly better than those who could not.[13]

More unique to an economic perspective is an emphasis on understanding market or market segment behavior. Economics typically does not take the view of any particular buyer or seller in the marketplace but rather makes simplifying assump-

---

[13]Andrew R. McGill, Michael D. Johnson, and Karen A. Bantel, "Cognitive Complexity and Conformity: Effects on Performance in a Turbulent Environment," *Psychological Reports*, 74 (1994), 1451–72.

tions for the purpose of making market predictions. It involves looking at both buyers and sellers in the aggregate. Understanding what types of customer behaviors are possible is less important than understanding what market behavior is probable. This view complements the manager's perspective in two important ways. First, it focuses on predictions or forecasts that are central to management decisions. Second, the customer information that it provides is integrated because of its focus on aggregates rather than on individual customers or groups. In many if not most cases, managers focus on entire markets or market segments when making strategy decisions. Even with the advent of "mass customization," frontline personnel and information systems are used to tailor product and service offerings to individuals while managers make market segment level decisions.

In contrast to both managers and economists, psychologists and psychological studies are generally interested in providing rich descriptions of the dynamics of individual or small group behavior. Psychology illustrates the types of customer behaviors that are possible in the marketplace. The approach taken in psychology, especially judgment and choice research, is to provide a more process-oriented perspective of how customers perceive, evaluate, and decide. This knowledge of process and dynamics helps managers to understand not only what is possible, but how they might adapt to, influence, or change customer information processing and processes.

Naturally, a better understanding of customers lies at the heart of this integration. Customers perceive, judge, and decide from a psychological perspective as well as consume from an economic perspective. Both purchase and consumption are important to managers as they comprise the two major acts in a customer's repurchase cycle. This tripartite view is used throughout the text to take advantage of the complementarity that exists in economic and psychological research and identify its value to managers.

Customer Orientation, Market Orientation, and Total Quality Management

Just how does a customer orientation differ from similar approaches and perspectives, most notably a market orientation and total quality management (TQM)? All three approaches are ultimately aimed at improving business performance and directly or indirectly involve customers and concepts such as customer satisfaction. A market orientation focuses more equally on customers and competitors in business decision making and strategy development. Importantly, it involves recognizing that there is more to developing a comprehensive business strategy than just being customer oriented. A customer orientation focuses disproportionately on customers and the processes of customer acquisition, satisfaction, and retention. Taking a long-run perspective, a customer orientation recognizes that although competitors may come and go, without customers there is no market to orient on.

The difference between a customer orientation and TQM is more a matter of evolution and focus. Under TQM, "you continuously endeavor to fulfill or exceed the demands and expectations of the customers at lower and lower costs in all processes which continuously are being improved and to which everybody is committed."[14] Compared with a customer orientation, TQM takes a more internal, process improvement focus. As described earlier, this focus on process improvement may even be at odds with a customer focus. TQM is also "total," in that all processes are being continuously improved. This approach makes sense when almost all of a firm's basic processes are inefficient or otherwise in need of improvement, which was an apt description of many firms in the early to mid-1980s. As internal processes have improved, it has become more important to use a customer orientation to identify specific internal processes that justify further improvement from a cost–benefit standpoint. Thus, a customer orientation provides a primarily external orientation that builds on, and provides focus to, existing internal quality improvement efforts.

Summary

Long-run business success requires that firms attract, satisfy, and retain their customers through the delivery of high-quality products and services. The quality literature identifies two important steps in this process: understanding customer needs and driving variance out of the processes that deliver these needs. The philosophy of a customer orientation builds on this perspective by emphasizing three organizational goals:

- Attain customer information to understand customers' root needs and values, how they are served by current products and services, and how they will likely be served by future products and services;
- Disseminate customer information to prepare the entire organization to translate customer needs into effective actions; and
- Implement change to follow through and provide customers with new and improved products and services.

A customer orientation involves more than just understanding customer needs. Firms must learn to communicate this understanding throughout their organizations and follow through in the delivery of high-quality products and services. Understanding customer needs and wants only provides a target of desired product or service specifications; proper communication and production or maintenance processes are required to provide these specifications.

The customer orientation advocated here provides tangible benefits to firms in profit and nonprofit, product and service, and business-to-business as well as end-user markets. Although relatively simple, it remains difficult to achieve. A lack of shared vision, a lack of leadership, myopic practices, organizational barriers, and an inability to "understand the whole" all make a customer orientation difficult. This book integrates managerial, economic, and psychological perspectives to identify

---

[14]Bo Bergman and Bengt Klefsjö, *Quality: From Customer Needs to Customer Satisfaction* (Lund, Sweden: Studentlitteratur, 1994), 21.

tools, methods, and processes that help organizations achieve a customer orientation. Managers are primarily interested in understanding what particular customer information is needed to make effective decisions. Whereas an economic perspective helps these managers to understand what market or market segment behavior is probable, a psychological perspective helps them to understand what types of customer behavior are possible. Together, the economic and psychological perspectives provide a better understanding of the purchase and consumption cycle that managers aim to both create and sustain over time.

Discussion Questions

1. How customer oriented are companies such as Honda, Disney, and McDonald's?
2. How customer oriented is your company, division, or organization?
3. What specific factors facilitate or inhibit your ability to be customer oriented?

CHAPTER **2** # Market Action

Each year companies gather volumes of data to learn about their customers. In chapter 3 we examine various types of customer information as well as the research methods used to obtain it. Prior to discussing the information itself, however, it is important to examine managers' information needs. Research is wasted unless raw data is transformed into information for managers to use as a basis for making decisions and taking market action. In this chapter we explore the nature of managers' information needs and the role that customer information plays in their decision making.

Central to our discussion is the nature of the decision problems facing managers. After describing these problems, the four phases of customer orientation are introduced as an organizing framework. The four-phase framework highlights the process-related decisions and action steps required to become customer oriented. The framework is illustrated using the radical example of Sweden Post, a former government service monopoly that evolved into a customer-oriented company in a short period of time.

Managers' Information Needs

Managers require different types of information to make different types of decisions. Of particular interest are three types of customer-related decisions: (1) market strategy decisions, (2) monitoring-based market action decisions, and (3) problem-driven market action decisions. Although these decisions may overlap and interact in practice and the same information may be used for more than one type of decision, important differences remain.

MARKET STRATEGY DECISIONS

Developing an effective strategy requires that managers and corporate leaders understand just what business or set of related businesses they are in. This understanding must come not from the firm's own perspective, but from the perspective of its customers. Recall, for example, that Xerox views itself as a "document processing" company, whereas Schlumberger provides "information" to the petroleum industry. Similarly, sports franchise owners are in the entertainment business, whereas both airlines and automobile manufacturers compete in the transportation business.

Strategic decisions are also made as to where the company should be headed and just how customer focused it should be. Most, but not all, companies are in dire need of increasing their customer orientation. However, this increased focus on customers must be balanced against a firm's internal process perspective, employee satisfaction, and owner satisfaction. For example, a firm may correctly decide that it is not yet ready to implement a customer satisfaction program. And in some unique cases, customer satisfaction may not be an issue if a pure monopoly exists and customers have absolutely no choice but to use a particular company's or agency's products and services. Even in the case of the Internal Revenue Service, however, customers may choose not to comply if they are dissatisfied with the quality of their tax services. A more likely situation in which customer satisfaction is temporarily less important than other organizational goals is one in which customer demand is so abundant that others issues are more critical, such as improving internal manufacturing and delivery processes to cut costs and maintain or improve objective quality measures such as defect rates.

This is the "understanding of the whole" described in chapter 1. One framework for understanding this whole is the balanced scorecard,[1] the principle idea of which is to give top managers information from multiple perspectives in a highly integrated form in order to assess a firm's performance and strategy in an integrated fashion. This includes an assessment of how the firm is doing from a customer perspective, a financial perspective, an internal or process perspective, and an innovation and learning perspective. The goal is to bring together often disparate and competing perspectives and guard against meeting some objectives at the expense of others. Although the balance between a customer orientation and other organizational goals is touched on throughout this book, our focus is on customers.

MONITORING-BASED MARKET ACTION DECISIONS

A second class of customer-related management decisions utilize information collected on an ongoing basis. Using the repurchase cycle as our frame of reference, customers continuously go through a process of purchase and consumption. At the purchase stage, customers process information, evaluate options, and select an alternative. At the consumption stage, customers consume or experience the product or service, evaluate their experience, and develop a predisposition to purchase or not purchase that product or service again. Managers use customer information to monitor prepurchase perceptions and attitudes and postpurchase customer satisfaction.

Prior to purchase or repurchase, customers typically go through an information processing phase that involves the perception, judgment, and choice of a particular product or service offering. Prepurchase monitoring research can involve perceptual studies of a brand's or category's position among a set of competing brands

[1]Robert S. Kaplan and David P. Norton, "The Balanced Scorecard—Measures that Drive Performance," *Harvard Business Review* (1992), Reprint No. 92105.

or categories. The perceptual mapping and clustering techniques described in chapter 6 are important tools that managers use to identify the perceived similarities and differences among competing brands or categories, the nature of competition in a market, and new product or service opportunities.

Prepurchase monitoring also takes the form of attitudinal studies of customer preferences. This may involve purchase likelihoods for particular brands or more general studies of buying plans. One of the best known of the general studies is the Index of Consumer Sentiment. Developed at the University of Michigan's Survey Research Center, the Index monitors consumer confidence in the economy and resulting buying plans for major household durables (such as autos and major appliances). George Katona used decades of Index data to show that, even at an aggregate or macro level, psychological variables such as consumer confidence have a major impact on market behavior.[2] Katona's basic idea was that buying plans and subsequent behavior depend on both an ability and a willingness to purchase. When consumer attitudes and expectations about the economy drop, this both predicts and contributes to economic downturns. Because of its predictive power, aggregate consumer confidence information has proven extremely valuable to managers and analysts making product planning and production decisions.

The second general type of monitoring-based decisions are customers' postpurchase evaluations of products and services, including their reactions to particular service encounters, other consumption experiences with a product or service, and their overall satisfaction. A good customer satisfaction measurement system not only monitors customers as an asset and source of future profits but enables firms to benchmark against competitors, determine internal rewards and compensation, and make product and service improvements.

PROBLEM-DRIVEN MARKET ACTION DECISIONS

The third category of decisions includes those made as a reaction to a problem. These problems include unanticipated actions by competitors and sudden, unexpected drops in market share, profits, or distribution. The manager must analyze the situation, develop a set of options, and make a decision in response to the problem. Overall, becoming customer oriented means becoming more proactive and anticipating problems before they occur. Even competitive actions are, to some degree, predictable if one considers the competitor's past actions, current strategy, and capabilities. Yet as long as there are unpredictable forces in a market environment, problem-driven decision making will remain. Although, for example, "zero defects" is an admirable goal, it is nearly impossible to achieve in a service setting.

Managers make all three types of decisions around relatively homogeneous populations or groups of customers that we call market segments. Whether it is a product or service design, promotion, pricing, distribution, or segmentation decision itself, the focus is typically on segments rather than individuals. Some notable

---

[2]See George Katona, "Towards a Macropsychology," *American Psychologist*, 34 (2, 1979), 118–26. See also George Katona, *Essays on Behavioral Economics* (Ann Arbor, MI: The University of Michigan, Institute for Social Research, 1980).

exceptions include service settings in which managers have direct customer contact and industrial markets in which each individual is a potentially separate segment. The aggregate level of managers' decisions affects the tools and information needed to improve them. It may be misleading to base our views and strategy on a body of knowledge that applies more to individuals than to market segments. As one example, consider how often management strives to "meet and exceed" customer expectations. This assumes that a disconfirmation model of satisfaction, in which satisfaction is the difference between quality expected and quality received, is an appropriate market segment level model. Unfortunately, disconfirmation provides a relatively poor description of market level satisfaction.[3]

The Four Phases of Customer Orientation

The three goals introduced in chapter 1 (attain customer information, disseminate that information, and implement required changes) provide a solid conceptual and philosophical foundation for a customer orientation. Yet they fall short of providing managers with the concrete processes and action steps necessary to become customer oriented. Still needed is a process framework that incorporates the strategy and monitoring decisions outlined previously, helps managers to assess where their organizations stand in the process, and identifies what they must do to improve.

The four phases of customer orientation, presented in figure 2.1, is a relatively simple framework that (1) captures the general goals of a customer orientation, (2) gauges explicitly where a firm stands in the process, and (3) identifies specific challenges involved in moving the process forward. Although the phases are presented as conceptually distinct, they overlap in practice. Nevertheless, success in one phase is dependent on success in previous phases, making it important to consider them sequentially.

PHASE I: CUSTOMER STRATEGY AND FOCUS

In phase I a firm or business unit addresses or revisits the role of customers and a customer orientation in its overall strategy. To what degree is a customer orientation a strategic priority? Some firms may be at this phase because, in the past, other con-

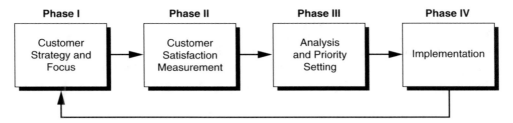

FIGURE 2.1 The Four Phases of Customer Orientation

[3]Michael D. Johnson, Eugene W. Anderson, and Claes Fornell, "Rational and Adaptive Performance Expectations in a Customer Satisfaction Framework," *Journal of Consumer Research*, 21 (March 1995), 695–707.

cerns have been a higher priority, such as removing sources of inefficiency in a production process. Others may find themselves at phase I because they have been too product (or service) focused in the past and are not as competitive as they once were. Still others may be at phase I because they are both profitable and growing but need to focus more on customers as a way to manage their growth. The bottom line is that firms are at phase I for a variety of reasons. What they have in common is the need to increase customer focus, whether it is to survive as an organization or remain focused as their organization continues to grow.

Included in phase I is the development of a market segmentation scheme. All subsequent efforts to improve customer orientation, from measuring and managing customer satisfaction to implementing product and service improvements, require an effective segmentation scheme. There is an inherent trade-off in the choice of a segmentation scheme that makes the process particularly difficult in some contexts. Market segments exist at the abstract level of desired product benefits and customer values (such as the "young at heart" segment). However, market segments are easier to define, locate, and reach at more concrete demographic and geographic levels (such as middle-income customers from a particular geographic region). Unless, however, the abstract and the concrete coincide, the manager trades off accuracy in a segmentation scheme for ease of use.

PHASE II: CUSTOMER SATISFACTION MEASUREMENT

When an organization decides to be more customer focused, several of the challenges discussed in chapter 1 may arise, from competing interests within the firm to organizational and structural barriers. From a customer perspective, however, the main challenge a firm faces at this point is installing a customer satisfaction measurement system. There are several desirable properties of such a system. It should link internal perspectives and processes (internal quality) with customer perceptions of product or service quality and subsequent perceptions of satisfaction (external quality). It should also be linked to key customer behaviors such as complaint behavior and customer retention. Finally, the measure of satisfaction should itself be meaningful; observed changes in the measure should be the result of underlying changes in product or service quality and not just random fluctuations.

Satisfaction models and measures exist at both a micro and a macro level. The four-phase framework focuses primarily on micro-level models, in which a firm monitors satisfaction with particular products or services within particular market segments. The recent emergence of national satisfaction indices in Sweden, Germany, and the United States offers a macro-level view of satisfaction, in which firms and entire industries are comparable. Chapter 8 details the process of satisfaction modeling and measurement at a micro level, and macro-level satisfaction is the topic of chapter 9.

PHASE III: ANALYSIS AND PRIORITY SETTING

Unfortunately, many firms are much better at collecting customer satisfaction data than they are at turning these data into information and using it to set priorities. This is the next major barrier faced by firms taking a customer orientation. There are two principal issues involved in overcoming this barrier. The first is the development of a systematic method for taking satisfaction and performance data and turning it into a set of priorities for product and service improvement. Unless market research information affects the decisions that managers make and how they do business, it is of little value. The second is making sure that the priorities that emerge from this process are achievable. Managers and employees must have the authority and resources at their disposal to achieve the action implications that emerge from their customer satisfaction measurement system and priority-setting process.

As an example, a retailer may have a problem with long lines in the early hours after opening in the morning. The priority-setting process may find that, to improve service quality, management should increase both the number of employees available to wait on customers and their service hours. If, however, there are constraints outside the manager's control (such as union contracts or limited physical capacity), then the solution may not be achievable or "implementable" in the next phase.

PHASE IV: IMPLEMENTATION

In phase IV the firm must succeed at following through and implementing the priorities set in phase III. There are several product/service design tools and internal process improvement methods that may be useful at this stage, such as Quality Function Deployment (QFD), which uses the "house of quality" approach to document customer needs and wants and connect these to their means of accomplishment within an organization.[4] Customer priorities are used as input to the house of quality for a particular product or service (or product/service group) being targeted at a particular market segment. Say that a segment of customers wants better handling in a line of sport utility vehicles. The house of quality then translates these objectives into engineering characteristics and targets. In ensuing "houses," the engineering targets are translated into design requirements, design requirements are translated into needed parts characteristics, and parts characteristics are translated into key process or production operations. Detailed discussions of this design and translation process are provided in chapters 10 and 11.

One final feature of the four-phase model is that the process of customer orientation, like quality improvement in general, is continuous. When phase IV objectives are completed, the company must reassess its strategic position, make the necessary changes in its satisfaction measurement system, set new priorities, and implement them. The primary value of the four-phase model is the diagnostic information it provides. It identifies important challenges or barriers facing a company as it continuously improves itself in the eyes of its customers. As mentioned, the model is not a performance scorecard; firms may be at phase I because they are underperforming and need to change or because they are performing well and want to continue doing so.

Some case examples help illustrate the value of the four-phase framework. A medium-sized manufacturing company markets a range of polyethylene piping for construction, agricultural, and recreational markets. Historically a manufacturing and sales organization, the company has experienced several years of double-digit growth.

---

[4]John R. Hauser and Don Clausing, "The House of Quality," *Harvard Business Review* (1988), Reprint No. 88307.

Obtaining customers and keeping them has not been a problem in the past. But as the company's markets have grown and competition has increased, customers have started to defect and at least some of the company's management recognizes the need to change. To continue its track record of growth and compete effectively, the company must focus more on its customers.

The company is clearly in phase I as it struggles to adapt to a changing market-place. The most immediate challenge facing the company is obtaining buy-in from management and other departments, especially sales and manufacturing, regarding the need to be customer focused. To move to phase II the company must then implement an effective customer satisfaction measurement system. If such a system is implemented prior to corporate buy-in from a strategy standpoint, or without a shared vision of the importance of such a system, the results could be disastrous. One possible result is an "information war," in which one department or camp (such as marketing) uses satisfaction data as leverage over other departments (such as manufacturing and sales). Rather than meeting goal 2 of a customer orientation—disseminating customer information throughout the organization—the information is used as a weapon within the organization.

Now consider the case of Cathay Pacific, the Hong Kong–based airline that finds itself at a different phase of the four-phase framework facing very different challenges. Traditionally a leader in the Asian market, Cathay is expanding into trans-Pacific flights and the growing Chinese market. Management at the airline has recognized the importance of being customer oriented, and customer satisfaction has become a cornerstone of its expansion goals. Unlike the manufacturing firm described previously, it has progressed through phases I and II to implement a large-scale customer satisfaction measurement system. The system annually collects tens of thousands of in-flight and post-flight surveys in which customers rate the airline on a host of quality-related attributes, overall satisfaction, and likelihood of retention. Unfortunately, although the system produces mountains of data, it has little effect on management decisions. Relatively few priorities have been set and implemented using this data. Thus, the primary challenge facing the airline is to improve the process by which it uses customer data to make decisions and set priorities (phase III).

Sweden Post provides a third example. This Swedish government monopoly-turned-limited company has progressed through all four phases of the model and now finds itself revisiting phase I. Because it illustrates the entire four-phase approach, its case history is presented in detail.[5]

The Transformation of Sweden Post

In the late 1980s Sweden's economy and its traditional social democracy were floundering. Facing increased European and global competition, Sweden had aspirations of joining the developing European Union. It was about this time that several competitive initiatives began including the establishment of a national customer satisfac-

---

[5]References for this section include *Sweden Post Annual Report 1992* and Marie Blomqvist and Claes Fornell, *Customer Satisfaction*, IPRA Gold Paper (1993). While this case describes actual events at Sweden Post, details of the specific satisfaction model and decision priorities presented here have been changed to preserve confidentiality.

tion index for Sweden.[6] First reported in 1989, the Swedish Customer Satisfaction Barometer compares the major industries in Sweden on a single 0- to 100-point customer satisfaction index. Sweden Post (SP) was a driving force in the development of the index because, as Swedish markets were opening up, traditional government monopolies such as SP saw the need to reinvent themselves and be more adaptive to customer needs.

The national index helped SP to benchmark itself on other industries and see just how well or poorly it was doing. It quickly realized that its customer satisfaction was low compared with more competitive product and service industries. SP began a formal process of improving its customer orientation. The initiative began from the top down as expressed by its Director General Ulf Dahlsten:

> Sweden Post is, over a short period, being transformed into a modern corporation, with the focus on customers and financial results. The time of the old government organization is past—the monopoly-protected organization that had no need to pay attention to either customers or competitors.[7]

THE TRANSFORMATION PROCESS

Internally, the transformation of SP into a more competitive company involved a four-step process. This process encompassed not only the four phases of customer orientation but organizational and legal changes as well. Step 1 was the initiation of a more customer-oriented approach to its businesses in which the customer is at the center of the organization's focus. Rather than view itself as a postal service, SP changed its mission statement to focus more on the benefits it provides customers, specifically to "deliver communications, parcels, and payments." Step 2 was a formal strategic market planning stage in which the organization was guided through a series of business plans while setting profit, customer satisfaction, and employee satisfaction goals. Steps 1 and 2 of this process correspond to phase I of the four-phase framework. SP then installed a sophisticated customer satisfaction and priority setting system to constantly monitor customers and identify areas in need of improvement.

Step 3 was the initiation of a radical total quality program of restructuring the organization to remove barriers to improving quality and satisfaction. Fully 67% of SP's costs were personnel related. A primary focus of the internal process improvement initiative was thus to decrease the total number of employees from more than 70,000 in 1990 to approximately 67,300 in 1991 and 62,100 in 1992. Finally, in step 4, SP underwent a legal transformation, in which Sweden Post Public Service Corporation became Posten AV, a limited company.

Of particular interest is SP's initiatives to be more customer oriented. This process involved all five of SP's specific business areas: (1) Post Girot, a cash-handling and payment transmission service (business and private sectors); (2) Sweden Post Banking and Counter Services; (3) Sweden Post Letters and Light Parcels (business and private sectors); (4) Sweden Post Parcels (business and private sectors); and (5) Sweden Post International, a new business designed to provide all services in-

---

[6]Claes Fornell, "A National Customer Satisfaction Barometer," *Journal of Marketing*, 56 (January 1992), 6–21.
[7]*Sweden Post Annual Report 1992*, p. 2.

volved in conveying letters and parcels worldwide (business and private sectors). Figure 2.2 presents SP's own customer satisfaction index, which is also on a 0–100 scale, for each of these major business areas in both business and private sectors where they apply.

Before we describe the system that produces these index numbers, we make several interesting observations from the figure. First, unlike other organizations whose goal is to have 100% satisfied customers, SP's goal for its businesses is an index score of 80 out of 100. This *does not* indicate that the organization is striving to underachieve. Rather, it indicates that SP has developed a sophisticated measurement tool as well as a good understanding of what is being measured. This will become clear when we describe customer satisfaction measurement later in the text.

A second observation is that SP is doing a better job satisfying customers in its financial service divisions than satisfying those in its letter and parcel delivery divisions. This provides general guidelines for where to focus further quality improvements. Finally, the organization is doing a better job satisfying its private sector customers than satisfying its business customer segments, in which Sweden Post is facing the most direct competition both domestically and abroad.

THE MEASUREMENT PROCESS

Particular care was taken in the development of SP's satisfaction measurement system. The system provides constant monitoring of past, present, and future customers. Using mail surveys (naturally), these customers evaluate SP businesses on multiple quality measures as well as multiple satisfaction measures. The survey results are used to measure the attributes and benefits that drive satisfaction and construct a customer satisfaction index (CSI). This CSI is modeled separately for each of the market segments using a multistage or systems approach. The first part of the system links the

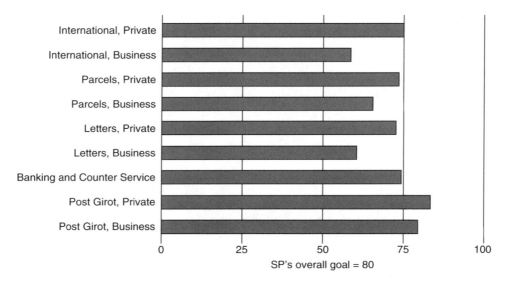

FIGURE 2.2   Sweden Post's 1992 CSI Scores

attribute items measured in the customer satisfaction questionnaire to the underlying benefits customers derive from the product or service. By explicitly modeling desired customer benefits, potential areas for quality improvement are viewed from the customers' perspective. As emphasized previously, viewing product and service quality through the "lens" of the customer is critically important. It is the key to avoiding a myopic focus on particular products, services, or organizational perspectives.

The second part of the system links desired customer benefits to the satisfaction index that is also modeled using multiple survey items. Statistical analysis is used to derive the impact that each of these benefits has on satisfaction. This enables SP to focus improvements in product or service quality where the impact is greatest. Recall that this is a major point of differentiation of a customer orientation from a process of total quality management (TQM). Whereas TQM more generally strives to improve inefficiencies in internal processes, customer satisfaction measurement systems focus a firm's efforts where the payoff is greatest. Finally, the model links the satisfaction index to critical performance measures within the firm, including customer complaint measures, customer loyalty, and financial returns. This enables the organization to see the bottom-line impact of efforts made to increase quality and subsequent satisfaction.

Modeling customer satisfaction in the center of this system of relationships is critically important. It enables us to see how the actions a firm takes to provide customers with desired product or service benefits translate into satisfaction. It also enables us to see the impact that this satisfaction has on key performance variables. While stand-alone measures of satisfaction may help from a benchmarking standpoint, they do not "close the loop" from actions to performance.

Figure 2.3 (page 22) illustrates more specifically a customer satisfaction measurement system for private-sector letter delivery services. Qualitative research is used initially to determine the nature of the "lens" through which customers view the product or service. This includes both the customer benefits that are salient to customers and the specific attributes of the service through which the benefits are manifested. At a benefit level, SP's customers want dependable delivery, "close" or accessible service, and a dynamic service that adapts to their specific problems. At the more concrete attribute level, "dependable" translates into service that is "on time, fast, and consistently so." Being "close" translates into SP having multiple locations that are close to customers and hours that make these locations accessible, and customers receiving personal or friendly service. Being "dynamic" translates into having service personnel who listen to customer problems and whose attitude is to be flexible and solve these problems.

A satisfaction survey asks customers to rate Sweden Post on the various performance attributes. Customers also provide several measures of their overall satisfaction, loyalty, and incidence of complaints. Statistical analysis is used to estimate the contribution or impact that each customer benefit has on satisfaction, the effect of satisfaction on key consequences (such as customer complaints and loyalty), and the importance of each concrete questionnaire item or attribute toward improving particular customer benefits.

A good satisfaction measurement system does more than simply measure customer satisfaction (phase II); it provides a customer-driven basis for setting priorities and making quality improvement decisions (phase III). Priorities are set using two

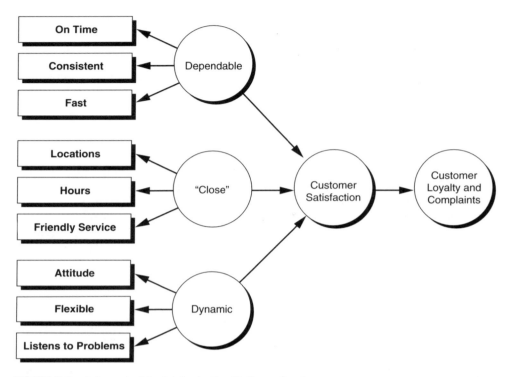

FIGURE 2.3 A Sample Model for Letter Delivery Service

important sources of information. The first is the impact the various benefits and attributes in the model have on satisfaction. The impact measures reflect whether improving a product or service on a particular benefit or attribute has any payoff in terms of increasing satisfaction. The second key source of information is the level of performance on particular benefits and attributes. That is, how is a product or service actually performing?

An increasingly popular way to combine this information is through a strategic satisfaction matrix (also called quadrant analysis). This matrix involves considering at least four possible scenarios. If a benefit or attribute has a relatively large impact on customer satisfaction and SP is performing well on that dimension, then it will be important to continue to excel. It is a competitive strength in the eyes of customers. If a benefit or attribute has an impact on satisfaction and SP is not performing well on that dimension, then it is a high priority for improvement. Improving the product or service on the benefit or attribute will have a tremendous payoff in the eyes of customers.

If, in contrast, a benefit or attribute does not have an impact on satisfaction and SP is performing well on that dimension, it is a low priority. Although SP may want to continue its current level of performance, it is less important to show any improvement. Finally, if a benefit or attribute does not have an impact on satisfaction and SP's performance is poor, it is again a low priority. This is not what the customer is looking for the product or service to provide and not an area where SP should invest scarce resources to improve satisfaction.

A phase III matrix for SP is illustrated in figure 2.4 using some attribute-level information. The highest-priority items for quality improvement in this example are in the high impact/weak performance category, where SP should increase the speed of its letter delivery, do a better job of listening to customer problems, and provide friendlier service. It is also important for SP to continue to play to its strength, which from the high impact/strong performance category includes consistent, on-time delivery. In the low impact/strong performance category there are two general possibilities: One is that, although the attributes are salient, performance is so strong that further improvements are not valued by customers; and the other is that the attributes are not as important to customers as previously thought, so less emphasis can be placed on providing convenient locations and hours. In the low impact/weak performance category, although SP does not perform particularly well on the general attitude of its service personnel or their flexibility in handling customer problems, customers do not look to SP to provide these services. The significance of a strategic satisfaction matrix is explored further in chapter 8.

Sweden Post: Lessons Learned

Implementation of this customer satisfaction measurement and management system over a period of years has enabled SP to increase its customer orientation and profitability. Viewed from the four phases of customer orientation framework, the key to phase I is that there was general buy-in that something had to be done. Top management recognized that customers are an asset that is built up over time, and that costs incurred to increase or maintain this asset are an investment in the future of the company. The keys to phases II and III are that SP implemented a solid customer satisfaction measurement system that enabled it to both benchmark its performance and identify specific product and service improvement priorities. Finally, in phase IV, SP was motivated and able to make needed product and service improvements.

Low Impact Strong Performance convenient locations convenient hours	High Impact Strong Performance on-time delivery consistent delivery
Low Impact Weak Performance general attitude flexibility	High Impact Weak Performance fast delivery listens to problems friendly service

FIGURE 2.4 Strategic Satisfaction Matrix for Sweden Post Letter Delivery Service

To continue to improve, Sweden Post must revisit its strategic objectives, make refinements to its measurement system, set new priorities, and implement those priorities. Problems have certainly been encountered along the way. For example, like many organizations, SP tried to support too many programs at the same time. The internal total quality program aimed at cutting costs was more or less competing for resources and attention with the customer satisfaction program aimed at increasing customer retention and revenues. After years of not-so-peaceful coexistence, the total quality program was abandoned.

An important consequence of having both programs operating simultaneously was that, even though customer satisfaction rose, employee satisfaction steadily declined as people were laid off in an effort to reduce operating costs. With continued economic woes in Sweden, employees are concerned about their job prospects. One solution is to expand SP's portfolio and use the displaced workers in new businesses. The important point is that the four-phase process is continuous and involves revisiting phase I in an ongoing process of assessing customer focus vis-à-vis other corporate goals.

Summary

Managers use customer-related information to make important market strategy decisions, monitor the effects of market programs, monitor customers' consumption experiences, and solve unanticipated problems. A customer orientation creates a proactive decision-making environment, in which strategy development and customer monitoring increase relative to "fire fighting." An examination of these decisions makes it clear that, while managers are interested in every possible customer, their decisions and information needs are more aggregate in nature. It also illustrates the challenges faced when translating the general goals of a customer orientation (from chapter 1) into a more action-based customer orientation process.

The four phases of customer orientation is a framework that helps organizations to identify where they stand in the process and what they must do to improve. In phase I, the firm must balance customer goals within an overall corporate and marketing strategy. Balanced performance measures are particularly useful for setting strategic priorities at this phase where customer, employee, owner, and other stakeholder satisfaction goals are simultaneously considered. Phase II requires the firm to invest in and implement a system that monitors customers as an asset. As is demonstrated in subsequent chapters, the satisfaction models and methods used in companies vary tremendously. It is important that firms take the time to evaluate this system carefully. In phase III, satisfaction survey data are analyzed and used as input to a priority setting process. Rather than sitting on surveys that cost hundreds of thousands of dollars to produce, managers need a system that helps them to turn data into information and turn information into market decisions. Finally, phase IV requires the firm to follow through and implement their priorities.

Rather than a scorecard of business performance, the four phases identify the challenges on the road to becoming customer oriented. The Sweden Post case uses this framework to demonstrate how a state-run monopoly can become customer oriented in a relatively short period of time. It also illustrates how problems may occur along the way—for example, when two major quality initiatives compete for limited resources. The downsizing and employee dissatisfaction that resulted, in the face of steadily increasing customer satisfaction, put the organization back at phase I in a continuous process of balancing multiple stakeholder needs.

Discussion Questions

1. Where is your company, division, or organization in the four phases of customer orientation? What are the particular hurdles that need to be overcome to reach the next phase?

2. Critically evaluate the tools or processes that your company, division, or organization currently uses in each of the four phases. What are the strengths and weaknesses of these tools or processes?

3. What makes the Sweden Post case similar to and different from the market conditions currently facing other organizations (including your own)?

CHAPTER # Understanding and Anticipating Customer Needs

Customer and market researchers continue to view their task in a limited light. Firms keep abreast of the "voice of the customer" using reactive surveys, clinics, and focus groups, which are themselves myopic. When this research is used as a substitute for rather than an input to market decisions, a narrow focus on customers' current preferences and "me-too" products results. This narrowness stems from marketing's inherent paradox. The essence of marketing remains relatively simple: Focus on customers and satisfy those customers more effectively and efficiently than others do. It is, at the same time, an inherently abstract, vague, broad, and elusive concept that requires a deep understanding of customer needs and values.

Understanding these root needs and values requires flexible and creative research efforts. It also requires decision makers who can integrate a vast array of market knowledge to identify both current unmet needs and future market opportunities. Primarily, it requires an open and proactive approach to customer research. Firms that succeed in uncovering root needs hold the key to developing fundamentally new markets with products and services capable of surprising and delighting the toughest customers.

The Goal of Customer Research

As described in chapter 1, marketing scholars have long emphasized the importance of being customer rather than product oriented as the essence of the marketing concept. Although the concept seems obvious and its value indisputable, it remains elusive and poorly understood. The key is to develop a thorough understanding of root customer needs and wants. Too often, however, this customer focus is translated mistakenly into customer slavery. Rather than providing input to market decisions, reactive customer research may drive these decisions. Firms may blindly provide products and services that customers say they want. Because customers are typically only familiar with current products and technologies, this slavery results in a plethora of me-too products.

One reaction to this customer slavery is to advocate "expeditionary" or imaginative marketing over formal market research.[1] Advocates urge firms to ignore the formal and potentially inaccurate research surrounding new product concepts and thus avoid the trap of being too close to customers. They argue instead that a better understanding of market knowledge is gained through fast-paced, low-cost, multiple product launches. Metaphorically, firms should concentrate on increasing their "times at bat" rather than their "hit rate."

Although the customer trap is very real, proactive market research does significantly increase a firm's hit rate. *The danger is not one of getting too close to customers; the real danger is not getting close enough.* Customer and market research must come to grips with the inherently abstract nature of root customer needs much in the way that firms themselves must understand their own skills or competencies. This research must also understand the links between concrete product and service attributes and more abstract customer needs and personal values.

Viewed in this light, the *primary* goal of customer research is to understand customers' root needs and values, how they are served by current products and services, and how they will likely be served by future products and services. This is the "attain customer information" goal from our discussion of a customer orientation in chapter 1 (see figure 1.1). This goal makes explicit that in the long run, it is far more important to understand the degree of excitement, value, achievement, or freedom that one's customers desire in their lives than it is to understand the remote control features they currently want in an entertainment system or the color of interior they currently prefer in an automobile. From a customer's perspective, a firm's current products and services are just one possible means to an end. Firms that focus on root needs and values can develop totally new markets with either new or existing technologies.

Reactive Research

Just as firms become focused on the products and services that they currently produce, deliver, or maintain, they become focused on research applications that obtain customers' reactions to existing products and services. Potentially flexible methods such as one-on-one interviews, focus groups, surveys, and clinics too often focus on existing, concrete products and services rather than their value-serving benefits and

---

[1]Gary Hamel and C. K. Prahalad, "Corporate Imagination and Expeditionary Marketing," *Harvard Business Review* (July–August 1990), 81–92.

consequences. Auto companies routinely use exterior and interior design, power train, feature, drive, and market acceptance clinics in their product development processes. This research formalism gives the impression of a customer orientation. Yet much of the research involves measuring customers' reactive responses to concrete prototypes or vehicles. Its value depends completely on whether the vehicle's product concept serves customers' root needs and values better than the competition does.

Take Ford's success with the Explorer. Ford's product development team saw the value of combining the sportiness and durability of a sport utility vehicle with the comfort and drive of a family sedan, thus filling the needs of a large target market better than competitors. Importantly, this product concept could not be defined at the concrete level of an existing vehicle type. Rather, it represented a hybrid. Honda's successful use of product concepts in developing the Accord is another case in point.[2] Although design and drive clinics provide important feedback and forecasts, their value is minimal unless built on a solid understanding of root customer needs.

The Kano model in figure 3.1 helps illustrate the limited scope of reactive customer research. The horizontal axis describes a product or service provider's degree of achievement, or ability to provide customers with various product attributes. The vertical axis describes the degree of customer satisfaction, from very dissatisfied to very satisfied, which results from providing these attributes. Kano describes three categorically different types of concrete attributes that influence customer satisfaction: (1) basic attributes that customers expect, but do not necessarily voice in traditional

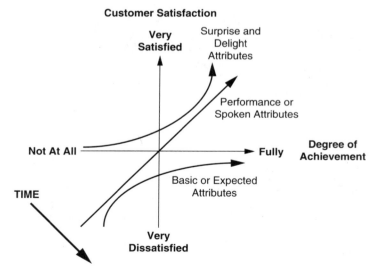

FIGURE 3.1 The Kano Model

---

[2]Kim B. Clark and Takahiro Fujimoto, "The Power of Product Integrity," *Harvard Business Review* (November–December 1990), 107–18.

research methods; (2) performance attributes which are typically voiced in interviews, focus groups, and surveys; and (3) excitement or surprise and delight attributes, which again are poorly elicited by traditional methods.[3]

Much of the customer research that firms conduct or commission focuses on but one of Kano's three classes of concrete attributes. Surveys, clinics, and focus groups in which customers react to current products and services elicit volumes of data on performance attributes (those product and service attributes on which incremental improvement is appreciated). However, they often fail to uncover attributes that customers expect from a product and that, if ignored, lead to significant dissatisfaction. They also provide limited insight into those unexpected or "excitement" attributes that surprise and delight customers. Customers expect a hotel room to be clean and adequately stocked; they appreciate a surplus of towels, a particularly firm mattress, or a larger than average bath; and they are surprised and delighted when they discover a whirlpool or a sauna in their room or receive complimentary cookies and milk. Reactive market research would likely uncover a preference for firmer mattresses or more comfortable chairs. Yet recognizing that a firmer mattress is only one possible means to an end, such as a "better night's sleep," opens the door to a broad range of satisfaction-producing product and service features.

The model also hypothesizes different functional forms for the three types of attributes. Providing basic attributes has the potential only to eliminate dissatisfaction, whereas not providing these attributes has a huge impact on dissatisfaction. Providing performance attributes increases satisfaction in a linear fashion, and surprise and delight attributes have the potential to increase satisfaction at an increasing rate. Over time, as Kano's model points out, surprise and delight attributes become performance attributes and performance attributes become basic attributes. For example, each generation of desktop computers (286, 386, 486, Pentium) seems "fast" when first introduced yet becomes commonplace and even "slow" as new generations arrive.

The point is that reactive research is limited in scope even when methods such as focus groups are used. This may seem surprising because focus groups, the "hot" research method of the 1980s, have become the standard solution to many customer research problems. Skilled focus group moderators can probe beyond concrete product attributes or features to uncover the benefits and consequences that drive customers' product attitudes and preferences. Yet even focus groups fail to delve deep enough. Participants only reveal those product benefits that they are comfortable discussing among a group of strangers. Proper protocol also limits the use of direct, probing questions. Asking participants very directly why they like this or that about a product or service increases the likelihood of canned, socially acceptable answers.[4] The face validity of focus groups is also a double-edged sword. Far too often focus group data are "cooked" or edited early on to support a particular view. Although valuable for a subset of product and service categories (especially those consumed in a social setting), focus groups are not a market research panacea.

---

[3]Noriaki Kano, Nobuhiku Seraku, Fumio Takahashi, and Shinichi Tsuji, "Attractive Quality and Must-Be Quality," presented at the 12th Annual Meeting of the Japan Society of Quality Control, B1–B21.

[4]Richard A. Krueger, *Focus Groups: A Practical Guide for Applied Research* (Newbury Park, CA: Sage Publications, 1988).

In contrast, traditional interviews and survey methods are finding new and important customer research applications. One-on-one or small group interviews, including laddering techniques (described subsequently), help researchers to understand important product and service attributes and the customer benefits they provide. In some contexts, interviews are even more effective and efficient at uncovering salient attributes than are focus groups.[5] Interviews have become a particularly important source of information when constructing customer satisfaction models such as the Sweden Post model described in chapter 2. Likewise, surveys have become increasingly important as a means of continuously monitoring customer satisfaction.

Nevertheless, the tendency toward myopic customer research remains a concern. This is not surprising considering that many research firms develop their own expertise and economies of scale using particular methods. Some firms specialize in telephone surveys, others in focus groups, and still others in satisfaction measurement systems that are sold as solutions to every manager's problems. This stems in part from the level of expertise required and the economies of scale involved. There are also significant organizational barriers to change. Research entrepreneurs with new methods or ideas for improving a firm's understanding of customer needs and satisfaction drivers are often ignored. Their proposals and ideas are critically evaluated and rejected by entrenched research departments or research firms with strong historical ties to an organization. The bottom line is that customer and market research itself often fails to be customer oriented.

Proactive Research and the Information Pyramid

A proactive approach to market research rests on two key principles: First, market research should include all available information pertinent to understanding customers. Second, market research is only for decision support; it is not a decision substitute. When market decisions become a slave to research output, marketing myopia results.

Take, for example, consumers' negative reactions to prototypes of unfamiliar products. After receiving a negative reaction to its prototypes for small televisions back in 1960, General Electric concluded that there was insufficient demand for the product. Sony, in contrast, looked beyond consumers' expressed preferences. Their market research focused on two important trends that would affect the pattern of television viewing: the increasing penetration of large televisions into American homes and the proliferation of television channels. This research suggested that a need would soon exist for a second, more portable television elsewhere in the home. "Though senior Sony executives have been heard to declare 'I don't believe in market research—it doesn't help us develop new products,' the company actually does make heavy use of market research—not the conventional kind, but an amalgam of fact-finding and social forecasting."[6] The Sony experience demonstrates that an understanding of root needs often requires a more open approach to market research.

---

[5]Abbie Griffin and John R. Hauser, "The Voice of the Customer," *Marketing Science*, 12 (1, 1993), 1–27.
[6]Christopher Lorenz, *The Design Dimension* (New York: Basil Blackwell, Inc., 1986), pp. 34–35.

The information pyramid, presented in figure 3.2, captures the range of customer information required to manage and develop products and services effectively. At the bottom or concrete level of the pyramid are the wide range of basic, performance, and surprise and delight attributes of a product or service described previously using the Kano model. At an intermediate level are the more abstract consequences and benefits that the concrete attributes provide the customer. Although reactive research uncovers some of these benefits, it only goes so far. At the top, the most abstract level, which is beyond the scope of reactive research, are the latent customer needs and personal values that provide the ultimate motivation for the purchase and consumption of products and services.

Two observations are critical here. First, the pyramid is based on parallel concepts of abstraction and translation. Abstraction is a process whereby concrete information is a means to an increasingly abstract end: Concrete product and service attributes are a means to provide customers with certain consequences and benefits that in turn serve their personal needs and values. Translation is a process of design that starts with customer values or benefits and translates them into concrete products and services. The point is that the relationships in the pyramid run in both directions, from the concrete to the abstract (for the customer) as well as from the abstract to the concrete (for the firm).

Second, when the concreteness–abstractness of important customer information is taken into account, the limitations of reactive research become even more obvious. Reactive research generally ignores the customer needs and personal values at the top of the pyramid. Moving beyond current product or service offerings to understand customers' root needs is the key to current as well as future business success. This is due to the relative permanence and stability of customer needs. Although customers' preferences for mint green shorts or turbo-charged engines may be fleeting, their preference for distinctive apparel or vehicle performance is more constant. Uncovering this information is not necessarily easy. It requires creative and flexible research techniques. Customers can tell you what they want; they can even project years down the road. But only if you observe rather than just look and ask the right questions.

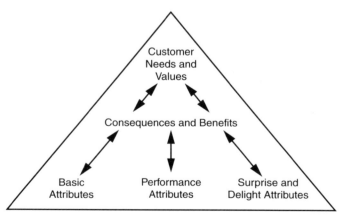

FIGURE 3.2 The Customer Information Pyramid

A proactive approach to customer research draws on a variety of creative and flexible research tools to understand as much of the customer information pyramid as possible. Many of these methods are either so basic that they are easily forgotten or are on the fringe of accepted industry or academic practice. Six alternative methods are illustrated here: (1) history and fundamental national factors, (2) unobtrusive measures, (3) value segmentation, (4) laddering, (5) comparing noncomparables, and (6) projective techniques. This list is far from exhaustive and is simply meant to illustrate some less common yet valuable approaches to customer research.

HISTORY AND CULTURAL FACTORS

History and culture provide important and often overlooked starting points for understanding root customer needs and values. When doing business in Japan, the importance of understanding Japanese history and culture has become a given. One such comparison was critically important to an American pharmaceutical firm seeking new markets in Japan (see table 3.1).[7] The comparison underscored an inherent emphasis on homogeneity, purity, and stability in traditional Japanese society.

TABLE 3.1   Japanese and U.S. National Fundamental Factors

	Nation	
Fundamental Factor	*Japan*	*United States*
Race	Homogeneous	Heterogeneous
Length of History (since first Constitution)	1387 Years	215 Years
Population Density	1.31 people per acre	0.011 people per acre
National Shock on Technological Level	Major Exposure to Western Culture in 1863/WWII	None
World War II	Loss (Bottom)	Victory (Glory)
Historic Life-Style	Static	Mobile
Historic Stability	Peaceful	Less Peaceful
Historic Food	Mainly Rice	Much Meat
Nation Formation	Naturally Formed	Won Independence
Language	Japanese	English
Religion	Shinto, Buddhism	Christian and Others

Source: Tsuda Hideo, *Japan 1990: An International Comparison* (Tokyo, Japan: Keizai Koho Center, October 31, 1989).

---

[7]Junya Ishamaya, *"For a Better Understanding of Japanese Market Requirements,"* term paper, University of Michigan Business School (1991).

This explains Japanese and U.S. customers' varying perceptions of, and preferences for, headache remedies. Whereas U.S. customers value a remedy tailored to their particular type of ache or pain, Japanese customers value purity and homogeneity in available remedies. One concrete implication is that Japanese customers prefer analgesic tablets in a bubble pack rather than a plastic bottle so that each tablet can be personally inspected for uniformity and purity.

The great strength of historical and cultural perspectives such as this is that they are an important place to start. The danger is that one must be careful not to overgeneralize from such comparisons. There are important market segment differences within a given culture that may be overlooked, and historical and cultural observations are a matter of perspective.

UNOBTRUSIVE OR NONREACTIVE MEASURES

Unobtrusive or nonreactive measures include a wide range of physical trace, archival, and observational information.[8] Because this information is collected in an unobtrusive fashion, or without the respondents being aware that they are being measured for a particular purpose, their responses are not a reaction to being measured. Using physical traces, such as the number of times a display or store shelf is cluttered, one can infer the popularity of specific products and areas in a retail establishment. Archival data includes everything from newspaper reports to sales records to census data. Creative use can also be made of both simple and contrived observations in market research settings. Doyle's classic character Sherlock Holmes personifies the art of observation. The passage in exhibit 3.1 (page 34) illustrates this when Dr. Watson decides to pay a visit to his old friend.

Another example of a simple observation is that of a music store owner who keeps track of all customer requests that involve selections of compact disks or cassettes not available in the store. It is just as important for the store owner to keep track of what could be sold that is not available as of what is available and being sold. Contrived observations include the use of confederates (employees from another part of an organization disguised as customers) and hidden recording devices. Although there are potentially serious ethical concerns over the use of contrived observation, it has become commonplace. One example is concealing microphones in automobiles to gauge customer reactions to interior design features. Another is the use of hidden cameras in vending machines to gauge nonverbal reactions to free samples for edible packaged goods.

VALUE SEGMENTATION

Another method whose use was limited in the past but is increasing quickly is value segmentation. This involves identifying clusters or segments of customers who have similar values, where values are defined as customers' enduring beliefs. These root values are identified using value surveys that make no mention of particular products

---

[8]Eugene J. Webb, Donald T. Campbell, Richard D. Schwartz, Lee Sechrest, and Janet Belew Grove, *Nonreactive Measures in the Social Sciences*, 2d Ed. (Boston: Houghton Mifflin Company, 1981).

EXHIBIT 3.1

The Unobtrusive Observations of Sherlock Holmes

One night—it was the 20th of March, 1888—I was returning from a journey to a patient (for I had now returned to civil practice), when my way led me through Baker Street. As I passed the well-remembered door, which must always be associated in my mind with my wooing, and with the dark incidents of the Study in Scarlet, I was seized with a keen desire to see Holmes again. . . . With hardly a word spoken, but with a kindly eye, he waved me to an armchair, threw across his case of cigars, and indicated a spirit case and a gasogene in the corner. Then he stood before the fire, and looked me over in his singular introspective fashion.

"Wedlock suits you," he remarked. "I think, Watson, that you have put on seven and a half pounds since I saw you."

"Seven," I answered.

"Indeed, I should have thought a little more. Just a trifle more, I fancy, Watson. And in practice again, I observe. You did not tell me that you intended to go into harness."

"Then how did you know?"

"I see it, I deduce it. How do I know that you have been getting yourself very wet lately, and that you have a most clumsy and careless servant girl?"

"My dear Holmes," said I, "this is too much. You would certainly have been burned, had you lived a few centuries ago. It is true that I had a country walk on Thursday and came home in a dreadful mess; but, as I have changed my clothes, I can't imagine how you deduce it. As to Mary Jane, she is incorrigible, and my wife has given her notice; but there again I fail to see how you work it out."

He chuckled to himself and rubbed his long nervous hands together.

"It is simplicity itself," said he; "my eyes tell me that on the inside of your left shoe, just where the fire-light strikes it, the leather is scored by six almost parallel cuts. Obviously they have been caused by someone who has very carelessly scraped round the edges of the sole in order to remove crusted mud from it. Hence, you see, my double deduction that you had been out in vile weather, and that you had a particularly malignant boot-slitting specimen of the London slavey. As to your practice, if a gentleman walks into my rooms smelling of iodoform, with a black mark of nitrate of silver upon his ring fore-finger, and a bulge on the side of his top-hat to show where he has secreted his stethoscope, I must be dull indeed, if I do not pronounce him to be an active member of the medical profession."

Source: Arthur Conan Doyle, *The Adventures of Sherlock Holmes: A Scandal in Bohemia* (originally published in *The Strand* between July 1891 and December 1892).

or services. Early attempts at value segmentation used surveys based on Maslow's need hierarchy or Rokeach's instrumental and terminal values. The more recent list of values (LOV) survey, developed at the University of Michigan's Survey Research Center, has participants rank order and/or rate the importance of nine fundamental values: self-respect, security, warm relationships with others, sense of accomplishment, self-fulfillment, sense of belonging, being well respected, fun and enjoyment in life, and excitement (see table 3.2).[9] Participants can then be segmented or clustered into groups on the basis of the homogeneity of their value rankings.

Ranking these values requires some soul searching on the part of respondents. The result, however, is an important glimpse into the future. Unlike concrete product and service preferences, values are by their nature enduring customer beliefs. Although value trends and life-cycle changes must be considered, their relative stability gives us important insights into customers' future preferences and provides a basis for matching emerging technologies and core competencies to segment needs.

To illustrate, the results of a LOV survey of business executives is presented in table 3.3 (page 36). Analysis of the executives' responses revealed two primary segments. Both segments ranked self-respect highly. Segment 1 ranked warm relationships with others and fun and enjoyment in life higher than did segment 2. In contrast, segment 2 ranked security, sense of accomplishment, and being well respected as relatively more important. Excitement and sense of belonging were low on both lists. The implications are considerable. Whether developing executive education sem-

---

TABLE 3.2 Sample List of Values Survey

Following is a list of nine personal values in random order. These values affect our sense of well-being and, indirectly, our purchase and consumption of various products and services. Please rank the values from 1 to 9, where 1 represents the value that is most important to you, 2 represents the value that is next more important to you, and so on. Indicate your response in the space to the right of the value.

Value	*Rank*
Self-Respect	_____
Security	_____
Warm Relationships With Others	_____
Sense of Accomplishment	_____
Self-Fulfillment	_____
Sense of Belonging	_____
Being Well Respected	_____
Fun and Enjoyment in Life	_____
Excitement	_____

---

[9]Lynn R. Kahle, Sharon E. Beatty, and Pamela Homer, "Alternative Measurement Approaches to Consumer Values: The List of Values (LOV) and Values and Life Style (VALS)," *Journal of Consumer Research*, 13 (December 1986), 405–9.

TABLE 3.3 LOV Survey of Business Executives

	Average Value Ranking (1 = Most Important)	
Value	*Segment 1*	*Segment 2*
Self-Respect	1.6	2.8
Security	6.8	4.0
Warm Relationships with Others	3.7	7.4
Sense of Accomplishment	4.3	2.8
Self-Fulfillment	3.8	3.4
Sense of Belonging	7.3	7.2
Being Well Respected	6.3	3.7
Fun and Enjoyment in Life	4.2	6.5
Excitement	6.5	7.2

inars, communications systems, or luxury automobiles, understanding these customers' values provides insight into the products and services these customers will ultimately prefer. Executives that place a greater value on warm relationships with others than on a sense of accomplishment, for example, will likely prefer future communication technologies that facilitate "accessibility" and relationship building.

Value surveys and segmentation provide a direct look at the top of the customer information pyramid, where core market segment differences exist. Another advantage of value segmentation is that it consolidates a firm's segmentation strategy. Firms such as General Electric, 3M, and Dow Chemical compete in hundreds of product market segments as defined by the particular product category, type, model, part, or material sold. Moving to a value segmentation scheme consolidates the number of necessary segments to a handful of fundamentally different customer needs. This streamlines the research process and creates synergy across applications. For example, it may become clear that an adhesive compound used in an agricultural setting provides a particular benefit, such as weather resistance, that is highly valued by the same core value segment in other industrial or consumer applications, such as construction or sporting goods.

LADDERING

Value ladders, or means–end chains, are another valuable, under-utilized, and easy-to-learn research tool.[10] This "laddering" is the demand side equivalent to "the five whys" system of production problem solving. In lean production firms workers are taught to systematically trace problems back to their root causes by continuously ask-

---

[10]See Thomas J. Reynolds and Jonathan Gutman, "Laddering Theory, Method, Analysis, and Interpretation," *Journal of Advertising Research*, 28 (1, 1988), 11–31. For further examples see Jacob Jacoby and Jerry Olson, *Perceived Quality of Products, Services and Stores* (Lexington, MA: Lexington Books, 1985).

ing why a problem occurs.[11] On the consumption side, customers can provide similar insight into product consequences and root customer values.

The researcher begins with some concrete product or service attributes and asks customers, in a progressive fashion, what the consequences of each attribute are and what needs or values each consequence serves. The goal is to delve far beyond existing product specifications to their consequences and, ultimately, to root values. Unlike focus groups, these means–end chains or ladders are constructed one respondent at a time and then analyzed and aggregated. Although not as "efficient" in a data collection sense as interviews or focus groups are, uncovering customers' root needs and values is the method's primary goal; it is not a by-product.

A simplified ladder for mountain bikes in figure 3.3 illustrates the value of the technique. Mountain bikers, like many athletes, rank sense of accomplishment highly.

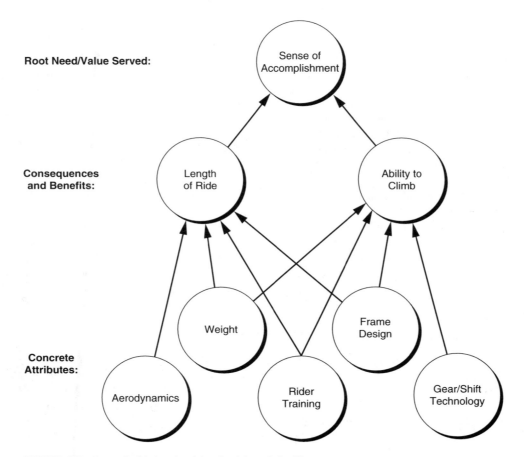

FIGURE 3.3 Sample Value Ladder for Mountain Bikes

---

[11]James P. Womack, Daniel T. Jones, and Daniel Roos, *The Machine that Changed the World* (New York: Harper Perennial Press, 1991).

Mountain bikes and mountain biking have many concrete attributes, including bike weight, aerodynamics, frame design, gear/shift technology, and rider training. When asked to indicate the primary consequences of these attributes, riders say that they affect their ability to climb hills and take long rides. When asked why they like to climb hills or take long rides, they express the feelings of personal accomplishment and satisfaction they bring. Interestingly, the ladder reveals that rider training has a major effect on both intermediate consequences. This suggests that bicycle manufacturers should consider training programs as an integral part of their product offerings.

COMPARING NONCOMPARABLES

Having customers "compare noncomparables" is another simple though nontraditional way to gain important insights into root needs and values. It helps managers understand not just high-level benefits and customer values but also those concrete attributes that are either basic or capable of exciting customers. Whereas managers are more comfortable viewing the market from within a particular category, this method forces managers to explore the space that exists between category boundaries.

Customer input into the nature of this space is critical. When asked to compare brands from the same category, or apples and apples, customers concentrate on concrete attributes and their relative importance. When asked to compare apples and oranges, customers freely use abstract benefits and personal values as choice criteria and even point out salient concrete attributes that are often ignored or taken for granted. For example, in a study conducted in the early 1980s, respondents were asked to compare and choose among products from completely different product categories.[12] When they compared a television with a bicycle, people remarked that it was easier to use the television with friends and family. As an entertainment option, an individual bicycle has certain social use limitations not shared by a television. It is not surprising that markets subsequently developed for state-of-the art tandem racing and mountain bicycles as well as improved children's seats and trailers. When asked to compare a motorcycle with an auto, people remarked that while the motorcycle is less "convenient," riding one provides far more "freedom." At the level of root customer values, a new product or technology that provides this freedom with the day-to-day convenience of an auto should find a slew of eager buyers.

PROJECTIVE TECHNIQUES

Projective techniques have customers project their feelings, attitudes, or preferences into a third party, through an alternative medium, or forward in time. Haire's classic study illustrates the third-party technique using a "shopping list" format.[13] When instant coffee was having problems in the introductory stage of its life cycle, researchers asked customers directly about the problem. A typical response was that they did not like the flavor. Haire then asked a group of customers indirectly to read a shopping

---

[12]Michael D. Johnson, "Consumer Choice Strategies for Comparing Noncomparable Alternatives," *Journal of Consumer Research*, 11 (December 1984), 741–53.

[13]Mason Haire, "Projective Techniques in Marketing Research," *Journal of Marketing*, 14 (April 1950), 649–56.

list and describe the shopper using only the list. Two alternative lists were presented to customers that were exactly the same except that one list contained Nescafé instant coffee and the other contained Maxwell House drip ground coffee. The Nescafé shopper was more likely to be described as a lazy individual who was unable to plan household purchases. This uncovered some important social norms that existed for instant coffee buyers, which traditional research methods would not otherwise elicit.

Of increasing popularity is the use of projective techniques that move customers forward in time to, for example, evaluate customer preferences for products that are not yet available. Dubbed "information acceleration," this projection involves an extensive interview procedure whereby customers are given information, from news reports to lifestyle information, as to what their world will be like in the future.[14] Customers are then asked questions about their preferences and attitudes for a future product such as an electric vehicle or a videophone. This technique is also a useful source of forecasts for existing product categories. In one such case, five-year forecasts of beverage consumption (beer versus soft drinks versus coffee and so on) were obtained by having customers describe their future daily purchase and consumption patterns *after* they had been interviewed and instructed to consider just how their environments, life and family situations, and careers will likely change. This relatively simple and cost-effective interview procedure resulted in estimates that were very consistent with industry expert projections.[15]

Summary

The primary goal of customer research is to understand customer needs and wants and their relationship to both current and future products and services. Yet traditional customer research focuses disproportionately on customers' reactions to existing concrete products and prototypes. The result is a research process that is potentially myopic and capable only of revealing current preferences rather than future market opportunities. Although customers cannot tell one exactly what products or services they will prefer months or years from now, a more proactive approach to customer research will point one in the right direction.

The customer information pyramid illustrates the scope of important customer information and points out the limitations of reactive research methods. Although traditional focus groups, interviews, and surveys provide valuable information for market decisions, it is important to expand one's arsenal of customer research methods and tools to capture all the important information in the pyramid. Six alternative methods or sources of data include history and cultural factors, unobtrusive measures, value segmentation, laddering or means–end chains, comparing noncomparables, and projective techniques.

---

[14]Glen L. Urban, "Information Acceleration and Pre-Production in New Product Forecasting of Buyer Durables" (presented at the American Marketing Association's 1992 Advanced Research Techniques Forum, Incline Village, NV).

[15]Junius Brown, Glen Janssens, Dean Hoglund, Patrick Vaughn, and Brian Young "*Predicting Beverage Consumption for 1995*," term paper, University of Michigan Business School (1990).

History and cultural factors are a good place to start understanding market segment differences. Unobtrusive measures tap the wealth of information that already exists in our environment but often goes ignored, including archival data, physical traces, and simple observations. Value segmentation goes right to the top of the customer information pyramid by having people evaluate the importance of different personal values in their lives. Laddering helps researchers to understand connections within the pyramid from concrete attributes to intermediate level consequences and benefits to abstract customer needs and values. Comparing noncomparables explores the possibilities between existing product and service categories by having people make choices between or among alternatives from different categories. Projective techniques have people project their own feelings and inhibitions into a third party, for example, through a "shopping list" study or forward in time through "information acceleration."

The main point is that understanding and anticipating customer needs is not a guessing game, nor is it a process of trial and error. Rather, it is proactive and involves using a variety of research information as input to market decisions. It entails adopting a broad definition of research that encompasses seemingly unorthodox as well as traditional methods. Customers can tell you the root of what they want. They can even provide a glimpse of the future, but only if one adopts an open and creative approach to research. Firms that fail in this regard will find themselves following the leader and building products that are perpetually out of date rather than creating new markets.

Discussion Questions

1. Discuss the pros and cons of the various research methods and sources of customer information described here. What are the primary strengths and weaknesses of each method or information source?

2. What customer information problem or problems are you currently facing in your firm, division, or organization? Which of the research methods and sources of customer information discussed here might help you solve these problems and why?

PART II: THE PURCHASE AND CONSUMPTION EXPERIENCE

CHAPTER 4

The Customer Experience Model

In part 1 we examine the goals of a customer orientation, the customer-related decisions that managers make, and the information used in these decisions. An understanding of customers and customer behavior must, however, delve much deeper. In part 2 we take a rigorous look at customers through both new and established paradigms, theories, models, concepts, and empirical findings. We begin by examining the important processes of customer acquisition and retention and use them to develop a parsimonious model of customer behavior called the *customer experience model.* The emphasis throughout this section is to identify research that is rigorous yet practical. As the demands of business executives continue to increase, a research perspective is an essential means to comprehend our rapidly changing economic world.

Customer Acquisition and Retention

The most relevant areas of customer behavior for managers are the processes of customer acquisition and retention. Without customers a business organization has no inherent value. These customers are of two general types: new and existing customers. Customer acquisition includes the attraction of new (or former) customers away from competitors as well as the attraction of customers into a market. Customer retention is primarily a process of satisfying customers, creating customer loyalty, and turning that loyalty into repeat purchases. This ranges from the repeat buying of a particular brand of soup to purchasing another financial investment from the same broker or brokerage house to signing another contract with an industrial parts supplier or service vendor.

There is an important distinction between loyalty and retention. Although loyalty typically leads to retention, it is not the same thing. Customer loyalty is a predisposition toward purchasing and/or using a particular product, manufacturer, or service provider again. This can be reflected by a high perceived likelihood of repurchase or a stated willingness to pay a higher price. As detailed at the end of this chapter, however, when the time comes to make an actual repurchase decision, a variety of factors can prevent loyal customers from being retained.

The distinction between acquiring new customers and retaining old customers lies at the heart of the distinction between offensive and defensive strategy in figure 4.1.[1] Almost all firms employ some combination of an offensive strategy for acquiring customers and a defensive strategy for retaining customers. Offensive marketing focuses on increasing market size and/or share where customers enter a market or switch from a competitor to buy a firm's brand. Defensive marketing involves reducing customer exit or switching. A firm can increase customer retention, or decrease turnover, in two ways: increase customer satisfaction to build loyalty and create a predisposition toward retention, and increase switching barriers, making it difficult to purchase or use another product or service. Examples of switching barriers include frequent flyer programs, a "cash toward purchase" credit card program, or tie-in products such as a particular brand of software that only functions properly in that same brand's hardware.

Making investments in customer satisfaction to increase customer retention depends critically on the adoption of a long-run rather than short-run perspective. Managers who take a short-run view of their costs, revenues, and profits have a difficult time committing resources to increase customer satisfaction. They look for relationships between, for example, satisfaction and revenues or profits that simply do not exist in the short run. Firms that take a long-run perspective look on customer satisfaction as an investment in an asset.

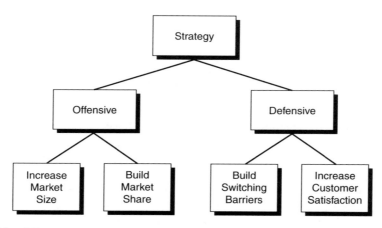

FIGURE 4.1 Offensive and Defensive Strategy

[1]Claes Fornell, "A National Customer Satisfaction Barometer: The Swedish Experience," *Journal of Marketing*, 56 (January 1992), 6–21.

SATISFACTION, RETENTION, AND PROFITS

The asset value of customer satisfaction and retention is a direct result of the economics of acquisition and retention. Research by Reichheld and his associates at Bain & Company details the economic impact of customer retention on a firm.[2] They found that the profitability of customer retention is attributable to two economically related dimensions of retention. The first is the effect of retention on different sources of customer-related costs and revenues. Customer costs tend to be "front-loaded," or to occur early in a firm's relationship with a customer, whereas profits tend to be "back-loaded," or to accrue only after a customer is retained for some time. The second dimension is the compounding effect of customer retention over time.

Regarding the first dimension, Reichheld describes six key factors that affect overall costs, revenues, and resulting cash flows over time:

1. *Acquisition costs.* The marketing costs of customer acquisition, which include incentive programs, prospecting costs, and the creation of internal customer accounts and records, occur early in a firm's relationship with a customer. Low response rates to direct mail programs, for example, create huge marketing expenditures in the credit card industry.

2. *Base revenues.* Each time period in which a customer is retained, a firm receives a base revenue from that customer. This revenue stream is naturally more even for nondurable products and services than for major durables.

3. *Revenue growth.* Revenue growth is the increase in revenues from an individual customer that occurs over time. This increase comes from two sources: cross-selling additional products or services and an increase in purchase volume. Given continued customer satisfaction with an insurance provider, for example, the different types of insurance purchased from that provider will tend to grow over time. Customers will not only insure their house but come to insure their automobile, life, and family with the same company. Revenue also grows through an increase in the volume of a product or service purchased. Annual revenues per customer in the auto service industry, for example, triple over the first five years a customer is retained.[3]

4. *Operating costs.* At the same time, operating costs tend to decrease as the repurchase cycle with a customer continues. Product and service providers come to know a customer and learn, for example, what problems tend to occur on the customer's car, how they like their meals prepared in a restaurant, how they like to be treated in a hotel, or even when, where, and how they like parts delivered to their plant.

5. *Customer referrals.* Customer referrals also tend to grow the longer a customer is retained. The word of mouth generated from a positive purchase and consumption experience generates additional revenues from friends and family.

6. *Price premiums.* Existing customers tend to pay a price premium compared with new customers because they are less likely to take advantage of price discounts such as through a coupon, loss leader, or "bonus miles" program.

---

[2]Frederick F. Reichheld, *The Loyalty Effect: The Hidden Force Behind Growth, Profits, and Lasting Value* (Boston: Harvard Business School Press, 1996).
[3]Reichheld (1996), p. 43.

The overall result is a per-customer profit stream that increases over time. Figure 4.2 illustrates this income stream from Reichheld's research on credit card providers. Initially card companies lose $80 per customer in acquisition costs. Only after the customer has been retained for a few years is this loss recouped, and only after the customer has been retained for several years is the customer highly profitable. The longer the customer is retained, the more profit the customer generates. Reichheld finds a similar profit pattern for other industries including automobile insurance, automobile service, industrial distribution, industrial laundry services, and life insurance.

The second economically related dimension of retention is the compounding of retention over time. This effect is less intuitive and best understood by an example. Consider a customer whose probability of retention in a given year is 0.75. The probability that this customer will defect in a given year is then 0.25. On average, a company will retain this customer for 4 years (1/defect rate). As the probability of retention grows to 0.80, the average customer tenure grows to 5 years. As the probability of retention grows to 0.85, the average customer tenure grows to almost 7 years. If the retention rate grows to 0.95, the average customer tenure reaches 20 years. Increases in customer retention thus compound to increase average customer tenure at an *increasing* rate. As retention rates increase, even small increments in a firm's customer retention rate have a huge impact on the average length of customer tenure and resulting revenue streams. This relationship is illustrated in figure 4.3.

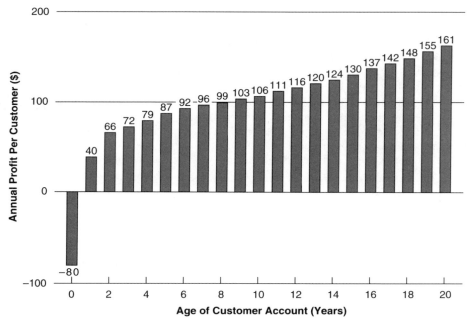

FIGURE 4.2   Customer Life-cycle Profits in the Credit Card Industry (from Reichheld 1996)

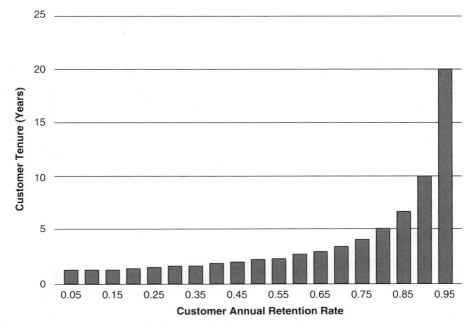

FIGURE 4.3 The Compounding Effect of Customer Retention

The combination of changing customer costs and revenues over time and the compounding of customer retention over time explain why it is so profitable to satisfy and retain customers. Recent research in both Sweden and the United States suggests that the profits from customer satisfaction and retention are not unique to the particular industries that Reichheld studied. Some of this research uses data from the Swedish Customer Satisfaction Barometer (SCSB) introduced in chapter 2. Analysis of the 77 firms in this database that report profits (from automobile and personal computer manufacturers to banks and department stores) shows that a 1-point increase in customer satisfaction per year (on a 0 to 100 scale) over a five-year period has a net present value of $7.48 million.[4] This represents 11.5 percent of the firms' current return on investment (ROI). These findings are conservative in that only a limited time period was studied and the asset value of the companies was relatively small (approximately $600 million per firm).

Studies using data from the American Customer Satisfaction Index (ACSI) also support the link between customer satisfaction and both accounting profits and shareholder value for major U.S. firms (see chapter 9 for details on the Index).[5] As in Swe-

---

[4]Eugene W. Anderson, Claes Fornell, and Donald R. Lehmann, "Customer Satisfaction, Market Share, and Profitability: Findings from Sweden," *Journal of Marketing*, 58 (July 1994), 53–66.

[5]See Claes Fornell, Michael D. Johnson, Eugene Anderson, Jaesung Cha, and Barbara Everitt Bryant, "The American Customer Satisfaction Index: Nature, Purpose, and Findings," *Journal of Marketing*, 60 (October 1996), 7–18.

den, the ACSI has a positive effect on ROI. In terms of market value, a 1-unit increase in the ACSI (on a 0- to 100-unit scale) is associated with a $654 million increase on average in the market value of equity above the accounting book value of assets and liabilities. Stock trading strategies based on either the SCSB or the ACSI have also delivered portfolio returns well above market returns.

The bottom line is that it is costly to rely on customer acquisition while customer retention is profitable. However, although the economics of customer retention has created a strategic shift from offense to defense, this does not imply that offensive marketing is unimportant. Nor does it imply that defensive marketing is myopic. In highly competitive markets where technology is changing rapidly, customer satisfaction and retention requires that companies become new product, service, and technology leaders that reinvent themselves constantly. Again, a favorable purchase and consumption experience only predisposes a customer to buy from a firm again. It guarantees nothing.

Several factors have intensified the shift from offense to defense. One is the more mature nature of many markets, especially the market economy in the United States. As markets have become more mature, there are fewer truly new customers to be had. Another related factor is the global increase in competition, which limits producers' ability to create niche markets or monopolies through segmentation or differentiation strategies. Whether it is pasta in a supermarket or minivans in a motor mall, customers have many high-quality choices in most market segments and subsegments. This increase in attractive choice alternatives has decreased barriers to customers switching and, as a result, increased the relative importance of customer satisfaction. One of the factors contributing to the global increase in competition is the lowering of trade barriers, which again increases customer choice, reduces switching barriers, and increases the importance of customer satisfaction in a defensive strategy.

The Customer Experience Model

The preceding discussion highlights two customer processes or experiences that must be thoroughly understood in an overall strategy of customer orientation: the set of perception, judgment, and choice processes involved in a purchase or repurchase decision; and the consumption experience itself, the customer's satisfaction with this experience, and the predispositions and behaviors that result.

The customer experience model in figure 4.4 provides a straightforward integration of these purchase and consumption processes using four key components: (1) the primarily psychological component of customer information processing and choice, (2) the economic and psychological component of product or service consumption and its evaluation, (3) the customer knowledge component, and (4) the market information component.

The information processing and consumption/satisfaction components together capture the important elements of a repurchase cycle. The information processing component is useful in describing both the purchase and repurchase processes, and the consumption/satisfaction component bridges the gap between purchase and repurchase. Thus the relationship between these components is recursive or circular.

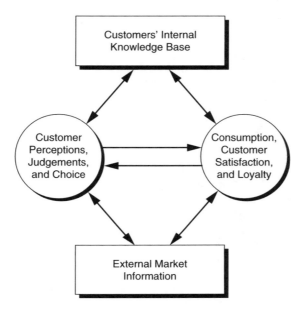

FIGURE 4.4 The Customer Experience Model

The market information and internal knowledge components explain changes in behavior as the purchase and consumption experience is repeated over time. With regard to customers' internal knowledge base, individuals perceive, learn, and store information or gain knowledge throughout the purchase and consumption cycle. This knowledge and stored information, in turn, affects what customers perceive and how they make decisions. It likewise affects how they consume and evaluate their consumption experience. Notice that the relationships from the repurchase cycle components to customer knowledge are bidirectional. This conveys the continuous interaction that occurs between customer knowledge and the elements of the repurchase cycle.

Customers also interact with external market information throughout a purchase, consumption, and repurchase cycle. As the market environment changes, new information is constantly being integrated with existing information when making purchase or repurchase decisions. Marketplace information also interacts with the consumption/satisfaction stage. Customers utilize available guidelines or warning labels on how to use or consume a product or service (such as how to use building materials or hazardous chemicals or how to operate an entertainment device) and word of mouth regarding consumption tips or warnings (such as what to order or not order in a restaurant).

The interaction in this case is a form of give and take. What customers take from the marketplace in terms of information they also give back, whether it is the prices they pay, the performance they receive, or the consumption tips they provide. As with the knowledge component, the relationships between the market information component and the repurchase cycle components are bidirectional, in that customers simultaneously draw upon and contribute to the vast amount of information available in the marketplace.

Customers' internal knowledge base grows in importance relative to external market information as the purchase and consumption cycle is repeated and customer experience grows. This is a fundamental premise of the Howard model of consumer behavior described in chapter 7.

DISNEY'S CUSTOMER ORBIT

The customer experience model provides a basis for constructing more detailed models of the purchase–consumption–repurchase cycle for individual products or services. One example is Walt Disney World's (WDW) model of the customer "orbit" depicted in figure 4.5. This model is used by managers and employees at WDW's Orlando, Florida resorts and attractions to understand the coproduction that occurs between customers and employees, improve customers' purchase and consumption experiences, and identify opportunities for repurchase.[6]

The purchase process begins when customers are initially attracted, such as through advertising or word of mouth, to visit a WDW resort or park. When responding to customer inquiries, employees must be able to explain to customers with

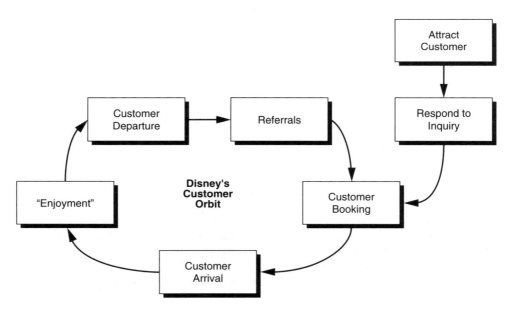

FIGURE 4.5 The Purchase–Consumption–Repurchase Cycle at Walt Disney World

---

[6]The materials for this section are based on two presentations: "Delivering Guest Satisfaction" by Terry Wick and "Operationalizing the Voice of the Customer in Disney's Educational Strategies" by Valerie Oberle, delivered at the American Marketing Association's Fifth Congress on Customer Satisfaction, Orlando, Florida, May 1995.

Repurchase Behavior

		Repeat	Switch
High		Satisfied Repeaters	Satisfied Switchers
Customer Satisfaction			
Low		Dissatisfied Repeaters	Dissatisfied Switchers

FIGURE 4.6 Four Customer Types

children in particular age groups which facilities would be best for their particular needs. This decision process and problem-solving stage culminates in a customer booking. The consumption process begins on arrival. Here WDW must ensure that systems are in place to make customers' arrival as friendly, smooth, and pleasant as possible so that their vacations start off on the right foot.

The heart of the consumption experience is the *enjoyment* of the characters, resorts, parks, and shops in WDW. Satisfaction measurement systems are used to constantly monitor and improve this experience. As with arrival, customer departure should be as friendly, smooth, and pleasant as possible. The orbit then explicitly recognizes the powerful source of market information provided by satisfied customers. The orbit leads to positive referrals, in which 85 percent of customers who visit would recommend WDW to others. Finally, the orbit recognizes the critical importance of retention through the booking of customers for repeat visits. To increase opportunities to continue the repurchase cycle, WDW now actively markets not only repeat vacation visits but family reunions, weddings, and conferences. Finally, having been through the experience already, customers themselves have stored knowledge to use when booking another visit or making the most of their next WDW experience.

Four Customer Types

The customer experience model separates the consumption process from the purchase process to highlight the distinction between customer satisfaction and retention. Though strongly related, their differences are important to understand. The four categorically different types of customers described in figure 4.6 further illustrate this distinction. These customer types vary on two dimensions: the customer's satisfaction with his or her experience in the consumption stage of the model and his or her decision to repeat or switch to an alternative product, service, or brand in the information processing and choice stage. Notice that all four components of the customer experience model described previously help explain these different categories of behavior.

In the case of the satisfied repeaters, customers are satisfied with their purchase and consumption experience and continue to buy the same brand. Take the example of a customer who always buys a particular brand and flavor of soft drink (Coke or Pepsi) or visits a particular fast-food outlet (Wendy's or McDonald's). From a market information standpoint, this customer is probably well aware of the wide variety of alternatives that exist and has tried many of them in the past. He or she goes through the purchase, consumption, and repurchase cycle itself relatively often if not daily. Through this process he or she has learned which soft drink or lunch alternative he or she prefers most. Customer experience and resulting knowledge are high and the purchase process has become habitual. Many customers in this situation have some degree of choice and have found the alternative or alternatives that best fit their needs.

In the case of the satisfied switchers, customers may again be satisfied with their purchase and consumption experience and be "loyal" or positively predisposed toward the brand they are currently using—yet they end up switching to a competitor when a repurchase decision occurs. Take the example of an automobile customer who loves his Audi. Similar to the case of the satisfied repeaters, this customer was aware of a wide range of market options, did his homework, and leased a vehicle with which he is satisfied. When it comes time to lease (or purchase) another vehicle, however, other factors may come into play. Variety seeking or changes in technology, for example, may be important to someone seeking a different driving experience. Competitors may also offer significant pricing or financing incentives that dramatically increase the perceived value of alternative makes and models. These factors may result in the Audi customer becoming a Lexus, Saab, or Cadillac customer in spite of a high degree of satisfaction and stated loyalty.

In the case of dissatisfied repeaters, a very different market environment likely exists. Although customers feel significant dissatisfaction with a product or service, they continue to repurchase and consume it. Perhaps the most common situation of this sort is when customer choice is limited or restricted. Take the example of a public or government agency that offers a single service option (such as letter delivery service, police services, tax collection) to a very heterogeneous population of customers. Because a monopoly exists, the agency has less incentive to increase satisfaction. Although customers understand that the service is not tailored to their specific needs, they have no other choice. Notice that for both satisfied switchers and dissatisfied repeaters, we cannot infer customer satisfaction and loyalty from their purchase behavior. As a result, satisfaction, loyalty, and retention must be measured separately to understand just how closely they are related.

Finally, in the case of the dissatisfied switchers, customers are dissatisfied with the product or service previously used and switch to an alternative or competitor. Consider here the case of a new resident in a community who is unfamiliar with the local restaurant options. From a market information standpoint, she has a variety of options available and an abundance of advertising and word of mouth experiences and recommendations. Market options and information are high, and personal knowledge and experience are low. The customer may be in a "trial-and-error" period in which, as new restaurants are explored, there is a significant chance that she will be dissatisfied and not go back. As she explores the market options and learns which restaurants she prefers, the dissatisfied switcher eventually becomes a satisfied repeater.

From our previous discussion we know that satisfaction and subsequent customer retention are highly profitable. Thus most customers fall in the Satisfied Repeater/Dissatisfied Switcher categories. As mentioned, however, it is important to understand those cases in which customer satisfaction and retention are not positively related in order to effectively manage customer retention. Another factor that may moderate the relationship between satisfaction and retention is customer involvement in the product, service, usage context, or purchase situation. If customers do not feel that the benefits exceed the costs of purchasing and learning how to consume a new product or service, then dissatisfied repeaters may again result.

Summary

The most relevant areas of customer behavior for managers are the processes of customer acquisition and retention. Obtaining, satisfying, and keeping customers is the key to long-run financial performance. Two important dimensions contribute to this economic effect: changes in costs and revenues as customers are retained and the compounding effect of retention over time. Satisfying and retaining customers helps firms to recoup their customer acquisition costs, grow their revenues, reduce operating costs, generate referrals, and enjoy price premiums. Equal increments in customer retention, meanwhile, increase a customer's tenure at an increasing rate.

The customer experience model provides a parsimonious model of customer behavior through the evolution of a purchase–consumption–repurchase cycle. The model distinguishes between decision processes and consumption experiences. It also distinguishes between external market information, which is essential early in a customer's learning process, and internal information or stored knowledge, which a customer comes to rely on as his or her experience grows. Subsequent chapters in this section detail the various components of this model. In chapter 5 we take up the economic and market information elements of the model; chapters 6 and 7 explore the information processing and knowledge development components. Chapters 8 and 9 then detail the important role that customer satisfaction plays in creating a customer-oriented organization at both micro and macro levels.

Discussion Questions

1. A major limitation of existing accounting systems is their failure to recognize which costs and sources of revenue apply to new as opposed to existing customers. How must accounting systems change to understand fully the economic impact of customer retention on a firm's profits?

2. Using the Disney "orbit" as an example, develop a detailed model of the purchase–consumption–repurchase cycle for a particular product or service. What are the implications of the model for improving customer satisfaction and retention?

3. Use the purchase–consumption–repurchase model developed in question 2 to create examples and descriptions of four customer types: satisfied repeaters, satisfied switchers, dissatisfied repeaters, and dissatisfied switchers. Again, what implications exist for increasing customer retention?

CHAPTER # Customers
in the
Marketplace

Customers perceive, evaluate, and make decisions regarding products and services in a complex information environment called the *marketplace*. This marketplace information is a major component of the customer experience model outlined in chapter 4. Much of the complexity of human behavior is the result of our pursuing relatively simple goals in relatively complex environments.[1] Similarly, the complexity of our behavior as customers is largely a function of the marketplace in which we operate. As participants in a market economy, customers do not make decisions in isolation. They are part of a market or population of individuals making similar decisions. In chapter 5 we develop an understanding of the nature of this marketplace activity within an economic framework. We explore the capability of an economic approach to explain and describe several key dimensions of customer and market activity from the simple predictions of supply and demand to customer expectations to customer satisfaction differences across industries.

Roots in Economic Theory

The roots of our understanding of customer behavior come from the study of economics. In traditional economic theory, customers are assumed to be utility-maximizing, rational individuals who are sufficient in number for a market to operate, have stable preferences for and perfect knowledge of the options available to them, and face no monetary or psychological costs associated with the gathering of information. Psychologists continue to criticize economic explanations of human behavior because of these assumptions. Increasingly, however, these assumptions have become a "straw man" or false target for researchers outside economics who seek to refute economic arguments.

One reason is that there has been significant relaxation of customer-related assumptions in economic models. Stigler's pioneering work on the economics of in-

---

[1]Herbert A. Simon, *The Sciences of the Artificial*, 2d Ed. (Cambridge, MA: MIT Press, 1981).

formation is a case in point.[2] Stigler introduced information search costs to explain the behavior of customers who seek to ascertain the lowest price for a product in a market. Assuming that customers know the distribution of possible prices in a market and that each "search" for a lower price involves some cost, Stigler posited that customers search for price information until the marginal cost of continued search equals the marginal benefit of finding a lower price. The economics of information model represents an important step forward as economic models have become increasingly flexible and capable of describing the complexity of behavior. Becker provides other detailed examples of how economic models can be expanded to explain a wide variety of human behavior.[3]

Another problem with criticizing the economic approach on the basis of individual-level assumptions is that it was never meant to describe individuals. The goal of economic theory is to explain regularities in market or aggregate-level behavior.[4] The individual-level assumptions in economics simply provide a parsimonious description of the nature of demand. Without them, literally thousands of assumptions would be needed to describe all the salient individual differences among customers in a market. Naturally, economic theory stands to gain as its assumptions become more descriptive of customers in the marketplace. The question is whether this increase in complexity increases predictive power.

Because many of the decisions that managers make involve groups of customers or market segments, the economic approach is quite valuable for our purposes. It is not a matter of economic models being right or wrong. Rather, we must ask, Do these models provide the best aggregate predictions available? Even if economic models provide superior predictions, however, it would be dangerous to rely solely on them. As detailed in chapters 6 and 7, individual-level psychological studies continue to provide a rich description of possible customer behavior.

NORMATIVE AND PREDICTIVE MODELS

Although we emphasize the predictive value of an economic approach, economic theory also provides a basis for normative models of how managers or customers should make decisions. The notion that individuals maximize utility took on normative implications when von Neumann and Morgenstern laid out a series of axioms of rationality from which expected utility maximization could be derived.[5] Researchers have since developed techniques and decision aids for assessing utility and making choices in a normative fashion.[6] Though complex and varied in its approach, the essence of

---

[2]George J. Stigler, "The Economics of Information," *Journal of Political Economy*, 69 (3, 1961), 213–25.

[3]Gary S. Becker, *The Economic Approach to Human Behavior* (Chicago: The University of Chicago Press, 1976).

[4]Milton Friedman, *Essays in Positive Economics* (Chicago: The University of Chicago Press, 1953).

[5]John von Neumann and Oskar Morgenstern, *Theory of Games and Economic Behavior* (Princeton, NJ: Princeton University Press, 1944).

[6]See Detlof von Winterfeldt and Ward Edwards, *Decision Analysis and Behavioral Research* (Cambridge: Cambridge University Press, 1986).

normative decision making is illustrated by a relatively simple and time-tested example. Exhibit 5.1 contains a letter written in 1772 by Benjamin Franklin, in which he describes to a friend, not what decision to make, but how to make it.[7]

Our primary emphasis, however, is on the power of economic theory and models to predict customer and market behavior. Perhaps the most fundamental prediction of microeconomic theory is the law of supply and demand. Given a set of supply conditions facing sellers (a supply curve) and a set of purchase conditions facing buyers (a demand curve), the law of supply and demand predicts that the market will reach an equilibrium where the quantity of a good sold and the price paid for the good are dictated by the intersection of supply and demand.[8]

In recent years economists have used laboratory markets in which supply and demand parameters can be controlled to test such basic economic predictions.[9] The results of these laboratory markets are convincing as prices paid and quantities sold converge to the equilibrium predictions of supply and demand. Whereas individual-level behavior may be anomalous and inconsistent with the assumptions of economic theory, this same behavior is far more rational and consistent with economic theory in the aggregate. Economic theory thus continues to provide the best predictions of how most markets behave.[10] We describe other economic predictions and their empirical support subsequently in this chapter, including a market's ability to learn and form accurate expectations and the effects of matching supply with demand on customer satisfaction.

Before exploring these topics, however, an important distinction must be made which pervades the information available in the marketplace and resulting predictions regarding both individual and market behavior. In early economic models, price and quantity varied while quality was held constant. This made sense when goods and services were relative commodities with few distinguishing characteristics. More recently, largely due to the revealed importance of product and service quality differences, the issue of heterogeneity in the quality of supply has become extremely important.

More than ever, today's marketplace reveals a range of product and service quality and differentiation that would have been hard to envision a hundred years ago. Quality information is fundamentally different from price information. Relatively speaking, price information is objective, whereas quality information is subjective. It is important, therefore, to study how market information environments have changed and what effect this has had on customers' knowledge and expectations regarding product and service performance.

---

[7]Source: J. Edward Russo and Paul J. H. Schoemaker, *Decision Traps: Ten Barriers to Brilliant Decision-Making and How to Overcome Them* (New York: Simon & Schuster, 1989), p. 129.

[8]See Edwin Mansfield, *Microeconomics: Theory and Applications*, 2d Ed. (New York: W. W. Norton & Company, 1975).

[9]For a review see Charles R. Plott, "Industrial Organization Theory and Experimental Economics," *Journal of Economic Literature*, 20 (1982), 1485–527.

[10]Charles R. Plott, "Rational Choice in Experimental Markets," in Robin M. Hogarth and Melvin W. Reder (eds.), *Rational Choice: The Contrast between Economics and Psychology* (Chicago: University of Chicago Press, 1987), 117–43.

EXHIBIT 5.1

Benjamin Franklin's Letter to a Friend

London, September 19,1772

Dear Sir,

In the affair of so much importance to you, wherein you ask my advice, I cannot, for want of sufficient premises, advise you what to determine, but if you please I will tell you how. When those difficult cases occur, they are difficult, chiefly because while we have them under consideration, all the reasons pro and con are not present to the mind at the same time; but sometimes one set present themselves, and at other times another, the first being out of sight. Hence the various purposes or inclinations that alternatively prevail, and the uncertainty that perplexes us.

To get over this, my way is to divide a sheet of paper by a line into two columns; writing over the one Pro, and over the other Con. Then, during the three or four days consideration, I put down under the different heads short hints of the different motives, that at different times occur to me, for or against the measure. When I have thus got them all together in one view, I endeavor to estimate their respective weights; and where I find two, one on each side, that seem equal, I strike them both out. If I find a reason pro equal to some two reasons con, I strike out the three. If I judge some two reasons con, equal to some three reasons pro, I strike out the five; and thus proceeding I find at length where the balance lies; and if, after a day or two of further consideration, nothing new that is of importance occurs on either side, I come to a determination accordingly.

And, though the weight of reasons cannot be taken with the precision of algebraic quantities, yet when each is thus considered, separately and comparatively, and the whole lies before me, I think I can judge better, and am less liable to make a rash step, and in fact I have found great advantage from this kind of equation, in what may be called moral or prudential algebra.

Wishing sincerely that you may determine for the best, I am ever, my dear friend, yours affectionately.

B. Franklin

From Caveat Emptor to the Federal Trade Commission: The Changing Information Environment

The economic approach has left an important mark on how we view customers in the marketplace. Economic ideas and theory entered western culture "at a time when business dealings were supposed to be controlled by a moral code that prohibited one man from profiting at the expense of another."[11] That is, the economic system of the Middle Ages, with the influence of the church, put a moral obligation on sellers to stand by their products or wares and the representations or advertisements made about them.

Proving largely unrealistic, this view was replaced by economic theory and its laissez-faire, or "hands-off," approach to interactions between buyers and sellers. In English common law, on which the U.S. legal system is based, this resulted in a philosophy of *caveat emptor*, or "let the buyer beware." Emphasis was then placed on the buyer's obligation to inspect any wares being purchased no matter what the cost of the inspection. This policy made a great deal of sense in an environment where buyers and sellers were generally capable of the same level of understanding of the objects of trade. Until relatively recently, goods were not terribly complicated and rarely involved finished products as we now know them. Buyers bought seeds to grow their own grain, wood to make their own homes, and cloth to stitch their own clothes.

Caveat emptor became more problematic as markets began to change rapidly from the middle of the nineteenth century and throughout the twentieth century. This age of consumerism was marked by a growing middle class and an increasing variety of consumer goods. These goods also became more complex with many hidden qualities. Today, for example, few consumers have a detailed knowledge of how a microwave oven, a fax machine, a personal computer, or an automobile really work.

The result is that trust in sellers in the marketplace has become more important. Other factors contributing to this trend include the increasingly impersonal nature of markets and the growth in disposable income (and resulting political power) of consumers. The legal ramifications have been significant as caveat emptor has been largely put to rest. In the United States, changes in the market environment resulted in the establishment of the Federal Trade Commission (FTC) in 1914, whose primary purpose is to oversee buyer–seller transactions.

The FTC's mandate has resulted in important and explicit information remedies designed to make the knowledge of buyers and sellers more equal. This includes the mandatory disclosure of specific product information such as health warnings on cigarettes, the disclosure of information in standard units of measure such as octane ratings on gasoline, encouraging a wider range of product and service providers to advertise including doctors and lawyers, encouraging explicit comparisons of competing products or services through comparative advertising, and mandating prior substantiation of ad claims as when a car is touted as being quieter than the competition.

---

[11]Guy Routh, *The Origins of Economic Ideas* (New York: Vintage Books, 1977), p. 29.

TYPES OF MARKET INFORMATION

The end result is that a wealth of information regarding the potential performance of products and services is available to customers as they adapt to an increasingly complex marketplace. As noted, we can generally distinguish between price and performance information. Price information is relatively objective in the sense that it is concrete. Unlike most performance information, it represents a major cost element that customers can use to compare products and services from very different categories as they make purchase and budget allocation decisions. Although a new satellite dish and a new automobile can be described as having different performance attributes, they are directly comparable on cost.

Performance information is fundamentally different from price. It varies from the concrete weight, size, and speed dimensions of a physical product to the abstract degrees of economy, convenience, or durability that a customer receives. This continuum of concrete to abstract performance is central to the customer information pyramid developed in chapter 3. Performance information also varies with respect to the customers' ability to ascertain or evaluate information at any given point in time or level of personal experience. We can classify this performance or quality information into three types: (1) search information, (2) experience information, and (3) credence information.[12]

Like price information, search information includes that performance information that a customer can readily observe prior to purchase. Examples of search information include the fit and feel of an article of clothing, the freshness date and ingredient list on a food product, and how an automobile handles in a test drive. Experience information is that which customers can readily obtain or evaluate after purchasing or consuming a product or service. This includes, for example, the quality of a restaurant's food or whether a pair of pants is truly "wrinkle-free" after washing. Finally, credence information is that which may not be readily observed even after some degree of purchase and consumption, such as the durability of an automobile, the long-run health risks of food products, or the "quality" of a doctor's advice.

As the examples illustrate, products and services are not easily classified into these categories. Rather, most of the products and services that we purchase and consume contain elements of each. Although some information can be obtained relatively easily prior to purchase or consumption, other information emerges only over time. Both marketers and third-party information providers try to fill this information void through promotional material and other information sources such as *Consumer Reports* and user group sites on the World Wide Web.

In summary, the purchase environment facing customers has changed radically and continues to do so. This change affects the complexity of the information facing customers and their ability to understand and predict the consequences of purchase and consumption decisions. This, in turn, affects how quickly information is disseminated into a market and what the subsequent customer demand will be. When prod-

---

[12]See Philip Nelson, "Information and Consumer Behavior," *Journal of Political Economy*, 78 (March/April 1970), 311–29, and Michael R. Darby and Edi Karni, "Free Competition and the Optimal Amount of Fraud," *Journal of Law and Economics*, 16 (April 1973), 67–88.

uct or service performance is difficult for customers to understand and predict, promotional strategies are often aimed at communicating the key underlying benefits that a product or service provides.

Learning in the Marketplace: The Nature of Expectations

Our discussion of the diversity of information available to customers in the marketplace raises another important issue. Through experience, customers accumulate more information about the price and performance of products and services. This accumulated information and experience enables customers to predict or expect some level of price and performance. As described in the customer experience model (chapter 4), these expectations affect how customers process information and how they evaluate their consumption experience.

EXPECTATION MODELS

There are several relatively simple mathematical models that describe the nature of customer expectations. Although originally developed in a price context, these expectation models help us to understand differences between price and performance information as well as important differences between individuals and market segments. The four prominent models in table 5.1 view price or performance expectations in a current time period $t(P^e_t)$ as some function of observed price or performance information in previous periods (P_{t-1}, P_{t-2}, and so on) as well as prior expectations (P^e_{t-1}).

The simplest, called the cobweb model (equation 1), suggests that price (performance) expectations are based on the observed market price (performance) in the immediately preceding period.[13] Price or performance expectations are based completely on the customers' (or sellers') immediately previous experience. This may well describe customers with limited experience. If a customer's first and only expe-

---

TABLE 5.1 Alternative Expectations Models

Cobweb model:
$$P^e_t = P_{t-1} \qquad (1)$$
Extrapolative expectations model:
$$P^e_t = (1-p)P_{t-1} + pP_{t-2} \qquad (2)$$
Adaptive expectations model:
$$P^e_t = bP_{t-1} + (1-b)P^e_{t-1} \qquad (3)$$
Rational expectations model:
$$P_t = P^e_t = P^*_t \qquad (4)$$

---

[13]The cobweb model gets its name from the prediction that under certain supply and demand conditions, specifically when demand is steeper or more inelastic than supply, the model predicts long-run market instability where price and quantity fluctuate increasingly from period to period in a cobweb-like fashion.

rience is a bad one, they may assume that their second will be the same. While intuitive, the cobweb model is not generally supported.[14] One obvious reason is that limited customer experience is not the norm, as most of the products and services that we purchase and consume we have purchased and consumed many times before.

The other three expectation models all take more of these previous experiences into account. According to the extrapolative expectations model (equation 2), buyers and sellers expect price (performance) to change by some constant factor times the most recent change. Price or performance expectations are essentially a weighted average of observed price or performance over the last two market periods. The size of the coefficient p determines the relative effect of price (performance) in periods $t–1$ and $t–2$ on expected price (performance) in time t. This model is similar to the cobweb model in that expectations are relatively biased toward more recent price or performance information.

The adaptive expectations model (equation 3) provides an important alternative to both the cobweb and the extrapolative models. It predicts that current expectations are developed by adjusting one's previous expectations by how wrong those expectations were. Expected price (performance) in any given period t is a weighted average of last period's expectation and the observed or actual price (performance) in that period. The b coefficient, which varies from 0 to 1, represents the adaptive coefficient of expectation, or the degree to which expectations are adjusted on the basis of recent price or performance information. As long as $b < 1$, the model makes use of all previous relevant data.

Most important for our purposes is that this model is consistent with the psychological processes that customers use to integrate or average past and current information, specifically the process of anchoring and adjusting.[15] Customers mentally anchor their evaluations or expectations on some salient piece of information, in this case an existing evaluation or expectation, and adjust that evaluation or expectation to incorporate new information. The anchor is that which customers hold in memory and recall in order to update or adjust as additional information is obtained.

The managerial implications of this model are straightforward. The size of the adaptive coefficient of expectation tells us how quickly customers change their minds. When expectations are very adaptive (b is high), customers are not as heavily influenced in their expectations by a firm's past price or performance levels. When expectations are not as adaptive (b is low), past price or performance levels buffer or prevent customers from relying completely on current price or performance information.

Take the example of two appliance manufacturers, one whose past performance quality has been low and the other whose past quality has been high. Now both firms are producing indistinguishably high-quality products. If customer expectations in this market are very adaptive, then primarily the more recent information will affect the expectation or image the customers form such that both manufacturers are now expected to provide high-quality products. If customer expectations in this market are

---

[14]Michael D. Johnson and Charles R. Plott, "The Effect of Two Trading Institutions on Price Expectations and the Stability of Supply-Response Lag Markets," *Journal of Economic Psychology*, 10 (2, 1989), 189–216.

[15]Amos Tversky and Daniel Kahneman, "Judgments under Uncertainty: Heuristics and Biases," *Science*, 185 (1978), 1124–31.

less adaptive, then the past performance differences between the firms will not be completely compensated by more recent performance equality. When the adaptive co-efficient is small, it may take years of high-quality product production or service delivery to make up for poor past performance.

From an economic perspective, all the models outlined here may be limited in a situation in which markets are relatively stable. A stable market is one in which price and quality are not undergoing fundamental change. In such a case, all existing information available to economic agents, including all past price or performance information in a market, may be equally important in predicting future price or performance. This includes those quality signals that managers send to create more accurate expectations using advertising and brand images. Any forecast that is biased toward more recent information should produce forecasting errors and market pressure to provide more accurate forecasts. The rational expectations model, introduced into the economics of pricing literature by Muth,[16] has been used to model price as well as performance expectations in such a fashion. Its impact on economic theory and research has been immense.

In its simplest form (equation 4), the model states that buyers and sellers use all relevant information available in a market such that the observed price in a given time period equals the market's price expectation, which in turn equals the prediction made by the relevant economic theory (the law of supply and demand), where $P*_t$ is the equilibrium price or performance level in time period t. An attractive feature of the model is that learning is continually taking place in the market. But unlike the models in equations 1–3, the rational expectations model is clearly a model of market expectations. It does not provide a psychological description of how individual customers form price or performance expectations. As customers are limited information processors, it is unlikely that they use all past performance or price information in an unbiased fashion when forming, storing, retrieving, or updating an expectation. The other models are much more plausible from an individual standpoint in that they require the integration of a smaller amount of information or an averaging of existing beliefs with more recent information.

THE NATURE OF EXPECTATIONS: ADAPTATION AND AGGREGATION

These expectation models provide various snapshots of how customers accumulate knowledge and make predictions. When a customer's experience is limited, his or her knowledge and expectations are naturally biased toward this experience (as in the cobweb and extrapolative models). As limited as the experience may be, it is salient and important to a customer who had a poor experience with his or her first computer or first visit to a bank. As a customer's experience increases, he or she naturally draws on this experience (as in the adaptive model). His or her knowledge of what to expect from a computer manufacturer or financial institution will reflect both recent and earlier experience.

---

[16]John F. Muth, "Rational Expectations and the Theory of Price Movements," *Econometrica*, 29 (July 1961), 315–35.

The models are valuable in another way. Recall that psychological and economic models describe different levels of aggregation—psychological models better describe individuals and economic models better describe market segments or populations. Existing research on adaptive versus rational price expectations provides a clear illustration of this phenomena. Recall that the rational expectations model was developed for a market level, and the adaptive model is more consistent with an individual's information processing limitations and abilities. Individuals vary widely in both the judgmental anchors they use and the adjustments made depending on the information they have, the mood they are in, and the prejudices they form. They also perceive, forget, and ignore information in a selective manner.[17] Aggregate expectations, on the other hand, change or adapt very slowly and are relatively stable over time. As Katona argues, "many factors cancel out when the attitudes and behaviors of very large groups are compared."[18] Individual-level anchors and adjustments tend to wash out making market-level expectations far more stable or "rational" than individual-level expectations.

Therefore, the rational expectations model proves useful when describing aggregate-level expectations, and the adaptive model is useful when describing individuals. Not surprising is that both experimental and survey studies find considerable variance in the price expectations of individual buyers and sellers. Some are relatively optimistic and others are relatively pessimistic. These individual-level optimistic and pessimistic forecasts are best described using the adaptive expectations model. In contrast, these same studies find that market-level or aggregate price expectations are very accurate and more consistent with the rational expectations model.[19]

Even at a market level there remains a considerable difference between price and performance information. Because a significant amount of performance information is experience or credence information, or that which is only revealed slowly over time, performance expectations may operate differently than price expectations. Like aggregate price expectations, aggregate performance expectations are relatively rational because idiosyncratic individual differences cancel out. Unlike aggregate price expectations, aggregate performance or quality expectations remain adaptive as changes in product or service performance or quality are revealed more gradually over time.[20] Put simply, when firms change prices, customers adapt relatively quickly to the new price levels. However, when firms improve quality, this information is disseminated more gradually and it takes customers longer to adapt their perceptions and expectations to this new quality level.

[17]Burkhard Strumpel, "The Role of Behavioral Research," *The 1979 Founders Symposium, The Institute for Social Research: Honoring George Katona* (Ann Arbor, MI: Institute for Social Research, 1979), 51–59.

[18]George Katona, *Essays on Behavioral Economics* (Ann Arbor, MI: University of Michigan, Institute for Social Research, 1980), p. 60.

[19]Albert Hirsch and Michael Lovell, *Sales Anticipations and Inventory Behavior* (New York: Wiley & Sons, 1969). See also Michael D. Johnson and Charles R. Plott, "The Effect of Two Trading Institutions on Price Expectations and the Stability of Supply-Response Lag Markets," *Journal of Economic Psychology*, 10 (2, 1989), 189–216.

[20]Michael D. Johnson, Eugene W. Anderson, and Claes Fornell, "Rational and Adaptive Performance Expectations in a Customer Satisfaction Framework," *Journal of Consumer Research*, 21 (March 1995), 128–40.

Customer Satisfaction in the Marketplace: The Matching of Supply and Demand

Perhaps the ultimate value of an economic approach lies in its capability to explain differences in customer well-being or satisfaction. Alderson captured the essence of our use of economic arguments to explain the marketing process and its effects on customer satisfaction when he stated the following:

> An advantageous place to start for the analytical treatment of marketing is with the radical heterogeneity of markets. Heterogeneity is inherent on both the demand and supply sides. . . . The marketing process matches materials found in nature or goods fabricated from these materials against the needs of households or individuals.[21]

This deliberate matching process involves two general activities. The first is that of a heterogeneous customer population who, through experience and problem solving, identifies products and services that best meet their needs from among a heterogeneous array of offerings. The other is that of a heterogeneous population of firms who, through market research and problem solving, market products and services to those customers who place the highest value on their offerings. This matching process, illustrated in figure 5.1, describes most competitive industries in our economy. It predicts that when specific customer segments with their unique needs are matched with firms that tailor their products and services to these needs, customers' perceptions of performance or quality increase, as does subsequent customer satisfaction.

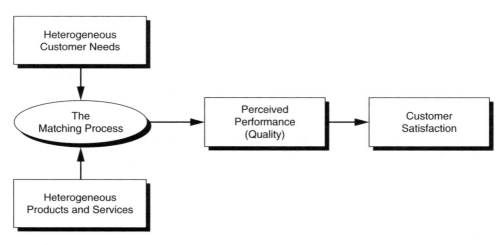

FIGURE 5.1   The Market Matching Process

[21]Wroe Alderson, "The Analytical Framework for Marketing," in Delbert Duncan (ed.), *Proceedings: Conference of Marketing Teachers from Far Western States* (Berkeley, CA: University of California, 1958), 15–28.

Consider the consequences of an impaired matching process. One possible constraint is customer learning. It takes some time for customers to find the particular offering or set of offerings in a product or service category that best meets their needs (recall the trial and error learning of dissatisfied switchers from chapter 4). Private-sector firms, government agencies, and nonprofit organizations all facilitate this learning process through target marketing and communication, information remedies (such as health warnings or nutrition information), and third-party sources (such as *Consumer Reports*). This learning process may require extensive problem solving in the case of more expensive and infrequently purchased products and major services. In contrast, learning is more a matter of trial and error in the case of less expensive nondurables and services. Here we would expect satisfaction to increase as the matching process becomes more mature.

In mature markets customer learning is not the major problem affecting the matching process; rather, it is the inability of products and services to provide a suitable match. This occurs in two ways. One is through the lack of competition in markets. When customers do not have a sufficient number of alternatives or options from which to choose at affordable prices, the likelihood of a match between supply and demand is restricted. The extreme case is when options are limited by the existence of a regulated public sector monopoly or government agency. Here there may be only a single choice no matter what differences exist in customer needs.

The other major limitation is the degree to which offerings are inherently able to differentiate themselves and thus provide a predictably different array of options for predictably different people. To be differentiated, a firm or industry must be able to tailor its offerings to conform to a particular customer's or market segment's needs. Products conform to customer needs largely through their physical means of production. Alternatively, services conform to customer needs through a production process that encompasses more of the human resources of the firm and customers themselves. This results in a greater degree of uncertainty in the production of services when compared with products.[22] Product-oriented industries are thus inherently more capable of differentiation than service-oriented industries.[23] Services are simply harder to standardize, and this standardization is necessary to differentiate an offering and target it to a particular population of customers.

The economic predictions for customer satisfaction are clear. Customer satisfaction should be highest in markets in which customers have a large degree of choice among predictably different options, namely competitive product-oriented industries (such as durable and nondurable products). Perceived quality and satisfaction should be lowest in those industries in which choices are limited and a large service component is involved, as in many public sector agencies (such as the local telephone company or police department). Competitive service and retail industries should be

---

[22]Christian Grönroos, *Strategic Management and Marketing in the Service Sector* (Cambridge, MA: Marketing Science Institute, 1983).

[23]Claes Fornell and Michael D. Johnson, "Differentiation as a Basis for Explaining Customer Satisfaction Across Industries," *Journal of Economic Psychology*, 14 (December 1993), 681–96.

more intermediate in quality and satisfaction. Although a large degree of choice exists in the retail, banking, and insurance industries, it remains difficult for customers to judge confidently which provider best suits their needs.

Research based on the Swedish Customer Satisfaction Barometer (SCSB), which examined the time period 1989–1992, supports this prediction. The results reveal that product-oriented industries averaged 66.5 on the 0–100 SCSB scale, and satisfaction for services was lower at 63, and lower still for government agencies at 59.[24] The more recent American Customer Satisfaction Index (ACSI), which measures satisfaction across thirty-five major U.S. industries, reveals similar differences.[25] As depicted in figure 5.2, durable and nondurable product industries lead the ACSI with an average index score of 80, followed by competitive service industries (transportation, communications, utilities, retail, finance, insurance, and other services) at 75, and public sector agencies (police services, sanitation services, and the Internal Revenue Service) at 64. These studies illustrate how an active market matching process increases customer satisfaction. They also show that the observed differences in customer satisfaction across industries, such as those revealed in the SCSB and ACSI, are meaningful.

This is not to say that customers, as a whole, will always be better off in a competitive and relatively unregulated marketplace. There will continue to be markets in which government regulation is critical to ensure equity and customer protection. At the same time, reliance on competitive market forces as a means to improve the lot of customers is on the rise, and for good reason. Even government agencies are being reinvented to operate more like competitive industries in order to better meet customer needs.[26]

An important ramification of the results in figure 5.2 is that it is possible for public sector agencies to effectively benchmark on private sector firms and industries as targets for quality improvement. Public sector agencies are service industries, so private sector services provide realistic benchmarks and targets for improvement. In Sweden, where such macroeconomic benchmarks have been in place since 1989, many public sector agencies have improved their customer satisfaction to a level that either meets or exceeds private sector services.[27]

---

[24]Ibid.

[25]National Quality Research Center, *1994 American Customer Satisfaction Index Baseline Report: National, Sector, and Industry Indices* (Ann Arbor, MI: National Quality Research Center, University of Michigan Business School, October 1994).

[26]For example, section 1 of President William J. Clinton's executive order of September 11, 1993 states the following:

> In order to carry out the principles of the National Performance Review, the Federal Government must be customer-driven. The standard of quality for services provided to the public shall be: Customer service equal to the best in business. For the purposes of this order, "customer" shall mean an individual or entity who is directly served by a department or agency. "Best in business" shall mean the highest quality of service delivered to customers by private organizations providing a comparable or analogous service.

[27]Michael D. Johnson, "Comparability in Customer Satisfaction Surveys: Products, Services, and Government Agencies," in *New Directions in Statistical Methodology* (Washington, DC: Office of Management and Budget, 1994).

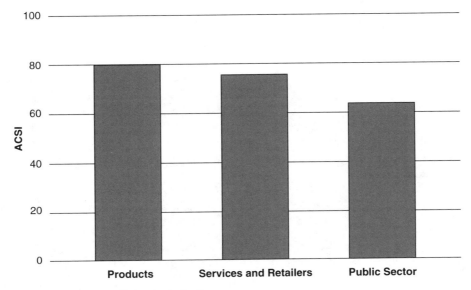

FIGURE 5.2 ACSI Results by Industry Type

Customer Dissatisfaction in the Marketplace: Exit or Voice?

We end our discussion of the economics of marketplace activity by examining the actions that customers take *in response to* customer satisfaction and dissatisfaction. The general consequences of this satisfaction and dissatisfaction are presented in figure 5.3 (page 66). To simplify matters, we examine a customer base that includes only two types of customers: satisfied and dissatisfied. We also ignore two potential types of customers described in chapter 4: dissatisfied customers who repeat (without voicing complaints) and satisfied customers who exit.

When customers are satisfied, customer retention is a likely result. When dissatisfaction exists, customers generally have a choice between "exit" and "voice."[28] One natural reaction would be for customers to show their dissatisfaction through exit, or leaving a firm's customer base. In more competitive markets, this exit may be to another firm in the industry. In less competitive markets, this exit may be to another industry (such as using a fax machine rather than the mail system to send a letter). Alternatively, customers may voice their dissatisfaction to a firm in hopes that their problems will be resolved or some restitution made. Customers who do voice their dissatisfaction then have two likely options: customer retention and exit, the choice of which often depends on whether the dissatisfaction is resolved.

---

[28] Albert O. Hirschman, *Exit, Voice, and Loyalty: Response to Decline in Firms, Organizations, and States* (Cambridge, MA: Harvard University Press, 1970).

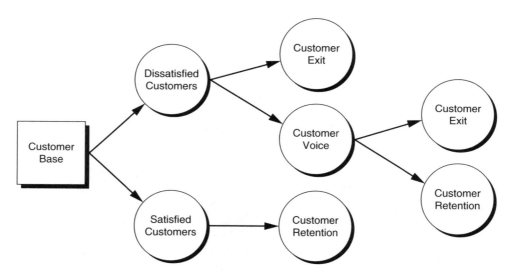

FIGURE 5.3 The Economic Consequences of Satisfaction and Dissatisfaction

This relatively simple system illustrates three important points. First, having a complaint management system that allows and even seeks out customer voice or complaints is critical to a firm's performance. Without such a system, customers will likely exit and be lost to a competitor. With such a system, the probability of retaining a customer is increased. Given the impact of customer retention on financial performance, this analysis underscores the benefit of complaint management systems. The benefits of having an effective complaint management system naturally depend on several factors, including the cost of such a system and the degree to which customers can, in fact, exit. The exit–voice consequences of customer dissatisfaction drive home the fact that customer complaints are an important source of information. When an organization is not customer oriented, complaints are simply bad news to be downplayed or ignored. But without such information, customers will flee silently to a competitor.

Second, the exit–voice framework provides us with a better understanding of the observation that complaining customers are among a firm's most loyal customers. These customers are, in essence, asking firms to listen to their concerns and foster their loyalty. Finally, just having a complaint management system is not enough. If the information provided by customers to a complaint management system is not used to actually resolve complaints, then customer exit given dissatisfaction will remain high.

Summary

An economic approach provides a solid foundation for understanding the marketplace within which customers behave. Economics and economic models, from the law of supply and demand to rational expectations, continue to provide excellent predictions of aggregate customer behavior. There has been a radical change in the marketplace over the last hundred years as differences in product and service quality, and the information customers use to judge this quality, have become considerable managerial issues. Importantly, several economic models and frameworks have emerged to foster our understanding of these differences.

Expectation models help us to understand how quickly customers adapt to changes in price and quality. Whereas customers adapt quickly to changes in price, adaptation to changes in quality take time. These models point out important differences between aggregate- and individual-level expectations as well, where aggregate expectations are more rational or stable over time and individual expectations are more adaptive or changing.

The matching of heterogeneous supply with heterogeneous customer demand is also fundamental to our understanding of basic differences in customer satisfaction within and across industries. Firms and industries that do a better job of matching a differentiated offering to a particular market segment's needs will have higher levels of perceived performance and customer satisfaction. This explains why customer satisfaction is highest for competitive product industries, lower for competitive services, and lower still for public agencies. Finally, exit–voice models underscore the consequences of dissatisfaction and help managers to understand the value of an effective complaint management system.

Discussion Questions

1. Pick a product or service of interest and develop a detailed list of all its important search, experience, and credence attributes and benefits. What attributes and benefits will have the greatest impact on customer expectations? What implications does this create for communicating information to customers in the marketplace?

2. The discussion suggests that differences in "market matching" explain observed differences in customer satisfaction across industries. Will similar differences in the market matching process explain differences in customer satisfaction across geographic regions or countries in an increasingly global economy? Why or why not?

CHAPTER # Customer Information Processing

A major premise in this text is that both economic and psychological perspectives provide managers with essential customer information. From an integrated economic–psychological perspective, economics tells us what behavior is probable and psychology tells us what behavior is possible.[1] Without a thorough descriptive understanding of customer information processing, it is difficult to comprehend even aggregate predictions and findings, especially in times of change. In this chapter we adopt a psychological perspective to develop a greater understanding of the complexity of this information processing. The emphasis is on the process dynamics of customer perception, judgment, and choice.

It is often as important to understand how a customer goes about evaluating and choosing a product or service as it is to understand what brand they eventually choose. An understanding of process may reveal a needed product or service improvement, such as the poor location of either a gauge on an instrument panel or an icon on a computer display. An understanding of process may also reveal the need to change a process, be it teaching customers to buckle up their seatbelts in an automobile or review their credit files to correct mistakes. A psychological perspective is similarly essential when individuals are the focus of market action. Take the case of industrial customers, including buyers of jet engines or robotics equipment, who are few in number. Here the market segment of interest may be an individual or a small group of individuals who make purchase decisions involving large market shares.

In chapter 4 we describe the customer experience model as a parsimonious model of customer behavior. Chapters 6 and 7 provide a detailed look at the psychological components of this model. How customers gather information, form perceptions, and categorize and store information is the focus of chapter 6, and chapter 7 examines the strategies and processes customers use to evaluate alternatives and make decisions.

---

[1]Karl-Erik Wärneryd, "Economic Psychology as a Field of Study," in W. Fred van Raaij, Gery M. van Veldhoven, and Karl-Erik Wärneryd (eds.), *Handbook of Economic Psychology* (Dordrecht, The Netherlands: Kluwer Academic Publishers, 1988), 2–41.

The Vehicle Purchase Process

The process that customers go through when purchasing a new motor vehicle helps both to illustrate the value of an individual process perspective and to identify important topic areas. The vehicle purchase process is typically composed of five distinct stages, as shown in figure 6.1.[2] Stage I is a perception and attitude formation stage that typically occurs over a period of several years. Customers begin forming perceptions and attitudes about the type of vehicle they will buy "next time" immediately after, if not during or before, the purchase process begins: "If we buy the station wagon now, next time around we can move to a sport utility vehicle." Through a casual processing of information from several sources, including word of mouth, advertising, and personal experience (riding in a friend's sport utility vehicle [SUV]), perceptions and attitudes are formed. This stage underscores the importance of information processing even though customers are not yet "ready to buy." The perceptions and attitudes that customers form affect which brands and models are considered later in the process.

In stage II the need to purchase a new vehicle is motivated, often by some triggering cue. It may be that a buyer's lease contract is about to expire, his or her current vehicle has broken down or become expensive to maintain, an unexpected bonus or tax refund is coming, or a drastically low sale price is offered. The customer starts

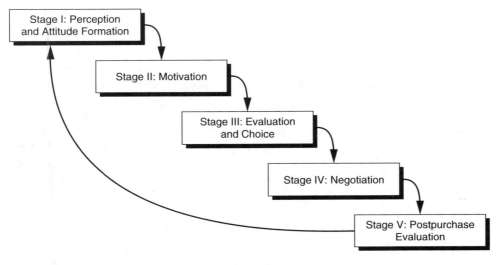

FIGURE 6.1 A Model of the Vehicle Purchase Process

---

[2]This process model represents a composite of several models developed over the years by students in my classes.

actively seeking and critically processing information on prospective vehicles. Stage III is an evaluation and choice phase, which can last anywhere from several hours to several weeks. Here customers spend time gathering information, visiting dealerships, and evaluating the choice alternatives using a variety of processing strategies. A common strategy is to eliminate a large number of alternatives based on relatively little information (such as focusing only on minivans with two rear doors or small sedans with dual air bags) to cut the problem down to size. When the choice is cut down to two or three vehicles (a Honda versus a Chrysler minivan), a more thorough evaluation of each vehicle's attributes and their trade-offs is used to make a final decision. Thus, an understanding of process reveals the minimum requirements that customers demand for a vehicle to even compete in their final consideration set.

Stage IV is when the customer and salesperson negotiate a final deal. It is regarded by many customers as the most negative stage in the whole vehicle purchase process. Identification and removal of this negative link in the process chain has been a major initiative among auto companies and retailers, many of whom now use nonnegotiable, single-price strategies for particular models (e.g., Ford Escort) or entire lines (e.g., Saturn). This is also a major selling point in new automobile "superstores," which sell multiple new and used brands and models at set prices.[3]

Finally, in stage V, customers continue to evaluate their decision after the sale. This often involves a process of resolving cognitive dissonance whereby negative aspects of either the vehicle or the purchase process are justified or resolved in customers' minds. Whatever is learned in stages I–V is naturally incorporated into customers' perceptions and attitudes. Stage V thus affects stage I as the process begins anew.

This five-stage process model provides a road map for vehicle manufacturers and dealers. It helps identify three categories of market actions that serve to improve a firm's customer orientation. First, it shows how products or services can be redesigned or improved. For example, the evaluation and choice stage may reveal that many customers simply eliminate a minivan because it does not have rear doors on both sides or does not have dual air bags.

Second, it outlines which types of information customers attend to at different stages, from more general advertising and word of mouth in stage I to more concrete vehicle information (e.g., engine and power train options) and third-party sources (e.g., *Consumer Reports*) in stage III. A better understanding of these information demands suggests ways to make information more user friendly. An example here is automobile superstores that now provide centralized kiosks with detailed information about available makes, models, repair records, and the location of each vehicle in the store's parking lot.

Third, it suggests how the process could be changed for the better. One example involves the motivating cues in stage II that lead to evaluation and choice. If manufacturers or dealers can anticipate these motivators, they can better influence what happens in subsequent stages. Knowing that a customer will soon hand in a lease car

---

[3]Kathleen Kerwin, "Used-Car Fever," *Business Week* (January 22, 1996), 34–35.

provides an excellent opportunity to present that customer with product improvement information and other incentives that may prevent them from shopping around. Another example is understanding customers' attitudes toward the negotiation stage in order to decide whether to replace this part of the process with a one-price strategy. Finally, understanding the postpurchase evaluation process underscores the importance of communicating with customers after the sale to identify and fix any problems that might arise.

The Information Processing Paradigm

The development of process models is an outgrowth of the information processing paradigm that has dominated cognitive psychology over the last few decades. This paradigm uses a particular analogy for studying the psychological processing of information. Humans are viewed as general-purpose symbol manipulators who perform a small number of basic operations on symbol representations to generate new symbols. These operations may involve the integration of information, the retrieval of existing information from a storage system (knowledge), or the use of existing symbols or information to form new knowledge. Outputs, as in the form of product perceptions or judgments of product quality, can be used as immediate inputs to choice or stored in memory for later use. In addition, the information processor's ability to perform operations on representations is limited; that is, people have a limited processing capacity.

The information processing approach draws on Newell and Simon's general framework of an information processing system, presented in figure 6.2.[4] Many of the essential features of an information processing system are contained in the customer experience model introduced in chapter 4. This general system has three primary components: an interface system, where information is either received from the environment through some receptor or transmitted back to the environment through some effector; the central processing unit, where symbols are manipulated; and a more permanent storage or memory unit.

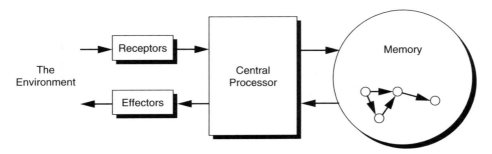

FIGURE 6.2 A General Information Processing System (from Newell and Simon 1972)

---

[4]Albert Newell and Herbert Simon, *Human Problem Solving* (Upper Saddle River, NJ: Prentice Hall, 1972).

The central processing unit has the capacity to both store information in and retrieve information from memory. The memory unit contains not only associations and concepts, but also memory for operations themselves or how to perform certain tasks. A common misinterpretation of the information processing approach is that humans are viewed in a mechanistic or computer-like way, as having physiologically separate central processors and memory units. Rather, the approach provides a metaphor for studying the dynamics of information processing, which has proved valuable in a wide range of contexts, from humans to computers.

Information processing models in a customer context have grown in both complexity and sophistication over the last three decades. Notable among these are the Andreasen, Nicosia, Howard-Sheth, Howard, Engle-Kollat-Blackwell, and Bettman models.[5] All these models retain the essential elements of the system in figure 6.2 and highlight several information processing properties and processes that deserve specific attention: (1) limited processing resources, (2) attention and involvement, (3) perception and cognitive representations, (4) information acquisition and memory, (5) categorization, and (6) judgment and choice strategies. The following sections detail the first 5 of these properties and processes while the sixth is the topic of chapter 7.

LIMITED RESOURCES

An important feature of human information processing is the limited capacity of our central processing capability. Information processing models refer to this central processor variously as short-term memory, shallow (as opposed to deep) processing, working memory or, more intuitively, "attention." In 1956 George Miller's influential study demonstrated that our limited capacity involves approximately seven items or chunks of information.[6] For example, subjects asked to recall a number sequence (e.g., 1 4 9 2 2 0 0 1 1 8 1 2) after having it read to them a single time are able to recall roughly seven numbers (plus or minus two). When, however, the numbers are organized around more meaningful chunks of information such as four-digit significant dates (e.g., 1492—when Columbus sailed the ocean blue, 2001—the title of a favorite book and movie, 1812—the date of Napoleon's march on Moscow and the title of Tchaikovsky's overture), all the information is easily recalled.

This illustrates an important information processing principle. We routinely use our existing knowledge (long-term or declarative memory) to help us perceive, organize, and recall incoming information. Our knowledge base helps us to overcome our processing limits. There are other ways that our cognitive processing adapts to information processing demand. One is simply to store the information in long-term memory (a.k.a. declarative memory or "deep" processing) by creating associations that attach meaning to a particular piece of information like a brand name. Another is to automatize a process through frequent and repeated execution or application of

[5]For a review of these models see Monroe Friedman, "Models of Consumer Choice Behavior," in W. Fred van Raaij, Gery M. van Veldhoven, and Karl-Erik Wärneryd (eds.), *Handbook of Economic Psychology* (Dordrecht, The Netherlands: Kluwer Academic Publishers, 1988), 332–57.

[6]George A. Miller, "The Magic Number Seven, Plus or Minus Two: Some Limits on Our Capacity for Processing Information," *Psychological Review*, 63 (1, 1956), 81–97.

a set of information processing steps, such as when typing words on a computer, playing sports, or driving a car. An important addition to the basic information processing framework in figure 6.2 has been *production memory*, in which information processing steps and subsequent actions are automatized through frequent application in a familiar context.[7] Consider your own lack of awareness of the process by which you type or drive a familiar route.

ATTENTION AND INVOLVEMENT

Paying attention is simply the allocation of our limited processing capacity to a stimulus, from advertising to warning labels on products to explanations of product or service features by sales representatives. The allocation of attention varies along two general dimensions. One is a selective aspect, in which attention is either allocated voluntarily to process or seek information or involuntarily to information that draws our attention. Although much of our allocation of attention and processing is planned or goal driven, in other cases the "squeaky wheel gets the grease."

A second dimension is the intensive aspect of attention whereby we pay more attention when involvement with a product or process is high and less attention when involvement is low. For example, involvement may be high when purchasing a new printer or going to an expensive restaurant but low when reordering printer paper or making a routine trip to an inexpensive restaurant. As these examples illustrate, the involvement construct is itself multidimensional and complex. Personal involvement with a purchase and consumption experience varies depending on a customer's personality, the situation or context, the product or service itself, and the type of customer communication used.[8]

Involvement and subsequent attention allocation affects the capability of marketing communications to persuade and change customer attitudes. Much of the research in this area involves Petty and Cacioppo's Elaboration Likelihood Model of persuasion, which describes two routes to persuasion: a high involvement or central route and a low involvement or peripheral route.[9] The use of low- versus high-involvement processing depends on a customer's level of motivation and ability to process information. When both ability and motivation to process information are high, as when customers have some expertise or knowledge of a product being purchased that is relatively expensive, involvement is higher and the central route is more likely. When either ability or motivation to process information is low, involvement is lower and the peripheral route is more likely.

Using the central route, attitudes are changed through critically evaluated attitude-relevant arguments. Using the peripheral route, attitudes are changed using cues and heuristics that are less critically evaluated and may not be directly relevant. For example, central route processing results in a more favorable evaluation of a product

---

[7]John R. Anderson, *The Architecture of Cognition* (Cambridge, MA: Harvard University Press, 1983).

[8]John H. Antil, "Conceptualization and Operationalization of Involvement," in Thomas C. Kinnear (ed.), *Advances in Consumer Research*, Vol. 11 (Ann Arbor, MI: Association for Consumer Research, 1984), 203–9.

[9]Richard E. Petty and John T. Cacioppo, "Central and Peripheral Routes to Persuasion: Application to Advertising," in Larry Percy and Arch Woodside (eds.), *Advertising and Consumer Psychology* (Lexington, MA: Lexington Books, 1983), 3–23.

when defensible arguments are made that a product is superior at delivering certain attributes or benefits. An example is a shaver that is demonstrated to be easier on the skin. Peripheral route processing results in a more favorable evaluation when multiple positive, albeit not necessarily defensible, statements are made and/or likable spokespeople are used. An example here might be a kitchen knife that, according to a famous model or sports star, "slices, dices, trims, cuts, saws, prunes, and severs." The action implication is that the quality of an argument made to customers is much more important under high involvement, where processing is more critical, than under low involvement, where processing is more passive. Although it is more difficult to change attitudes under high involvement, the resulting changes are more enduring.

PERCEPTION AND COGNITIVE REPRESENTATIONS

When attention is allocated to a stimulus, we form, store, and subsequently recall a perception. This perception, or *cognitive representation*, is how customers internally describe and think about products and services. The product and service attributes or aspects that form the basis of these internal descriptions vary in two fundamental ways: concreteness–abstractness and feature–dimensionality. Descriptive product and service attributes vary from the concrete to the abstract. As described in chapter 3, this concreteness–abstractness is the basis of the customer information pyramid and research techniques such as laddering. Recall that laddering involves a mapping of concrete attributes into more abstract consequences and benefits and a mapping of these consequences into even more abstract customer values or enduring beliefs. In the mountain bike example, the aerodynamics of the bike enable a biker to take longer rides, which in turn affect the biker's sense of accomplishment. In another example, shopping at small clothing stores has the consequence of possibly finding unique apparel. This unique apparel has the benefit of enabling one to "stand out" in a crowd, which ultimately enhances one's self esteem.[10]

Abstraction is important for several reasons. Describing products and services at a more abstract level, as on value, quality, or necessity, enables customers to directly compare relatively noncomparable, or dissimilar, items.[11] Diverse food products that contain different ingredients and are prepared in different ways (e.g., a cheeseburger and a salad) can be described and compared directly on their nutritional value and flavor. Likewise, financial investments that are different and thus noncomparable on their concrete descriptions (e.g., a real estate investment and a stock fund) are comparable at the more abstract level of risk and return.

Abstract attributes also integrate or summarize a large amount of concrete information. This summation process is central to the customer information pyra-

---

[10]Jonathan Gutman and Scott D. Alden, "Adolescent's Cognitive Structures of Retail Stores and Fashion Consumption: A Means-End Chain Analysis of Quality," in J. Jacoby and J. Olson (eds.), *Perceived Quality of Products, Services and Stores* (Lexington, MA: Lexington Books, 1984), 99–114.

[11]Michael D. Johnson, "Consumer Choice Strategies for Comparing Noncomparable Alternatives," *Journal of Consumer Research*, 11 (December 1984), 741–53.

mid, in which concrete information is summarized in the form of benefits and consequences, which in turn serve key customer needs and values. When information is integrated into a meaningful unit or chunk, such as a customer's overall evaluation of a brand, it becomes that which is recalled from memory for later use. Strategically, understanding what products and services provide at a more abstract level is the key to remaining adaptive and avoiding marketing myopia. As we demonstrate subsequently, understanding the difference between concrete and abstract perceptions is also central to the development of an effective customer satisfaction model.

A second major qualitative distinction among descriptive product and service attributes is that between continuous dimensions and distinct features.[12] Features are dichotomous or categorical attributes that products and services either have or do not have (e.g., dual air bags or a navigation system in a vehicle). Dimensions are attributes on which objects vary as a matter of degree (e.g., size, safety, or economy in a vehicle). Whether customers use features or dimensions is partly a function of how they choose to process information. Customers may describe food products that vary continuously in nutritional value in a simpler fashion as either "healthy" or "junk food," whereas investments that vary continuously on several risk factors may be categorized simply as "risky" or "safe."

At the same time, there is an inherent or natural degree of feature–dimensionality that varies directly with the abstractness of a customer's cognitive representation. Contrasting the perceptions of relatively concrete brands and more abstract product categories illustrates this difference. Figures 6.3 and 6.4 (pages 76 and 77) contain examples of two sets of stimuli, a set of twelve concrete candy bar brands and a corresponding set of twelve more abstract snack food categories.

The two types of spatial and treelike representations are produced using the same perceptual information. Customers are asked to judge the overall proximity of each pair of stimuli (e.g., Snickers and Three Musketeers, Snickers and Kit Kat) on a scale that varies from very dissimilar to very similar. The respondents are free to use whatever attributes they would naturally use to judge the perceived similarity of the brands and categories. The resulting data are then used as input to two types of perceptual scaling techniques, multidimensional scaling for figure 6.3 and hierarchical clustering for figure 6.4 (using an average linkage estimation method).

Multidimensional scaling solutions represent products and services as varying on a small number of continuous dimensions. The metric (typically Euclidean) distance separating any two products in the space captures the psychological distance between them. Brands or categories that are closer together in the space are perceived as more similar, and those that are further apart are perceived as more dissimilar. As brands, Three Musketeers and Reese's Peanut Butter Cups are perceived as very dissimilar. As categories, grapes and apples are perceived as very similar snack foods.

---

[12]Michael D. Johnson, Donald R. Lehmann, Claes Fornell, and Daniel R. Horne, "Attribute Abstraction, Feature-Dimensionality, and the Scaling of Product Similarities," *International Journal of Research in Marketing*, 9 (1, 1992), 131–47.

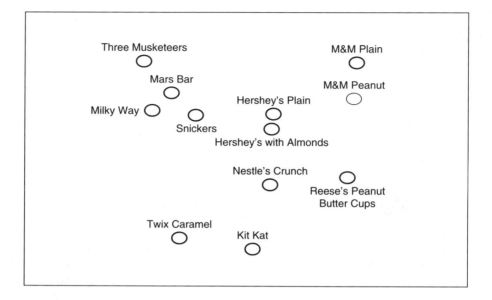

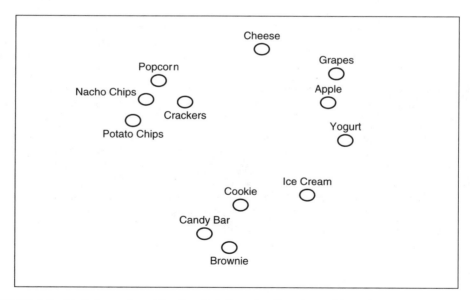

FIGURE 6.3 Multidimensional Scaling Solutions for Candy and Snacks

The hierarchical clustering schemes have a more featurelike structure. Stimuli are represented as external nodes in a tree. Perceptual distance is proportional to the lengths of the paths separating each pair of brands or categories in a tree.

Perceptual scaling methods have grown to include a variety of spatial, clustering-based, and hybrid approaches. Proximity-based methods, as in the candy bar and snack food examples, use overall proximity measures ranging from proximity ratings to brand-switching data (assuming that similar brands are more substitutable). Other methods use ratings of the brands or categories on a battery of attributes in a factor analytic approach or some combination of overall proximity and attribute ratings. Managers use these representations to understand customer perceptions, analyze the

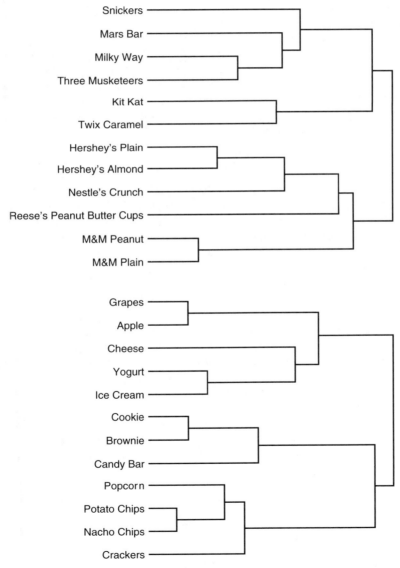

FIGURE 6.4 Hierarchical Clustering Schemes for Candy and Snacks

nature and structure of competition, develop new product ideas, and track the effectiveness of tactical changes in price, promotions, and other marketing mix variables.[13]

Spatial representations are particularly helpful in seeing the "big picture" using an intuitive, maplike format. Our own conception of distance is more consistent with that employed in spatial scaling.[14] Relating perceived distances among stimuli to the lengths of the paths separating nodes in a tree is less intuitive.[15] Anecdotal support for the intuitive superiority of spaces exists in the language managers use to analyze markets for strategy development: Products are "positioned" in spaces rather than "branched" onto trees. Similarly, managers strive to identify unique product "niches" in what is clearly a spatial metaphor.

Yet the treelike representations have their own advantages. Customer decision processes are often hierarchical, or "top-down": Decisions are first made among categories, then among subcategories, and then among brands in a subcategory. Hierarchical trees are more consistent with this hierarchical decision process. Trees also offer unique strategic advantages. They are superior at delineating a market's competitive structure, from the nature of competition among specific brands to the broader, more categorical competition among product types.[16]

Thus each type of scaling method provides managers with important insights into customer perception. Looking at the spaces in figure 6.3, it becomes clear that there is a categorizing or clustering of stimuli for brands and categories alike. At the same time, the underlying descriptive attributes are very different. For candy bars, it is difficult to imagine salient underlying dimensions. These dimensions are more salient for the categories in which the snacks vary on flavor (salty versus sweet) and healthiness (natural/healthy versus processed/unhealthy). In figure 6.4, the inherent features that distinguish the candy products are very interpretable as branches of the tree: Snickers, Mars Bar, Milky Way, and Three Musketeers are all nougat-centered bars from the same manufacturer, and Kit Kat and Twix both have cookie centers. The features or branches in the snack food tree are more categorical groupings along the flavor and healthiness dimensions.

These examples illustrate how cognitive representations change from brand-level stimuli to category-level stimuli. Foremost, they become more abstract. It is natural that more abstract or categorical stimuli are described using more abstract attributes, which, as noted, makes them easy to compare. As descriptive attributes become more abstract and summarize more concrete information, they also become more inherently dimensional or continuous. This is not to say that continuous attributes are necessarily abstract. There are many concrete attributes that are continuous (e.g., size, weight, height). Yet it is difficult to imagine an abstract, summary attribute that does not vary as a matter of degree, be it safety, durability, practicality, necessity, or fun.

---

[13]Paul E. Green, Frank J. Carmone, and S. M. Smith, *Multidimensional Scaling: Concepts and Applications* (Boston: Allyn and Bacon, 1989).

[14]Roger N. Shepard, "Psychophysical Complementarity," in M. Kubovy and J. Pomerantz (eds.), *Perceptual Organization* (Hillsdale, NJ: Erlbaum, 1981), 279–341.

[15]Michael D. Johnson and David A. Horne, "An Examination of the Validity of Direct Product Perceptions," *Psychology & Marketing*, 9 (3, 1992), 221–35.

[16]John O'Shaughnessy, *Competitive Marketing: A Strategic Approach* (Boston: Allen & Unwin, 1984).

This increase in dimensionality with attribute abstraction has direct implications for the use of scaling solutions. Like perceptions, scaling techniques themselves differ in abstractness. Spatial scaling is conceptually similar to other data reduction or summation techniques such as factor analysis or principle components analysis. The goal is to capture or explain perceptual differences among stimuli using a smaller number of more abstract or latent dimensions. In contrast, each branch of a tree can be interpreted as a different concrete attribute. This suggests that the capability of spatial scaling techniques to capture or explain customer perceptions should improve (relative to tree-based techniques) when categories rather than brands are analyzed. This prediction is well supported across a range of product and service stimuli.[17] Therefore, one practical implication is that spatial scaling is particularly valuable when studying the abstract perceptions of product categories, whereas tree scaling is particularly valuable when studying the more concrete perceptions of alternative brands.

In the end, perception is an inherently subjective phenomena that must be thoroughly studied in order to view the world from a customer's perspective. Perception is our interpretation of reality, which is affected by context and expectations as well as the actual features of a product or service itself. Perceptions may even depart from reality when expectations are strong. For example, two chocolate puddings may be exactly the same except for their color, one being lighter and one being darker, and rate identically in a blind taste test. Yet when customers can see that one is darker, it may be perceived as having a "richer taste" and "more chocolate flavor."

INFORMATION ACQUISITION AND MEMORY

The allocation of limited processing capacity to gather and process information can be described as a cost–benefit trade-off.[18] Customers obviously benefit when they acquire and use more information to make better decisions. These improved decisions come at the cost of acquiring and processing the additional information. Customers may trade off these costs and benefits either explicitly or implicitly over time, as through trial and error. There are at least three models of customer information acquisition and learning that are driven by cost–benefit considerations.[19] Although developed in a price context, they also apply to performance-related information. The models are compatible in that they involve very different situations.

The first is Stigler's economics of information (EOI) model introduced in chapter 5.[20] This model describes situations in which customers know the basic distribu-

---

[17]See Michael D. Johnson and Claes Fornell, "The Methodological Implications of the Cognitive Representation of Products," *Journal of Consumer Research*, 14 (September 1987), 214–28. Michael D. Johnson, Donald R. Lehmann, Claes Fornell, and Daniel R. Horne, "Attribute Abstraction, Feature-Dimensionality, and the Scaling of Product Similarities," *International Journal of Research in Marketing*, 9 (1, 1992), 131–47. Andreas Herrmann, *Produktwahlverhalten: Erläuterung und Weiterentwicklung von Modellen zur Analyse des Productwahlverhaltens aus marketingtheoretischer Sicht* (Stuttgart: Schäffer-Poeschel Verlag, 1992).

[18]Lee Roy Beach and Terence R. Mitchell, "A Contingency Model for the Selection of Decision Strategies," *Academy of Management Review*, 3 (July 1978), 439–49.

[19]Jouni T. Kujala and Michael D. Johnson, "Price Knowledge and Search Behavior for Habitual, Low Involvement Food Purchases," *Journal of Economic Psychology*, 14 (2, 1993), 249–66.

[20]George J. Stigler, "The Economics of Information," *Journal of Political Economy*, 69 (3, 1961), 213–25.

tion of prices available in a market, but not where those prices are located. Customers ascertain which sellers offer which prices using an overt search process as might occur when visiting different stores or entertaining sales calls. The search process continues until the marginal cost of additional searches exceeds the marginal benefit. The important point is that an overt search process is used to gather information and learn about the market environment. This model is particularly well suited to situations in which the benefits of search are significant because the customer has relatively little knowledge of the price or performance levels available (as when buying a large consumer durable such as a home or automobile).

An alternative to the EOI model is the low uncertainty (LU) model, which describes contexts in which consumers have considerable knowledge regarding which sellers offer which prices in a market. The greater the knowledge, or the lower the level of uncertainty, the lower the value of overtly searching for more information. In contrast to the EOI model, prior knowledge should limit search in this case.[21] This prediction is very consistent with a body of research that shows a general reduction in external information search as customers' prior knowledge or experience increases.[22] Many appliance purchases are made, for example, through appliance or department stores that vary predictably in the price and quality of their products and services. According to the LU model, customers should use this existing knowledge to limit their search behavior. The main difference between these two models, therefore, is that the search for more information increases knowledge in the EOI model, whereas prior or existing knowledge limits search in the LU model.

However, neither model is readily applicable to frequent, low-involvement purchase situations in which an overt information search process is unlikely. Consider that food purchase decisions are often made quickly with little overt processing of information at the point of purchase.[23] Here the customer already has considerable knowledge of the price or quality levels available, and the decision itself does not involve any great risk. There is little benefit to conducting an overt search for more information. A poor decision simply results in not buying the same brand again.

Learning in this situation is better described using an adaptive rationality (AR) model. Adaptive rationality separates current motives from current actions through an emphasis on experimental learning over time or purchase occasions as an alternative to an overt search process.[24] Price and performance information and knowledge are obtained from actual prices paid and performance received across purchase occasions. For example, when do you notice how much you paid for a box of cereal or a gallon of gasoline? This information is often considered only after a purchase decision has been made, be it the price of cereal at the breakfast table or gasoline as it is being pumped into your tank. This has also been called *incidental learning*, in

---

[21]Joel E. Urbany, "An Experimental Examination of the Economics of Information," *Journal of Consumer Research*, 13 (September 1986), 257–71.

[22]See Jouni T. Kujala and Michael D. Johnson (1993).

[23]Wayne Hoyer, "An Examination of Consumer Decision Making for a Common Repeat Purchase Product," *Journal of Consumer Research*, 11 (December 1984), 822–29.

[24]James G. March, "Bounded Rationality, Ambiguity, and the Engineering of Choice," *Bell Journal of Economics* (9, 1978), 587–608.

the sense that learning is a by-product of some other activity such as purchase or consumption.[25]

One implication of this type of learning is that customer knowledge is far superior for chosen brands. Another implication is that it is often difficult to create "new learning." When the perceived costs of acquiring more information exceed the perceived benefits, customers learn primarily through trial and error. Trial-and-error learning can be risky when performance information is only revealed over long periods of time, as in the case of credence attributes or when the consequences are much greater than perceived (e.g., using potentially harmful products). An example is consumers' use of nutritional information. It may take a lifetime to observe the benefits of changing one's food purchase and consumption habits to include low-fat and low-sodium products. Therefore, consumers may not have the incentive to exert a lot of effort to process complex nutrition related information because the benefits are not very salient. One solution within the cost–benefit framework is to lower the costs of information gathering and processing. Rather than present complex nutrition information, easy-to-process information (colored symbols or tags to indicate low-sodium or low-fat products) is more likely to affect purchase decisions.[26]

Information processing in the use of potentially harmful products is also better understood within a cost–benefit framework. When used improperly, products such as chemical drain cleaners or power tools have very negative and even life-threatening consequences. Unfortunately, these downside consequences, because they are infrequent albeit severe, are often unknown to potential users. Cost–benefit considerations prompt users of such products to read only as much of the product's instructions as they absolutely need to read to start using the product (as to unclog a drain). Yet manufacturers typically place warning labels in a separate location where they are easily ignored. Research suggests that warning information is more likely to be acquired, processed, and heeded when embedded in the procedure that customers must read to use the product.[27]

When information is acquired, it can be stored in memory. There are several theoretical models of memory, ranging from "multiple store" models (long-term versus short-term storage) to "depth of processing" models (deep versus shallow processing). The functional differences among these models are relatively minor for our purposes. There is, at the same time, a very useful memory concept that is common to many of these models: an associative network and its spread of activation.[28] An associative network views semantic concepts in memory as nodes linked to other

[25]Tridib Mazumdar and Kent B. Monroe, "The Effects of Buyers' Intentions to Learn Price Information on Price Encoding," *Journal of Retailing*, 66 (1, 1990), 15–32.

[26]J. Edward Russo, Richard Staelin, Catherine A. Nolan, Gary J. Russell, and Barbara L. Metcalf, "Nutrition Information in the Supermarket," *Journal of Consumer Research*, 13 (June 1986), 48–70. See also Alan S. Levy, Odonna Mathews, Marilyn Stephenson, Janet E. Tenney, and Raymond E. Schucker, "The Impact of a Nutrition Information Program on Food Purchases," *Journal of Public Policy & Marketing*, (4, 1985), 1–13.

[27]James Paul Frantz, "Effect of Location, Procedural Explicitness, and Presentation Format on User Processing of and Compliance with Product Warnings and Instructions," unpublished doctoral dissertation, The University of Michigan, Department of Industrial and Operations Engineering (1992).

[28]A. M. Collins and E. F. Loftus, "A Spreading Activation Theory of Semantic Processing," *Psychological Review* (82, 1975), 407–28.

nodes in a metaphorical network.[29] The meaning that we attach to any given concept or node in the network is derived from its associations or related nodes.

A simple example involving beverages appears in figure 6.5. The example shows some of the possible associations to two popular soft drinks, Coke and Pepsi. Coca-Cola, as a brand concept in memory, is defined by associations it has in common with Pepsi and other soft drinks (cold beverage, brown, sweet taste, caffeine, carbonated) as well as more unique associations (a distinctive bottle). Some of these associations are shared with other categories and brands, which themselves have their own network of associations.

When customers access information in this network or the network is stimulated, as through an advertisement, the effect is viewed as a spread of activation. Seeing an advertisement for Coke, the strongest or most immediate associations to Coke in the network are the most likely to be "activated," or brought to mind. Associations that are more indirect or farther away in the network are less likely to be stimulated, such as coffee, which shares at least some attributes with both Coke and Pepsi.

The concept of spreading activation in an associative network is useful because it is a relatively simple and universally applicable tool for understanding how memory works. A good example is the effect that comparative advertising has on customer perceptions. Comparative ads involve the explicit mention or comparison of more than one direct competitor in the same ad, whether it is the superiority of one chemical company's product over another's in a trade magazine or a comparison of ham-

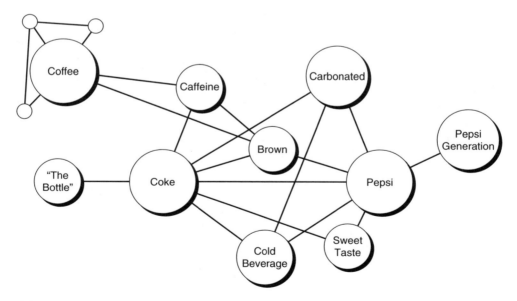

FIGURE 6.5 A Simplified Associative Memory Network

---

[29]This network is loosely hierarchical in that information that is common to an entire category is more likely to be associated or stored at the level of the category rather than the category member (e.g., all banks offer checking accounts).

burgers from two competing fast-food chains on television. Although comparative ads have sparked significant interest and controversy over the years, relatively few studies have systematically explored their effects in a natural setting, where actual customers are exposed to actual ads for actual products. The research that has been conducted is easily explained within a spreading activation framework.

Consider that brands from the same product category have more common than distinctive attributes or associations. As illustrated in figure 6.5, because both Coke and Pepsi are cola soft drinks, they have many common associations. To most customers their differences are minor relative to their similarities. This network of associations suggests that exposure to a comparative ad involving the brands should reinforce and increase their perceived similarity.[30] This is why market leaders avoid comparative ads—to minimize any perception of similarity to other brands. Me-too products, on the other hand, may benefit from the use of comparative ad campaigns. The notion of an associative network also suggests that as the number of distinctive associations increases relative to common associations, comparative ads produce less association and greater differentiation.[31] Comparing a Dodge Neon to a Ford Escort is one thing, but comparing a Neon to a Viper is quite another.

CATEGORIZATION

Central to the organization of knowledge in semantic memory is a customer's categorization of products and services in their environment. The classical view of categorization is that products or services either are or are not members of a category based on a number of necessary and sufficient conditions that define the category. It has become clear, however, that some brands are better members, that is, more prototypical, of a category than are others. An apple, for example, is more typical of the category fruit than is a kiwi. Rather than category membership being all or none, categories reflect a type of graded structure in which members of the category vary in their prototypicality.[32] This graded structure exists at both a general taxonomic level, across contexts or usage situations, as well as a context-specific or ad hoc level.[33] A kiwi, for example, is very typical of the type of fruit served at a cocktail party or used in a fancy dessert.

Graded structures have direct implications for understanding customer preferences. In many categories, customer preference is positively correlated with the perceived prototypicality of category members. Ford's Explorer is both popular and prototypical of midsize SUVs. In categories in which uniqueness is highly valued, however, as with sports cars or fashion clothing, more atypical members may be pre-

---

[30]Michael D. Johnson and David A. Horne, "The Contrast Model of Similarity and Comparative Advertising," *Psychology & Marketing*, 5 (3, 1988), 211–32.

[31]Beth A. Walker, John L. Swasy, and Arno Rethans, "The Impact of Comparative Advertising on Perception Formation in New Product Introductions," in Richard J. Lutz (ed.), *Advances in Consumer Research*, Vol. 13 (Provo, UT: Association for Consumer Research, 1986), 121–25.

[32]Eleanor Rosch, "Cognitive Representation of Semantic Categories," *Journal of Experimental Psychology: General*, 104 (September 1975), 192–233.

[33]Lawrence W. Barsalou, "Ad Hoc Categories," *Memory and Cognition*, 11 (May 1983), 211–27.

ferred. Therefore, though there tends to be a relationship between prototypicality and preference, in some cases it is positive and other cases negative.[34]

Recall that categories exist at various hierarchical levels of abstraction, from superordinate categories to more intermediate categories to subordinate categories. The sample hierarchy for vehicles in figure 6.6 contains four categorical levels, with vehicle as the most superordinate category, SUV as an intermediate category, and different sizes and brands of SUV as more subordinate categories. Psychological research shows that there is a particular intermediate level, called the basic level, where categorization is strongest. This means that category members at this basic level tend to be relatively more similar to each other than to members of other categories at the same level.[35]

Basic-level categories tend to be the first category distinctions customers learn and rely upon to process and understand products and services in their environment. They also tend to be the most abstract categories that customers can visualize. In the hierarchy in figure 6.6, SUV is a more basic-level category than either vehicle or midsize SUV. The managerial implication is that basic-level distinctions are more salient to customers and the easiest for them to use when processing market communications. Advertising and promotional messages that use more superordinate or subordinate distinctions may be more difficult for customers to comprehend and process quickly.

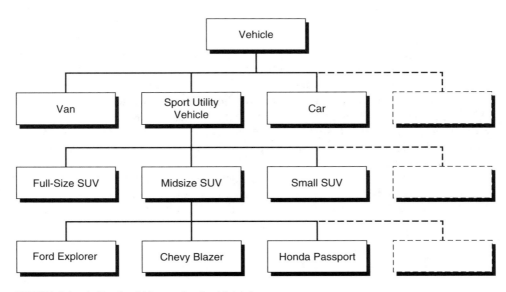

FIGURE 6.6 A Product Hierarchy for Vehicles

[34]James Ward and Barbara Loken, "The Generality of Typicality Effects on Preference and Comparison: An Exploratory Test," in Michael J. Houston (ed.), *Advances in Consumer Research*, Vol. 15 (Provo, UT: Association for Consumer Research, 1988), 55–61.

[35]Eleanor Rosch, Carolyn B. Mervis, Wayne D. Gray, David M. Johnson, and Penny Boyes-Braem, "Basic Objects in Natural Categories," *Cognitive Psychology*, 8 (July 1976), 382–439.

Summary

The action implications of an information processing perspective are many and varied. Understanding the process customers go through when gathering information, evaluating alternatives, and making decisions provides important feedback on how to improve products and services, provide needed information, and improve the process itself. A variety of models and tools are available to help us wade through this complexity, starting with the general notion of an information processing system and extending to perceptual, learning, and memory processes and choice strategies.

Models of perception and cognitive representation highlight systematic differences in how customers describe brands versus categories. Whereas categories tend to be described on more abstract and inherently continuous attributes, brands tend to be described on more concrete features. This has been shown to affect the ability of alternative spatial and tree-based scaling techniques to capture or explain customer perceptions. Customers' levels of involvement also affect how they learn from their environment and alter their opinions. Information search models contrast the overt search for information common in high-involvement situations and the more passive or adaptive learning of information common in low-involvement situations. Research on the elaboration likelihood model likewise reveals that high-involvement processing of information is both more critical and more likely to change customers' attitudes compared with low-involvement processing.

The information that is processed and stored in memory is productively viewed as a network of associations. The spread of activation in this network explains what stored information comes to mind when customers encounter a product, service, or promotional message. For comparative advertising, it suggests that the overriding effect of presenting two brands from the same category in the same ad is to foster an association between the brands. Finally, understanding how customers categorize products and services provides insight into customer preferences as well as the ease with which different types of information are processed.

Discussion Questions

1. Considering the model of the vehicle purchase process in Figure 6.1:
   a. How does the customer's level of involvement vary throughout the process?
   b. How do the customer's cognitive representations vary throughout the process?
   c. How does the customer's memory for and categorization of vehicles grow and evolve throughout the process?
2. What are some market action implications of these changes in involvement, cognitive representation, memory, and categorization?

7

Customer Choice

Having gathered various sources of information from the environment and recalled other information from memory, customers integrate this information to evaluate and choose among options. Several models or strategies have been advanced to describe this evaluation and choice process. The goal of this chapter is to introduce the reader to these strategies. First we examine the various choices customers face and strategies they use. We then turn to the important effects of risk on evaluation and choice.

Choice Strategies

Choice strategies must be considered in light of three categorically different types of choices that customers face. One is a choice among brands, or similar alternatives from the same basic- or subordinate-level category. The second is category-level choices, or choice among entire categories of possibilities. The third involves very specific or concrete alternatives from different basic-level categories. Each type of choice alternatives involves unique cognitive representations and resulting evaluation and choice strategies.

BRAND-LEVEL CHOICE

Brand-level choice alternatives come from the same basic level of categorization and are generally described using concrete attributes on which they are directly comparable. Automobiles are compared on leg room, number of airbags, and handling, and industrial adhesives are compared on ease of application, strength of bond, and durability. Generally, the strategies used to evaluate these alternatives vary in two respects: whether the processing is alternative or attribute based and whether the processing is compensatory or noncompensatory. Attribute-based processing strategies compare alternatives directly on descriptive attributes, whereas alternative-based strategies evaluate alternatives more holistically across descriptive attributes. Compensatory strategies involve trading off attribute information, where a high or good value on one attribute compensates for a low or poor value on another. Noncompensatory strategies involve the use of elimination rules, where alternatives that do not meet specific minimum values on one or more attributes are eliminated without consideration of other attribute information. Noncompensatory strategies do not allow for trade-offs among attributes.

A variety of brand-level strategies are described in table 7.1.[1] The first strategy listed is habitual choice, in which customers simply recall and repurchase a previously chosen alternative. We shall examine what happens to choice strategies as customer experience increases near the end of the chapter. For now, it is useful to keep in mind that past evaluations naturally influence current decisions, especially when the customer's level of motivation or involvement in the choice are low.

All the other strategies listed involve a more overt or explicit evaluation process that is more likely under higher involvement. The linear compensatory or additive strategy is an alternative-based strategy in which attribute values for each available alternative are first combined in a compensatory fashion into overall evaluations. The resulting overall evaluations are then compared to make a choice.

TABLE 7.1 Brand-Level Evaluation and Choice Strategies

Habitual choice: Recall and repeat the habitual choice.

Linear compensatory (additive) strategy: Add up or combine each attribute value for an alternative into an overall evaluation and then compare the overall evaluations of the different choice alternatives (alternative based, compensatory).

Conjunctive strategy: A brand must "pass" (equal or exceed) a set of attribute value cutoffs on key attributes (alternative based, noncompensatory).

Disjunctive strategy: A brand must "pass" (equal or exceed) a relatively high cutoff, or be very good, on at least one attribute (alternative based, noncompensatory).

Additive difference strategy: Customers determine the difference between any two alternatives on a given attribute, then determine their difference on another attribute, and so on. These attribute differences are combined or added up into an overall difference between the alternatives (attribute based, compensatory).

Lexicographic strategy: A brand is chosen that is best on the customer's most important attribute. If more than one brand is equal on this attribute, the second most important attribute is used to break the tie, and so on (attribute based, noncompensatory).

Elimination by aspects (EBA) strategy: Attributes or aspects are chosen with some probability that is proportionate to their importance to the customer. For each attribute selected, alternatives that are unacceptable or unsatisfactory on that attribute are eliminated (attribute based, noncompensatory).

Phased or hybrid strategies: Phased or hybrid strategies involve the use of more than one qualitatively different type of strategy for different alternatives or at different phases of the evaluation process. The particular combination of strategies is often constructed as the customer proceeds through the evaluation or choice task.

---

[1]Michael D. Johnson and Christopher P. Puto, "A Review of Consumer Judgment and Choice," in Michael J. Houston (ed.), *Review of Marketing 1987* (Chicago: American Marketing Association, 1987), 236–92.

The conjunctive and disjunctive strategies are noncompensatory and alternative based. Using a conjunctive rule, an alternative must pass minimally acceptable levels on a set of salient attributes. Using a disjunctive rule, an alternative must be outstanding on at least one attribute. These noncompensatory strategies may not result in a single acceptable alternative, in which case the cutoff values may be changed and the rules applied again.

The additive difference strategy is compensatory and attribute based. The difference between two alternatives on each of a set of attributes is considered. These attribute differences are combined or added into an overall evaluative difference between the two alternatives. Using a lexicographic strategy, in which processing is attribute based and noncompensatory, choice alternatives are compared directly on the customer's most important or salient choice attribute or criterion, and the highest ranking alternative is chosen. If more than one option ranks high, the customer compares the remaining alternatives on the next most important attribute and so on.

Using elimination by aspects (EBA), attributes are selected probabilistically according to their importance. Most but not all of the time (as when contextual or situational factors intervene), customers choose their most important attribute first, their second most important attribute second, and so on. Alternatives that are unacceptable or unsatisfactory on a chosen attribute are eliminated from further consideration. Finally, phased or hybrid strategies represent combinations of two or more of the qualitatively different strategies described previously. As in the vehicle purchase process in chapter 6, one common hybrid strategy is to use some sort of elimination strategy, such as EBA, to cut the choice problem down to size. When a smaller number of alternatives exists, a more compensatory additive or additive difference strategy is used to thoroughly evaluate the options.

Notice that these strategies vary in the amount of effort required and the potential for making errors. Generally, the compensatory strategies are more effortful because explicit trade-offs are required. They are also less likely to lead to a decision-making error because more information is considered. Figure 7.1 provides an example of four hypothetical round-trip flights to London used to illustrate the strategies and their differences. The flights are described on four attributes, the price of a coach class ticket, the airline's on-time record, the number of round-trip flights per day, and the airline's rated service quality.

	Price	On-Time Record	Flights Per Day	Service Quality
Northwest	$800	Good	2	Good
British Air	$750	Fair	1	Good
American	$800	Fair	1	Fair
United	$600	Poor	1	Poor

FIGURE 7.1 Hypothetical Attributes for a Round-Trip Flight to London

Following are portions of protocols or records of how a customer might apply each of the strategies listed in table 7.1. See if you can match each protocol to a strategy (not including habitual choice):

A. "The most important thing to me is that I am treated well on the plane. It is a long flight, and I can not afford first or business class. Of the four flights, Northwest and British Air rate the highest on service quality, so it is between these two. Now, price is the next most important factor remaining. I'll take the British Air flight because it's cheaper."

B. "I need a flight that costs less than $700 and flies every day. Northwest has two flights a day but costs too much. British Air flies every day but is still too expensive. American also flies every day but is again too expensive. United's flight is only $600 and flies every day, so that's what I want."

C. "Let's see . . . the Northwest flight is $800, on-time record and service quality are both good, and there are two flights per day, which is overall a pretty good deal. The American flight is also $800, on-time record and service quality are fair, and there is one flight per day, which is not as good overall as the Northwest flight, so I'll fly Northwest."

D. "Price, hmmm, the Northwest and American flights are really too expensive. That leaves the British Air and United flights. On-time record is fair in both of them, which is OK. Each one flies daily to London, which is also what I need. On service quality, I don't like being treated poorly, so I would eliminate the United flight. That leaves British Air."

E. "I'm looking at the British Air and the United flights. United is $150 cheaper. British Air has a better on-time record, however, and they both fly daily to London. British Air also has a higher rating on service quality. However, the $150 that I save is still more important to me than the service and on-time record, so I'll go with United."

F. "I want a flight that is either very inexpensive, less than $700, or has good service. The Northwest flight is more expensive than I'd like but has the service. The British Air flight is again too expensive but the service is good. The American flight doesn't offer the price or the service that I want, so that's out. The United flight has the kind of price that I want. So, now I have to decide among the two with good service and the one with a good price."

G. "Price is important, and the Northwest and American flights are just too expensive, so I would eliminate them on price. That leaves the British Air and United flights. For $750, the British Air flight has only a fair on-time record but is good on service quality. For $600, the United flight has a poor on-time record and poor service quality, but is overall a pretty good deal, so I'll fly United."

These examples illustrate several points. The observed differences in how information is processed are important yet subtle. They are subtle in that, although each strategy is distinct, there are similarities. The differences are important because they often lead to different choices using the same information. The information in the protocols also highlights instances in which important information is overlooked or not processed.

A wealth of research studies suggests several regularities in strategy use.[2] Customers often prefer attribute-based strategies because of the relative ease of making direct comparisons on the same attribute (such as comparing the airline flights directly on price). When information in the customer's environment or in memory is

---

[2]See Michael D. Johnson and Christopher P. Puto (1987).

organized by brand, however, processing is more alternative based. As their experience grows, customers are also more likely to recall the output of a previous decision (habitual choice). Furthermore, customers are likely to use a hybrid or phased strategy as the complexity of the choice problem increases, as when the number of attributes or alternatives grows. The overriding consideration is adaptation. Customers adapt their choice processing or construct a choice process that makes sense in a particular decision-making context.

CATEGORY-LEVEL CHOICE

Most of the research on evaluation and choice strategies has focused on brand-level choice alternatives that are directly comparable on their concrete attributes. Yet customers routinely encounter other types of choice alternatives. At a more basic level of categorization, customers choose among arrays of products and services from very different categories. Examples include choosing a type of beverage to consume at a restaurant (e.g., beer, wine, or soft drink) or the type of trip to take on a vacation (e.g., cruise, ski package, or sight-seeing tour).

These category-level alternatives are also directly comparable. As described in chapter 6, larger categories are naturally described using more abstract criteria on which they are directly comparable. Beverage categories are naturally described on healthiness, and vacation categories are naturally described on fun. Thus the primary difference between brand- and category-level choice alternatives is the level of abstraction of their choice criteria.[3]

Choice among category-level alternatives is generally described as a hierarchical or top-down process.[4] The EBA strategy in table 7.1 is a prime example of a hierarchical choice process. This strategy makes particular sense in the context of product category alternatives, because it is an efficient way to reduce a potentially large choice set.[5] Because individual alternatives are evaluated as part of a category, they do not have to be evaluated separately.

NONCOMPARABLE CHOICE

Customers also face choices involving individual alternatives from very different categories. Such alternatives are more noncomparable because they are naturally described using very different concrete, nonprice attributes on which they are not directly comparable. Whereas a particular stereo is described by its sound quality and power, a particular bicycle is described by its frame design and number of speeds. Noncomparable alternatives may arise for several reasons, such as when there is only one alternative available in a category or separate decisions are made to, for example, find a favored bicycle and a favored stereo before a choice is made between them.

---

[3]John A. Howard, *Consumer Behavior: Application of Theory* (New York: McGraw-Hill, 1977).

[4]Michael D. Johnson, "The Differential Processing of Product Category and Noncomparable Choice Alternatives," *Journal of Consumer Research*, 16 (December 1989), 300–309.

[5]Amos Tversky, "Elimination by Aspects: A Theory of Choice," *Psychological Review*, 79 (4, 1972), 281–99. See also John R. Hauser, "Agendas and Consumer Choice," *Journal of Marketing Research*, 23 (August 1986), 199–212.

There are two general strategies that customers use to compare noncomparable alternatives.[6] The first is some type of alternative-based strategy such as the linear compensatory strategy in table 7.1. Whether brands from the same or different categories are involved, a linear strategy can be used to holistically evaluate the options separately and then choose on the basis of their overall evaluations of worth or value.

The second strategy is attribute-based processing with abstraction. Here customers must first develop a more abstract representation of the options either by constructing abstract descriptions from more concrete attribute values or recalling more categorical information from memory. When a more abstract, comparable representation is available, then an attribute-based strategy is easily employed. In the example of the stereo and the bicycle, both can first be described more abstractly on fun, value, and necessity and then directly compared. A major resulting difference between noncomparable and product category choice is that the former is relatively bottom-up, in which customers move from the concrete to the abstract when describing and evaluating choice alternatives, whereas the latter is relatively top-down or hierarchical in nature.

Price, Quality, and Value

In the end, customers select an alternative that they perceive to offer the highest level of value (the benefits or quality received relative to the costs or prices incurred). Psychological studies tend to view price as simply another product or service attribute to be evaluated in the same manner as other nonprice attributes, as in the protocols for the flights to London. A more integrated economic psychology approach treats price as the cost against which performance quality is judged. Emery offers a relatively simple model of how customers map performance quality and price information together to form a perception of value, a variation on which is presented in figure 7.2 (page 92).[7]

The model presumes some objective level of both price and quality. Customers first translate the objective quality into a subjective level or category of quality, as when a product is judged to have superior, average, or poor quality relative to a similar category of goods (such as economy cars or imported beers). Objective price is likewise translated into a subjective price level or category, as when a product is judged to be expensive, reasonable, or cheap relative to a similar category of goods (a price that is expensive, reasonable, or cheap for an economy car or for an imported beer).

The customer arrives at a perception of value by then mapping or comparing his or her subjective perception of price with his or her subjective perception of quality. When the mapping is from a low price level ("cheap") to a higher quality level ("average or superior"), the result is a "good value." When the mapping is from a high price level ("expensive") to a lower quality level ("average or poor"), the result is a "poor value." When the mapping is at the same level (a "reasonable" price for

---

[6]Michael D. Johnson, "Consumer Choice Strategies for Comparing Noncomparable Alternatives," *Journal of Consumer Research*, 11 (December 1984), 741–53.

[7]Fred Emery, "Some Psychological Aspects of Price," in B. Taylor and G. Wills (eds.), *Pricing Strategy* (London: Staples Press Ltd., 1969), 98–111.

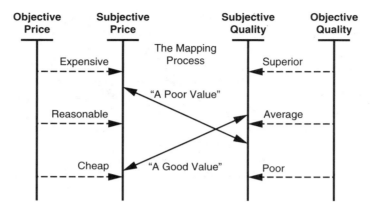

FIGURE 7.2 Emery's Mapping of Price and Quality into Value

an "average" quality product), the customer perceives a "fair value" or comparable exchange.

The model provides at least three implications. First, price and quality information are distinct and evaluated separately. Second, both price and quality are evaluated relative to price and quality levels for a similar category of goods. Third, these subjective perceptions are explicitly compared to form an evaluation of perceived value at some point in the decision-making or consumption process. For relatively inexpensive or frequently purchased products and services, this perceived value perception likely involves an overall evaluation of relevant quality dimensions. For more expensive or infrequently purchased products and services, customers may make separate price and quality evaluations and value comparisons for different components of quality. For example, the customer might ask, What level of warranty quality am I receiving and what am I paying for it? The mapping of price and quality at a component level is also likely in business-to-business situations, in which extensive problem solving is likely.

Risky Choice: Heuristics and Framing Effects

As most of the decisions customers make involve some degree of risk, it is important to understand how customers perceive risk and incorporate it into their evaluation and choice processes. Two notable heuristics, or "rules of thumb," that customers use to judge the uncertainty of events are representativeness and availability.[8] Using representativeness, a customer could estimate whether a particular supplier will deliver parts on time by how representative or similar the supplier is to a category of "reliable suppliers." An implication is that a customer expects even limited experi-

---

[8]Amos Tversky and Daniel Kahneman, "Judgment under Uncertainty: Heuristics and Biases," *Science*, 185 (September 1974), 1124–31.

ence with a product or service to be representative of a much larger experience base. For example, a customer may judge the quality of a restaurant by the one dining experience he or she had.

Using the availability heuristic, customers judge the probability of an event by the ease with which instances or examples of the event can be brought to mind or made available. The implication here is that customers judge probability on the basis of absolute rather than relative frequency. If a firm has used two advertising agencies over the years, where Agency A has produced three campaigns that were flops and Agency B has produced only one, Agency B may be viewed as less likely to produce a poor ad campaign. However, Agency A may actually have produced four times the number of campaigns as Agency B and thus have a higher probability of success (lower probability of failure). Although both representativeness and availability may result in some bias or inaccurate perceptions of probability and risk, they generally work.

Perhaps the most interesting phenomena to come out of research on risky choice is decision framing. A classic example of framing effects follows.[9]

- *Problem 1:* Imagine that the United States is preparing for the outbreak of an unusual Asian disease, which is expected to kill 600 people. Two alternative programs to combat the disease have been proposed. Assume the exact scientific estimates of the consequences are:

    —If program A is adopted, 200 people will be saved.

    —If program B is adopted, there is a 1/3 probability that 600 people will be saved and a 2/3 probability that no people will be saved.

  Which of the two programs would you favor?

- *Problem 2:* Same introduction as Problem 1, but with the following alternative presentation of programs:

    —If program A is adopted, 400 people will die.

    —If program B is adopted, there is a 1/3 probability that nobody will die and a 2/3 probability that 600 people will die.

  Which of the two programs do you favor?

One group of subjects is given problem 1 and a second group is given problem 2. Notice that the programs are exactly the same in the two problems. In problem 1, the programs are framed in terms of lives saved (gains). In problem 2, the programs are framed in terms of lives lost (losses). Most respondents prefer program A when framed as in problem 1 but are more likely to prefer program B when framed as in problem 2.

More generally, people are relatively risk averse when problems are framed as gains and more risk seeking when problems are framed as losses. The predominant explanation of this framing effect comes from Prospect Theory, which assumes that

---

[9]Amos Tversky and Daniel Kahneman, "The Framing of Decisions and the Psychology of Choice," *Science,* 211 (January 1981), 453–58.

all prospects are valued relative to a reference point.[10] Depicted in figure 7.3, this value function is concave for gains above the reference point, convex for losses below the reference point, and steeper for losses than for gains. The value function predicts, for example, that customers will prefer a sure gain of $100 to a lottery in which they have a 50/50 chance of winning $200 or nothing. It also predicts that customers will avoid a sure loss of $100 when the alternative is a 50/50 chance of losing $200 or nothing. Put simply, people want what is perceived as the larger of the two gains and the smaller of the two losses.

In an interesting business application of this framing effect, Puto had industrial buyers evaluate different purchase scenarios that required the rewarding of a contract to one of two competing suppliers.[11] One competitor submitted a guaranteed performance offer that cost less than the buyer's budgeted amount for the purchase (such as a guaranteed $90,000 price given a $100,000 budget), creating a "gain" frame or sure savings. The other competitor submitted a conditional offer in which one possible outcome was lower than the guaranteed offer and the other outcome was more than the guaranteed offer, though still at or under the buyer's budgeted amount for the contract—thus creating a probabilistic savings (such as a price of either $80,000 with a probability of 0.5 or $100,000 with a probability of 0.5). The decision frame was manipulated by altering the buyers' budgets in the procurement scenarios (such as changing the budgeted amount from $100,000 to $80,000).[12] When the budget is

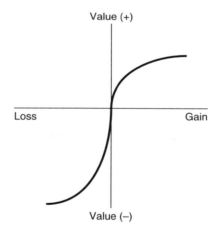

FIGURE 7.3 Prospect Theory's Value Function (from Kahneman and Tversky 1979)

---

[10]Daniel Kahneman and Amos Tversky, "Prospect Theory: An Analysis of Decision under Risk," *Econometrica*, 47 (2, 1979), 263–91.

[11]Christopher P. Puto, "The Framing of Buying Decisions," *Journal of Consumer Research*, 14 (December 1987), 301–15. For another example see William J. Qualls and Christopher P. Puto, "Organizational Climate and Decision Framing: An Integrated Approach to Analyzing Industrial Buying Decisions," *Journal of Marketing Research*, 26 (May 1989), 179–92.

[12]The dollar amounts and probabilities used here are not taken from the original study. They are simply meant to illustrate the manipulation.

higher, Puto found that the outcomes are more likely to be framed as gains. When the budget is lowered so that both competitors' offerings involve losses (purchases that are over budget), the outcomes are more likely framed as losses.

The study found that changing the budgeted amount had a significant effect on which supplier was awarded the contract. Consistent with Prospect Theory, a guaranteed offer was more likely to be chosen in the gain frame and the contingent or probabilistic offer was more likely chosen in the loss frame. Another interesting aspect of this study is that the manipulation of the reference point, which in this case was the budgeted amount for the contract, had more influence on buyers with less experience. More experienced buyers had developed preferred decision frames for evaluating the proposals which were independent of the budget levels.

Prospect Theory also has important implications for how customers mentally account for gains and losses.[13] Because of diminishing marginal value to equal gains in figure 7.3, it is advantageous to segregate or separate multiple gains mentally. This might include a series of added features or price discounts on an automobile. Because of diminishing marginal value to equal losses, it is likewise advantageous to integrate or lump together multiple losses mentally. This could include the lumping together of a series of costs or prices into a "package" price.

The Howard Model

Integrating all the various aspects of information processing and customer psychology is a difficult task. Yet this integration is necessary if we are to understand how customer behavior changes and evolves over time. The Howard model provides a useful integration of customer behavior over the product life cycle.[14] The model distinguishes among three qualitatively different stages and types of processing, extensive problem solving (EPS), limited problem solving (LPS), and routinized response behavior (RRB).

EXTENSIVE PROBLEM SOLVING

Extensive problem solving involves the evaluation of a new product or service category primarily at the introductory stage of its life cycle. At this point, customers have no strong category-level concept in memory and process extensive amounts of information to understand what the new category provides. When personal computers (PCs) were first introduced, IBM focused on the more categorical benefits of productivity and efficiency that PCs offered versus, for example, typewriters and adding machines. Customers did not have the knowledge base to fully evaluate the concrete attributes of the products in the category. Customer choice is more categorical and abstract at

---

[13]Richard Thaler, "Mental Accounting and Consumer Choice," *Marketing Science*, 4 (Summer 1985), 199–214. For a more recent example of the limits of mental accounting phenomena see Timothy B. Heath, Subimal Chatterjee, and Karen Russo France, "Mental Accounting and Changes in Price: The Frame Dependence of Reference Dependence," *Journal of Consumer Research*, 22 (June 1995), 90–97.

[14]John Howard (1977).

this stage. Moreover, relatively little of the information processed regarding brands and companies is recalled from memory; most of this information is obtained externally from the marketplace. Although EPS occurs infrequently compared with LPS and RRB, it is more time and information intensive.

Howard's three stages of problem solving also provide good descriptions of the purchase processes of industrial buyers.[15] In an industrial context, EPS is termed a *new buy* situation, such as might exist when a new technology becomes available for installation in a plant or office facility. Many individuals in an organization might be involved to gather an extensive amount of information to evaluate the new technology. Whether consumer or purchasing agent, the buyer in EPS takes on considerable risk as they are purchasing something new and relatively unknown.

LIMITED PROBLEM SOLVING

Limited problem solving occurs primarily in the growth stage of the life cycle. Customers know what the product or service category is and what benefits it provides but are still in the process of understanding all the concrete differences among the competing brands. Customers develop a more concrete knowledge of brands at this stage and begin to form brand concepts (stored images or expectations). Howard defines a *brand concept* as the subjective meaning of any homogeneous class of objects of which customers are aware. These concepts arise as associations in memory grow and become strong through the continuous process of moving through the repurchase cycle (as in the customer experience model).

Over time, information obtained externally from the marketplace is abstracted into an overall image or concept for a brand and stored internally in memory (as for Coke and Pepsi in figure 6.5). The core of LPS is the forming of these brand concepts through the use of decision strategies and the evaluation of consumption experiences. Therefore, decisions at this stage involve more concrete brands than abstract product categories. A customer's confidence in these brand concepts grows, or the level of perceived risk decreases, with each purchase and consumption experience. This is where products and services are effectively positioned within a category and a consideration set of acceptable brands or options is determined.

In an industrial context, LPS has been labeled a *modified rebuy*, where the buyer may be categorically aware of the technology, part, or service being purchased but is unfamiliar with any modifications that have occurred since the last purchase. Buying alternatives are typically known but changed in a way that requires some significant amount of information to be gathered and processed.

ROUTINIZED RESPONSE BEHAVIOR

Routinized response behavior occurs when customers have a significant amount of experience and knowledge to draw on. It is typical of the mature stage of a life cycle, where customers have iterated through the repurchase cycle repeatedly and de-

---

[15]Patrick J. Robinson, Charles W. Faris, and Yoram Wind, *Industrial Buying and Creative Marketing* (Boston: Allyn & Bacon, 1967).

termined which brand or brands best meet their needs. This is similar to a *straight rebuy* in an industrial setting, in which orders for frequently purchased materials are handled on a routine basis and involve relatively few people. Brand concepts and buying relationships are strong and have a large effect on which brands or suppliers are both considered and chosen.

The core of RRB is the integration of information that remains situation specific, and may only be available in the marketplace (such as price, availability, or freshness), with information that has been abstracted away from multiple purchase experiences and stored in memory as a brand concept. Within the context of the customer experience model, this suggests that the customer's primary source of information changes over the life cycle from externally based information available in the marketplace to internally stored information available in memory. The brand concepts that become strong at this stage include a loyalty component or predisposition to purchase a particular brand or brands.

The implication is that after these brand concepts are formed, they are difficult to change. Customers consider the risks of repurchasing the same brand to be low. Unless customers have a reason to believe that the situation has changed, and changed enough to warrant the additional effort required to seriously evaluate new brands and their attributes, they are likely to simply recall and repeat the habitual choice.

MANAGEMENT OVER THE LIFE CYCLE

Understanding how customer information processing changes over a product or service life cycle provides managers with a framework for revising their market strategies accordingly. This parallel evolution of customer behavior and management strategy is summarized in figure 7.4 using Howard's model of management over the life cycle.[16]

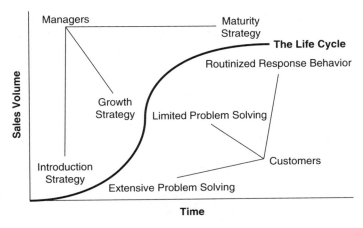

FIGURE 7.4 Howard's Model of the Life Cycle

---

[16]John A. Howard, "Marketing Theory of the Firm," *Journal of Marketing*, 47 (Fall 1983), 90–100.

From the customers' perspective, the amount of problem solving that occurs is correlated with the stage of a life cycle for many categories. As a product or service category grows from introduction through growth to maturity, customers become more routinized or habitual in their choice behavior. (Exceptions to this correlation would include some major durables for which limited or extensive problem solving is likely to persist over time.) From the managers' perspective, the correlation between life cycle stage and problem-solving stage underscores the need to develop three different strategies: an introduction strategy, a growth strategy, and a maturity strategy.

In the introduction stage, the customer is described in general terms as having relatively little knowledge and facing high risk. The primary strategic goals are to create awareness of the product or service category and its benefits (versus existing categories) and induce trial. For example, Apple computers created awareness, trial, and learning among future buyers by instituting its PCs in schools and other educational institutions. Similarly, Netscape has gained significant growth and popularity because it has allowed Internet users to download the software free of charge.

In the growth stage, customers have at least category if not brand knowledge and perceive a lower level of risk of purchasing in the category. The managers' strategic objectives are to differentiate their brands from competitors on important concrete aspects and grow. Apple stressed its superior interfacing between customers and its PCs. From a growth standpoint, manufacturers introduced a variety of machines to meet the particular needs of a growing and diverse population of buyers. The decrease in perceived risk has important implications for distribution strategies. As the customer benefit of point-of-purchase and sales information declines, less expensive distribution strategies emerge. In the PC market, manufacturers like Dell and Gateway developed successful mail-order distribution systems in this life-cycle stage.

In the mature stage, customers face little risk and know a lot about what to buy. Management strategy is twofold. First, in contrast to the relatively offensive strategy adopted in the introduction and growth stages, where the emphasis is on growing the market and market share, the emphasis here turns to a defensive strategy. Customer retention becomes a key goal to keep costs down and revenues up. Management objectives turn to creating customer satisfaction and fostering retention. Customer perceptions and evaluations of their consumption experience are monitored to make focused product and service improvements. The second aspect of a mature strategy is the consideration of how the firm can continue to grow and evolve by competing in new growth markets.

CASCADING STRATEGIES

One highly successful growth strategy that has emerged is a cascading strategy.[17] *Cascading* is generally described as a market evolution process that leverages life-cycle development. It involves progressive learning, in which a firm moves from smaller niche markets within product or service categories and a market segmentation strategy to larger mass markets and a market differentiation strategy. One ex-

---

[17]Christopher Lorenz, *The Design Dimension* (New York: Basil Blackwell, Inc., 1986).

ample is the cascading of Japanese vehicle manufacturers through different, albeit closely related, product markets, as illustrated in figure 7.5.

The first category is developed where the barriers to entry are small and the market segment's needs are not being met, as was the case for small economy cars in the United States when the Japanese manufacturers entered this market. These niche markets allow competitors without strong brand concepts to gain a foothold in a market and grow. As the market segment grows and approaches maturity (or before), the learning and expertise acquired in the first market is carried over into a new but closely related life cycle. In the U.S. market, for example, Toyota generally moved from marketing small cars to small trucks to medium-sized cars to medium-sized trucks. Notice that this cascading is from markets in which competition is weak (segmentation) to markets in which competition may be strong and requires doing similar things better than competitors (differentiation).

However, by the time a company like Toyota cascades into one of these larger markets, it has gained significant advantages that facilitate the growth of new business opportunities. Its brand concepts have become strong and well-known among potential customers, lessening the need for huge investments to create awareness and reducing customers' perceived risk. The organization has learned to produce and market a class of products effectively, whether it is vehicles or consumer electronics. It has also removed barriers to entry and efficiency that might normally exist through, for example, the establishment of a distribution network and an effective product or service development process.

The photocopier market provides another example: Xerox concentrated primarily on the medium to large photocopier segments, ignoring the small and seemingly less profitable personal photocopier segment. This provided a beachhead for foreign manufacturers to enter the small photocopier market, learn from their experience, and eventually challenge Xerox in its core segments. The experience and customer awareness gained and brand equity created in the small segments served to leverage success in the large segments. Imagine how successful Canon or Toyota might have been if, instead of the small photocopier or small car segments, their initial entries in these

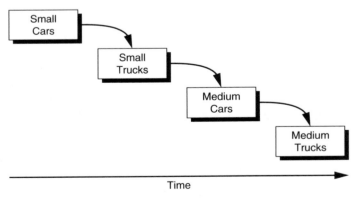

Time

FIGURE 7.5 A Cascading Strategy for Japanese Vehicle Manufacturers

categories were in the large photocopier or large vehicle markets, where U.S. competitors were strong.

Therefore, the key to a successful cascading strategy is to simultaneously leverage both the skills of a firm and customer knowledge and experience through the introduction of related categories of products and services. Using Howard's stages, it is a process by which customers are pushed only from RRB to LPS, while avoiding the risks, investments, and lack of customer knowledge that exist in EPS, as new product and service categories evolve.

Summary

Customers use a variety of choice strategies when making purchase and repurchase decisions, ranging from habitual or routinized choices to overt evaluations of multiple alternatives on a variety of price and nonprice criteria. Even the more overt evaluation strategies vary in the error and effort involved in their execution. More compensatory strategies trade off the pros and cons of choice alternatives, and elimination strategies quickly and efficiently eliminate alternatives on the basis of some particularly important feature or dimension. When choice alternatives involve noncomparable alternatives or categories themselves, decision processing is at the more abstract levels of the customer information pyramid, where direct comparisons are possible.

The variety of choices and choice processing that customers use to evaluate options has direct implications for market action decisions. Choice strategy research, with its emphasis on process dynamics, identifies sources of both process satisfaction and dissatisfaction. As emphasized in chapter 6, this information is used to improve the quality of products and services as well as the purchase process. Noncompensatory strategies identify important barriers that prevent customers from thoroughly evaluating particular alternatives. Drawing on our discussion in chapter 4, process details also help managers to identify context variables that prevent satisfied customers from being retained.

Howard's model effectively and efficiently integrates the variety of customer information processing and choice strategies into three qualitatively different stages of problem solving: extended problem solving, limited problem solving, and routinized response behavior. These problem-solving stages provide managers with an action plan for adapting their strategies throughout the stages of a product or service life cycle. Early in the life cycle, customers evaluate primarily externally available market information to conduct more extensive problem solving. As a market grows and matures, more information is stored internally in memory and used to limit problem solving. Eventually, the strong brand and category concepts that emerge from the purchase–consumption–repurchase cycle enable customers to purchase products and services in a routine fashion. At this point it becomes particularly difficult to enter a customer's evoked or consideration set.

Market strategies must evolve and adapt to these systematic changes in customer behavior. The key to an introductory strategy is to emphasize the abstract benefits of a new product or service category as customers are engaged in more extensive, category-level problem solving. As the category grows and matures, the key is to establish concrete points of differentiation, satisfy customers through continued increases in product and service quality, and variety, and reinforce customers' repeat buying habits. The strategic implications of these changes extend beyond any given product or service. As recent history shows, a cascading strategy is an effective means of leveraging strong brand concepts as well as organizational skills and capabilities into successive product or service life cycles.

Discussion Questions

1. Develop a list of specific contexts or situations in which customers encounter brand-level, category-level, and noncomparable choice alternatives. How will customers' choice processing differ in each of these contexts or situations, and what market action implications exist?

2. What are the strengths and weaknesses of Howard's three stages of customer problem solving (extensive problem solving, limited problem solving, and routinized response behavior)?

3. What are the strengths and weaknesses of cascading as a growth strategy?

C H A P T E R

Customer Satisfaction and Priority Setting

"And what is good, Phaedrus, and what is not good—
Need we ask anyone to tell us these things?"
—Pirsig (1974)[1]

Having made their purchase and consumption decisions, customers enjoy the fruits of their labor in the form of a consumption experience. Consumption is a quintessentially subjective experience that varies widely from customer to customer. As Pirsig's quote reminds us, customers are the best judges of their own experiences. The pragmatic implication is that measures of perceived quality and satisfaction must come from customers themselves; measures derived from inside an organization are insufficient (such as defect rates). As an output of their consumption experience, customers develop or update perceptions of product and service quality, expectations, and evaluations of customer satisfaction.

In this chapter we explore the antecedents and consequences of customer satisfaction. Understanding the richness and diversity of the consumption experience is itself a growing research area that provides an understanding of what products and services mean to customers and how this meaning evolves over the course of product ownership or service use. We focus on phase II (customer satisfaction measurement) and III (analysis and priority setting) of the four phases of customer orientation developed in chapter 2 (see figure 8.1).

---

[1]Robert M. Pirsig, *Zen and the Art of Motorcycle Maintenance: An Inquiry into Values* (New York: Morrow, 1974).

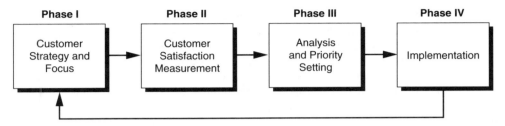

FIGURE 8.1 The Four Phases of Customer Orientation

The psychology of customer satisfaction provides an appropriate foundation for our discussion. This foundation is used to build a customer satisfaction model (CSM) in phase II as a way to measure and monitor satisfaction, the output of which is analyzed in phase III to make decisions and set priorities for market action. Phase II presumes, however, that a customer orientation is a strategic priority coming out of phase I; otherwise a sound customer satisfaction program may be wasted. Exiting phase I also presumes the existence of a sound market segmentation strategy; otherwise any satisfaction model rests on a shaky foundation.

The goal of the priority-setting process is to help optimize rather than maximize customer satisfaction. Financially there are diminishing returns to increased satisfaction. To achieve 100% customer satisfaction with a particular product or service is, in effect, a poor goal. The goal should be to set priorities and increase satisfaction until further increases cannot be justified on the basis of current and future cost and revenue considerations.

A Customer Satisfaction Framework

Customer satisfaction is better understood within a broad framework that ranges from what a firm does internally to improve quality to external perceptions of quality and customer satisfaction to the effect of satisfaction on repurchase decisions. This general framework is presented in figure 8.2.

A firm's internal product and service production and maintenance processes determine what customers actually consume and serve as the basis for forming subjective perceptions of delivered quality and value. Linking customer perceptions and

FIGURE 8.2 A Customer Satisfaction Framework

preferences back to these internal product and service production processes falls under the general topic of implementing quality improvement (covered in chapters 10 and 11). Past performance also serves as the basis for customer expectations. These quality and value perceptions and expectations, in turn, affect a customer's overall evaluation of their consumption experience to date, or customer satisfaction.

Increased customer satisfaction has immediate consequences for customer behavior and attitudes. These effects include a decrease in informal complaints to retailers or service providers, a decrease in formal complaints to management, an increase in customer repurchase intentions, positive word of mouth, and a decrease in sensitivity to price increases, all of which may be generalized into two key consequences: customer loyalty and complaint behavior. Customer loyalty is directly reflected, for example, in a customer's stated likelihood to repurchase from the same manufacturer or service provider the next time around as well as his or her willingness to repurchase at a higher price.

As argued previously, this loyalty is distinct from customer retention. Loyalty is a psychological predisposition toward repurchase; customer retention is the act of repurchase. This is illustrated in figure 8.2 by the contextual or environmental factors that intervene between loyalty and complaint behavior on the one hand and retention on the other. Following our discussion of exit and voice in chapter 5, the existence of a complaint management system and that system's capability to provide satisfactory restitution to customers affects ultimate customer retention. Loyalty and repurchase are closely related when the customer's situation and environment are relatively stable.

However, the customer's situation can change, as when a product or class of products is no longer needed. Alternatively, a competitor could offer such a great discount that the price differential offsets any difference in loyalty. Even "loyal" Pepsi buyers will buy Coke if the price is right (recall the satisfied switchers from chapter 4). If a competitor is more progressive in developing the latest technology into its products, the benefits of this technology may likewise offset any predisposition to buy a particular computer or telecommunications system.

As stressed throughout this text, the primary way to manage customer retention is through a process of constantly finding new and better ways to satisfy customer needs, thereby leveraging customer loyalty into repurchase behavior. This includes strategic investment in new technology, developing revolutionary products and services, and controlling costs to constantly provide customers with the highest possible value.

The Psychology of Customer Satisfaction

There has been a lively debate in the last decade over the psychological basis of satisfaction. This debate has centered on two particular conceptualizations of customer satisfaction: transaction-specific and cumulative satisfaction.[2] A transaction-specific perspective defines satisfaction as a customer's evaluation of a particular product experience or service encounter; satisfaction is a transient perception of how happy a

---

[2]Michael D. Johnson, Eugene W. Anderson, and Claes Fornell, "Rational and Adaptive Performance Expectations in a Customer Satisfaction Framework," *Journal of Consumer Research*, 21 (March 1995), 695–707.

customer is with a particular product or service at a given point in time. A cumulative perspective defines customer satisfaction as an overall evaluation of a customer's purchase and consumption experience to date. The latter definition is more consistent with existing views of satisfaction in related fields of study, especially economics and economic psychology, in which satisfaction is equated with a customer's postpurchase consumption utility.

The transaction-specific and cumulative perspectives offer different conceptualizations of the antecedents of, or factors that drive, customer satisfaction. Prominent among transaction-specific studies of customer satisfaction is the disconfirmation model. Prominent among cumulative studies of customer satisfaction is the performance model. Our goal is to identify a model that helps managers to set priorities and take market actions. This model must be able to both describe and predict customer behavior.

THE DISCONFIRMATION MODEL

In the context of a specific transaction, consumption episode, or service encounter, the disconfirmation or "gap" model views customer satisfaction as the degree to which perceived product or service performance confirms or disconfirms expectations. Satisfaction increases as performance exceeds expectations (a positive disconfirmation or gap) and decreases as performance falls below expectations (a negative disconfirmation or gap).[3] These transaction-specific "gaps" are aggregated into an overall level of customer satisfaction. As depicted in figure 8.3, the gap model predicts that as performance increases (holding expectations constant), there is a positive disconfirmation of expectations and satisfaction increases. As expectations increase (holding performance constant), there is a negative disconfirmation of expectations and satisfaction decreases.

Even among customer satisfaction researchers, there is disagreement over the specifics of the disconfirmation model.[4] One problem is the conceptual distinction

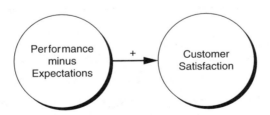

FIGURE 8.3 The Disconfirmation Model

---

[3]R. E. Anderson, "Consumer Dissatisfaction: The Effects of Disconfirmed Expectancy on Perceived Product Performance," *Journal of Marketing Research*, 10 (February 1973), 38–44.

[4]For example, see Ruth N. Bolton and James H. Drew, "A Longitudinal Analysis of the Impact of Service Changes on Customer Attitudes," *Journal of Marketing*, 55 (January 1991), 1–9. J. Joseph Cronin Jr. and Steven A. Taylor, "Measuring Service Quality: A Reexamination and Extension," *Journal of Marketing*, 56 (July 1992), 55–68. R. Kenneth Teas, "Expectations, Performance Evaluation, and Consumers' Perceptions of Quality," *Journal of Marketing*, 57 (October 1993), 18–34.

and relationship between service or product quality and customer satisfaction. Whereas some researchers view quality as an antecedent to satisfaction, others view satisfaction as an antecedent to a more general attitude regarding quality. A second issue pertains to the nature of the expectations used as a basis for disconfirmation. There is confusion as to whether expectations constitute a prediction as to what a consumption experience will be ("will" expectations), or a preference as to what a consumption experience should be ("should" expectations).

Practical applications of the gap model refer to customer expectations but then ask customers to provide attribute importance ratings. Consider the example of a savings and loan that has customers rate both customer expectations (e.g., "How important is it for you to receive individual attention?") on a scale from 1 (not at all important) to 5 (very important) and performance (e.g., "How does the savings and loan perform on its ability to provide individual attention?") on a scale from 1 (poor) to 5 (excellent). Figure 8.4 presents the average expectations and performance measures for ten drivers of satisfaction as well as a composite of all ten drivers. Later we describe several problems associated with asking customers directly for importance ratings. One common problem is illustrated here: Notice that the ratings do not effectively discriminate more important satisfaction drivers from less important drivers. All the importance ratings average near 4.5 on the 5-point scale.

To calculate the gaps, one simply subtracts the average expectations rating from the average performance rating for each satisfaction driver as well as the composite. Positive gaps are relative satisfiers, and negative gaps are relative dissatisfiers. These

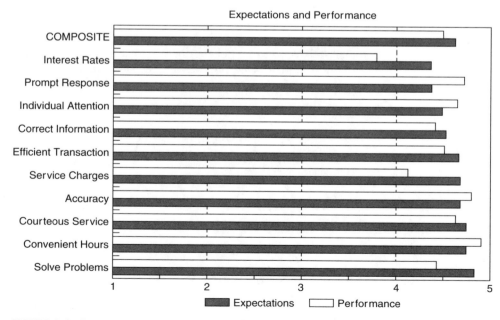

FIGURE 8.4 Expectations and Performance Ratings for a Savings and Loan

gaps are illustrated in figure 8.5 for the savings and loan example. In this case, prompt response and convenient hours are relative satisfiers, and interest rates, service charges, and ability to solve problems are relative dissatisfiers.

Resolving the problems with the disconfirmation model requires that we adopt clear and useful definitions of quality, satisfaction, and expectations. First, following an economic psychology perspective, satisfaction should be a cumulative or overall evaluation of a customer's consumption experience to date. It is this consumption experience that directly effects customer loyalty and subsequent retention. Second, perceived quality is a customer's perception of recent product or service performance. Because quality only captures recent performance information, it is necessarily different from satisfaction. Because recent as well as past performance information affects cumulative satisfaction, performance quality or value should also be an antecedent or driver of satisfaction. Third, an expectation is that which a customer predicts. Adopting a prediction-based definition of expectations is consistent with our discussion of alternative models in chapter 5, where expectations are predictions based on what has been learned about price and performance levels in the past. These definitions lead us directly to a performance-based model of customer satisfaction.

THE PERFORMANCE MODEL

In the performance model, expectations are essentially similar to a customer's image of a product or service, which captures the level of performance they can expect on the basis of past experience. This past experience includes a customer's own purchase

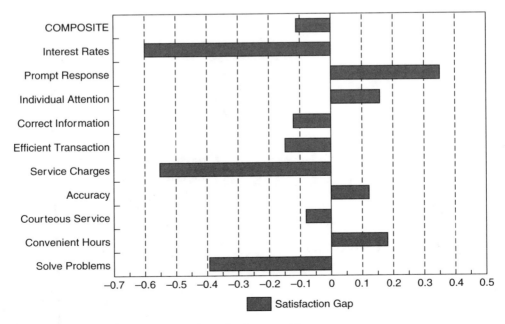

FIGURE 8.5 Satisfaction "Gaps" for a Savings and Loan

and consumption experiences as well as sources of information over which managers have more direct influence. Through communication and promotional strategies, managers inform, educate, persuade, and remind customers about pertinent performance information and potential product or service usage contexts. Sources of information over which managers wish they had more control, such as user group newsletters, Internet Web sites, and word of mouth, also influence customer expectations.

Although expectations are important, the primary antecedent or driver of satisfaction is perceived performance. This follows directly from the notion of a value–percept disparity, which says that the greater a product's or service's capability to provide that which customers need, want, or desire relative to the price or costs incurred, the more satisfied a customer should be with his or her purchase and consumption experience.[5] Thus, as shown in figure 8.6, performance has a direct positive effect on customer satisfaction. When building a CSM, this performance effect is broken down into a set of salient quality and price or cost components called *satisfaction drivers.*

The biggest difference between the performance model and the disconfirmation model concerns the role of expectations. Because expectations capture prior information or the image a customer has entering a consumption experience, these expectations anchor the customer's overall evaluation of satisfaction. These expectations contain important information as to how a product or service has performed in the past and is likely to perform in the future. This anchor is adjusted or updated over time in light of more recent performance information. Examples of this updating process include the extrapolative and adaptive expectations models from chapter 5.

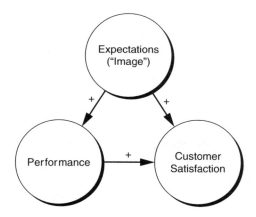

FIGURE 8.6 The Performance Model

[5]Gilbert A. Churchill and Carol Suprenant, "An Investigation into the Determinants of Customer Satisfaction," *Journal of Marketing Research*, 19 (November 1982), 491–504. David K. Tse and Peter C. Wilton, "Models of Consumer Satisfaction Formation: An Extension," *Journal of Marketing Research*, 25 (May 1988), 204–12. Robert A. Westbrook and Michael D. Reilly, "Value-Percept Disparity: An Alternative to the Disconfirmation of Expectations Theory of Consumer Satisfaction," in Richard P. Bagozzi and Alice M. Tybout (eds.), *Advances in Consumer Research*, Vol. 10 (Ann Arbor, MI: Association for Consumer Research, 1983), 256–61.

The implication is that evaluations of customer satisfaction are maintained in the vicinity of the expectations. That is, expectations have a positive effect on, or buffer, satisfaction rather than a negative effect, as the disconfirmation model predicts.[6] This effect is again consistent with the psychological process of anchoring and adjustment. The performance model also includes a positive effect of expectations on perceptions of performance. This represents primarily the capability of expectations or past performance information to predict current performance levels. The effect also encompasses the capability of strong expectations to affect perceptions of performance, as described in chapter 6. Recall that when expectations are strong, perceptions are more likely to depart from some objective performance level.

WHICH MODEL TO USE?

Overall there are important descriptive and predictive reasons for choosing the performance model over the disconfirmation model as a basis for modeling customer satisfaction. Descriptively there are obvious problems with the disconfirmation model, especially in the context of cumulative satisfaction. The definition of customer expectations has become ambiguous in this model, and it involves ignoring the absolute level of product or service performance. Not surprisingly, empirical studies generally support the performance model as being superior at predicting customer satisfaction.[7] These same studies generally support expectations as having a positive rather than negative effect on satisfaction, which is clearly consistent with the performance model and inconsistent with the disconfirmation model.

As a result, the performance model is simply a better predictor of customer loyalty and retention. Consider a relatively simple example involving a choice between two hotels, Hotel A and Hotel B. Both expectations and performance levels are higher for Hotel B than for Hotel A (holding price constant). However, performance has generally exceeded expectations for Hotel A (positive disconfirmation), and expectations have generally exceeded performance for Hotel B (negative disconfirmation). The disconfirmation model predicts that, in the future, customers will frequent Hotel A. The performance model predicts that, on the basis of the absolute level of performance, customers will frequent Hotel B. Most customers would visit Hotel B on their next trip consistent with the performance model.

We focus, therefore, on the performance model and a cumulative definition of customer satisfaction. Cumulative satisfaction is a better proxy for the overall evaluation that customers go through when making a repurchase decision. The question remains as to why the disconfirmation model remains popular. One reason is that "meeting and exceeding" customer expectations has become firmly embedded in many corporate cultures. Another reason is that the concept of exceeding expectations is intuitive and straightforward to explain to a variety of people in an organization, from top-level managers to frontline service personnel. The disconfirmation construct also

---

[6] Richard L. Oliver, "A Cognitive Model of the Antecedents and Consequences of Satisfaction Decisions," *Journal of Marketing Research*, 17 (November 1980), 460–69.

[7] See Youjae Yi, "A Critical Review of Customer Satisfaction," in Valarie Zeithaml (ed.), *Review of Marketing 1990* (Chicago: American Marketing Association, 1991), 68–123.

makes more sense when satisfaction is defined and modeled in the short run as being transaction specific. Expectations and performance quality are more likely to differ and result in a positive or negative disconfirmation for a given interaction with a product or service than they are over time (contrast one visit to a restaurant against a history of experience with a restaurant).

Although our emphasis is on modeling cumulative satisfaction, a thorough understanding of transaction-specific satisfaction remains a valuable source of customer information. Even though the disconfirmation model of satisfaction is more plausible in this context, it is incomplete. Oliver's model of customer satisfaction incorporates psychological phenomena described under both the disconfirmation and performance models to provide a better overall description of customers' reactions to more discrete episodes or transactions. Accordingly, performance, expectations, and disconfirmation all have some direct positive effect on customer satisfaction. Disconfirmation is itself modeled as a direct function of performance and expectations. This model has even been expanded to include the effects of positive and negative affect on transaction-specific satisfaction.[8]

WHEN ARE EXPECTATIONS IMPORTANT?

Whereas performance should always have a substantial effect on satisfaction in the performance model, the effect of expectations varies across product and service applications. The decision of whether to include customer expectations in a CSM depends on two factors: the strength of the expectations and the strength of the incoming performance information. Expectations are strong when based on a significant amount of experience and customers are very confident that their expectations are accurate. Expectations are relatively weak when there is little information available in memory to draw on. Performance information is strong when, for example, the customer has access to a significant amount of new information when purchasing, using, or consuming a product or service (as in Howard's extensive problem solving). Performance information is weaker in low-involvement situations, such as when purchase and consumption are more habitual and relatively little new information is processed (as in Howard's routinized response behavior).

Information may also be relatively weak or strong depending on whether the offering is a product or service. Product information is more tangible and thus relatively strong. When an engine fails to start or a part malfunctions, the evidence is undeniable. Expectations regarding the engine's or part's performance quality are easily refuted by the tangible facts. When a service is poor, however, the evidence is more ambiguous and debatable. The "rudeness" and "helpfulness" of a salesperson are more intangible and subjective. Customer perception varies from person to person.[9] Consider situations in which you and a friend have come away from a restaurant meal with totally different impressions of the service performance.

---

[8]Richard L. Oliver, "Cognitive, Affective, and Attribute Bases of the Satisfaction Response," *Journal of Consumer Research*, 20 (December 1993), 418–30.

[9]J. E. G. Bateson, "Do We Need Service Marketing?" in P. Eiglier, E. Langeard, C. H. Lovelock, J. E. G. Bateson, and R. F. Young (eds.), *Marketing Consumer Services: New Insights* (Cambridge, MA: Marketing Science Institute, Report No. 77-115, 1977), 1–29.

The matrix in figure 8.7 illustrates four possible scenarios involving the relative strength of customer expectations and performance information and the resulting size of an expectations effect.[10] Expectations should have their greatest effect on evaluations of customer satisfaction when they are strong and incoming performance information is relatively weak. We predict expectations to have little to no effect on satisfaction when expectations are weak and performance information is strong. When expectations and performance information are both strong or both weak, a more moderate effect should result.

The results of two recent studies support and illustrate these predictions. A study of Swedish firms using the SCSB data compared thirty-five product-oriented firms with thirty-seven service-oriented firms over a three-year period (1990–1992).[11] Presuming that the product firms are generally in the top half of the matrix in figure 8.7 (strong performance information) and the service firms are generally in the bottom half (weak performance information), we expect a larger positive effect of expectations on satisfaction for the services and a smaller positive effect for the products. Consistent with the framework, the service-oriented firms showed a strong positive effect of expectations on satisfaction and the product-oriented firms showed a smaller positive expectations effect.

A recent study of U.S. firms using the 1994 ACSI data examined the size of the expectations effect across approximately 46,000 customers for 200 firms competing in seven industry sectors.[12] Specifically, this study compared low-involvement/frequently purchased products and services (nondurable products and retailing) with high-involvement/infrequently purchased products and services (manufactured durables, insurance, and financial services). For the nondurables and retailers, customer expectations or brand concepts are strong relative to new information

		Expectations	
		Strong	Weak
Performance Information	Strong	Moderate Expectations Effect	Little to No Expectations Effect
	Weak	Strong Expectations Effect	Moderate Expectations Effect

FIGURE 8.7 The Effect of Expectations on Satisfaction

---

[10]This table represents an adaptation of a framework for the study of human covariation assessment proposed by Lauren B. Alloy and Naomi Tabachnik, "Assessment of Covariation by Humans and Animals: The Joint Influence of Prior Expectations and Current Situational Information," *Psychological Review*, 91 (1, 1984), 112–49.

[11]Michael D. Johnson, Georg Nader, and Claes Fornell, "Expectations, Perceived Performance, and Customer Satisfaction for a Complex Service: The Case of Bank Loans," *Journal of Economic Psychology*, 17 (2, 1996), 163–82.

[12]Claes Fornell, Michael D. Johnson, Jaesung Cha, Barbara Everitt Bryant, and Eugene W. Anderson, "The American Customer Satisfaction Index: Nature, Purpose, and Findings," *Journal of Marketing*, 60 (October 1996), 7–18.

processed. Here the positive effect of expectations on satisfaction should be relatively large. For the durables and major services, expectations or brand concepts are weak relative to new or incoming information. Here the positive effect of expectations should be smaller. Again, consistent with the matrix in figure 8.7, the study supported these predictions. Therefore, the importance of including an expectations component in a CSM is dependent on the relative strength of expectations versus performance information.

Building a Customer Satisfaction Measurement System

Customer satisfaction models have become an important analytical tool in the day-to-day management of products and services. They enable firms to monitor their customers, focus product and service improvements, provide performance benchmarks versus competitors, and provide compensation benchmarks for managers and employees. Satisfaction models also enable firms to estimate the positive impact of satisfaction on customer complaints, word of mouth, customer retention, and profits.

Customer satisfaction models are but one component of an overall customer satisfaction measurement system. Ideally, this measurement system should

- be standardized, sensitive, and flexible;
- measure and report satisfaction as an index of multiple measures;
- link satisfaction to a firm's controllables or inputs;
- estimate the consequences of an increase or decrease in satisfaction; and
- disseminate the information throughout an organization.

It is important that a measurement system be standardized for different products, services, and customers in an organization to ensure comparability. When different divisions use different systems, any observed difference in division performance may be the result of the system itself and not the customers' underlying perceptions of performance quality or satisfaction. The system should also be sensitive to or able to detect meaningful changes in satisfaction. Satisfaction measures are used to track performance, provide incentives and compensation, benchmark against competitors, diagnose quality problems, and predict subsequent performance. Using satisfaction measures for these purposes is problematic if observed changes or differences in satisfaction are simply the result of random fluctuations. The system should also be flexible, or able to adapt to changing market conditions and segmentation schemes.

An important way to provide a more sensitive measure is to construct a satisfaction index using multiple survey measures. Any single survey item is subject to various sources of measurement error or bias. Using multiple measures limits the error in satisfaction (reduces the confidence interval around the measure), resulting in a more sensitive measure. Another way to reduce error variance in a satisfaction measure or index is to use a more sensitive scale. Although simple "yes/no" satisfaction scales have become popular in many contexts, including services in which customer satisfaction information is collected quickly near the end of a transaction, such a scale is very insensitive. The customer has only two choices. Most customers repurchase from a product or service provider because they are relatively satisfied, so most all of the responses are "yes." Put differently, satisfaction and performance quality information is generally skewed such that most responses are toward the positive end of a rating scale. This renders simple yes/no questions as relatively uninformative.

This makes it critically important to use a more sensitive scale. For example, whereas a 5-point scale (where 1 = very dissatisfied and 5 = very satisfied) provides more sensitivity than a yes/no scale, a 10-point scale (where 1 = very dissatisfied and 10 = very satisfied) is even better. Best of all is a combination of multiple measures using a 10-point scale. Therefore, a satisfaction index based on a weighted average of three satisfaction measures, each of which employs a 10-point rating scale, provides greater sensitivity or accuracy than either a dichotomous satisfaction measure (yes/no) or a single 10-point scale. This, in turn, improves the accuracy with which a CSM estimation can identify the effects of various drivers on satisfaction and the effects of satisfaction on other performance measures.[13]

Conceptually, the construction of a satisfaction index is consistent with a cumulative view of the customer satisfaction construct. Because customer satisfaction captures a customer's overall consumption experience to date, it is an amorphous and abstract or latent construct that cannot be measured directly. Satisfaction, as a synonym for consumption utility, cannot be equated with or measured directly by any one scale item or measure. Any single scale item or measure is, at best, a proxy for satisfaction. When viewed as an abstract or latent construct, however, satisfaction is measurable as a weighted average or index of multiple indicators.[14]

In addition to an overall assessment of their own satisfaction, customers likely use multiple benchmarks or standards for evaluating their consumption experience over time, which provide natural multiple measures for a satisfaction index.[15] Prominent among these benchmarks are comparisons of quality received relative to an "ideal" product or service provider and comparisons of quality received relative to that which a customer expects or predicts (as in the disconfirmation model). From a measurement standpoint, cumulative customer satisfaction is not equated with any one of these measures. Rather, it is partially reflected in all of them.

An ideal measurement system and model should also help a firm to "close the loop" in two important ways. First, the system should link satisfaction to a firm's controllable inputs, or what can be done internally to improve quality and satisfaction. Second, as there are diminishing returns to satisfaction, the system should estimate the consequences of increasing or decreasing customer satisfaction for the firm. Previously, we generalized these immediate consequences into customer loyalty and com-

---

[13]Michael J. Ryan, Thomas Buzas, and Venkatram Ramaswamy, "Making Customer Satisfaction Measurement a Power Tool," *Marketing Research*, 7 (Summer 1995), 11–16.

[14]Michael D. Johnson and Claes Fornell, "A Framework for Comparing Customer Satisfaction Across Individuals and Product Categories," *Journal of Economic Psychology*, 12 (2, 1991), 267–86.

[15]Robert B. Woodruff, Ernest R. Cadotte, and Roger L. Jenkins, "Modeling Consumer Satisfaction Processes Using Experience-Based Norms," *Journal of Marketing Research*, 20 (August 1983), 296–304. See also Ernest R. Cadotte, Robert B. Woodruff, and Roger L. Jenkins, "Expectations and Norms in Models of Consumer Satisfaction," *Journal of Marketing Research*, 24 (August 1987), 244–49.

plaint behavior. The various links in this system become the building blocks or elements of a CSM.

Elements of a Customer Satisfaction Model

The elements of a CSM are introduced in chapter 2 in the context of the Sweden Post case. As this example shows, an ideal CSM adopts a systems approach in which inputs are linked to satisfaction and satisfaction is linked to its key consequences (such as loyalty and complaints). An outline of a more general CSM is presented in figure 8.8. From an input standpoint, the overall performance effect described previously is broken down into the various drivers of satisfaction. From the customer's perspective, the primary performance drivers or immediate antecedents to satisfaction are the more abstract performance benefits that a product or service provides, be it the "information" provided by a piece of technology, the "relationship" between a supplier and a customer, or the "dependability" of letter delivery.

Consistent with the customer information pyramid described in chapter 3, these abstract benefits comprise the "lens" through which customers view product or service performance. At a more concrete level, there are a variety of product and service attributes that effectively provide these benefits. A critical first step in the de-

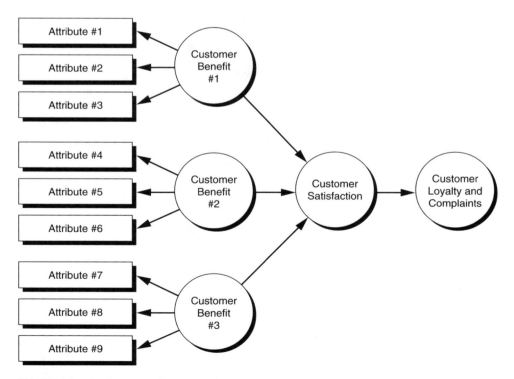

FIGURE 8.8 Outline of a Customer Satisfaction Model

velopment of a CSM is the use of qualitative research methods, such as the interview, focus group, and laddering techniques described in chapter 3, to build an initial cause-and-effect type model structure. The model outline in figure 8.8 resembles closely the output of a laddering process in which customers are interviewed to understand the important attributes of a product or service and the subsequent benefits or consequences these attributes provide.

In practice, focus groups and personal interviews are common sources of this qualitative data. Focus groups are particularly valuable when a product or service is purchased and consumed socially by more than one individual, as is the case for many consumer products, where there is potential synergy among focus group participants. Personal interviews are particularly valuable when a purchase or consumption is more individually based, as is often the case in industrial purchasing in which there is a key decision maker (such as a purchasing agent). Interviews facilitate a deeper probing into the consequences and benefits involved, as illustrated by the laddering technique.

The simplified example in figure 8.8 has four main components. At far left are the concrete attributes on which customers can readily assess a product's or service's performance using a satisfaction survey (such as whether a sales representative keeps appointments on time, returns phone calls, and provides needed information). These attribute ratings are used to measure the customer benefits. These benefits then directly affect overall customer satisfaction that, in turn, directly affects loyalty, complaints, and other organizational performance measures.

THE CONSEQUENCES OF SATISFACTION

The key consequences of satisfaction incorporated into a CSM depend largely on the history of the system. Whereas repurchase cycles for consumer nondurables are often days or weeks long, repurchase cycles for major durables take years. Therefore, much of the financial benefit of increased satisfaction, in terms of affecting retention and profits, is often lagged far into the future. As illustrated previously, contextual effects also muddy the relationship from customer satisfaction to retention. This creates a paradox as managers strive to understand and demonstrate the payoffs to increasing customer satisfaction. What is needed is a time series of satisfaction and hard performance measures (e.g., actual retention, return on assets) to demonstrate these relationships.

In those cases in which "hard" performance measures (actual customer retention and/or profit) are not yet available, a CSM should employ the next best thing. Using figure 8.2 as a guide, this would include measures of customer loyalty and complaint behavior. Customer loyalty, or customers' predisposition to buy from a particular manufacturer or service provider again, is a particularly straightforward and useful proxy for performance that can be applied flexibly across a variety of product and service contexts.

PRICE AS A SATISFACTION DRIVER

Another important modeling issue is whether price or some other cost-related factor should be included among the drivers of satisfaction. This question is difficult to answer on general terms and often requires a case-by-case decision. The qualitative research used as a starting point in developing a CSM often indicates whether price should be explicitly included. Drawing on our discussion of how customers learn price information in chapter 6, a general argument can be made based on the customer's level of involvement and experience with a product or service.

For relatively low-involvement products with which customers have a significant amount of experience, learning price information is more adaptive or incidental. Price is less likely to be explicitly considered as a separate factor to be compensated for by nonprice-related benefits when evaluating purchase and consumption. As in Emery's model of price and quality (see chapter 7), unless the relative value received (benefits received relative to costs incurred) is categorically "out of whack," price is not a particularly salient driver.

Contrast this with a situation in which a customer is laying out a large portion of his or her budget on a major durable product, such as a washing machine or automobile, or an industrial customer is purchasing large quantities of parts or raw materials. Involvement and problem solving are high and price is more likely to be considered explicitly in both the customer's evaluation of satisfaction and the modeling effort.

ESTIMATING IMPORTANCE WEIGHTS

One of the most important diagnostic pieces of information to come from a CSM is the estimation of attribute and benefit importance. There are at least six methods that might be employed[16]:

- Select poorly rated attributes and benefits as important.
- Select attributes and benefits that are poorly rated relative to customer expectations as important.
- Have a product or service development or management team assign importance weights.
- Benchmark on what competitors or admired peers feel is important.
- Ask customers directly for importance ratings.
- Statistically estimate importance as the impact of one variable on another.

The problem with using performance ratings is that a poor rating on an attribute or benefit does not mean that the attribute or benefit is important in increasing satisfaction. The problems with using performance gaps are documented previously in this chapter. Put simply, performance–expectation gaps are not the only benchmarks for evaluating satisfaction. Having a development or management team assign importance weights is obviously problematic because the input is not from the customer. Simply copying what competitors or peers outside your industry believe is important is also problematic. It assumes that benchmarked competitors or peers know what is important to their customers, that you share the same customer base, and that you are competing directly to provide customers with the same product or service benefits.

---

[16]Anders Gustafsson and Michael D. Johnson, "Bridging the Quality-Satisfaction Gap," in Anders Gustafsson, *Customer Focused Product Development by Conjoint Analysis and QFD*, (Dissertation No. 418, Division of Quality Technology, Linköping University, Linköping, Sweden, 1996), 55–88.

More popular is the use of direct importance ratings, in which customers indicate how important an attribute or benefit is on a rating scale (e.g., from "not important" to "very important"). Unfortunately, this approach assumes that customers know what attributes and benefits are important to them and even understand what you mean by "important." Consider the savings and loan example in figures 8.4 and 8.5. Would a decrease in the negative gap for interest rates necessarily improve customer satisfaction? Even if customers know what is important to them, are they willing to tell you?

In the end, direct importance ratings often result in status quo or socially acceptable answers and poor discrimination (in which a large number of importance ratings are skewed toward the "very important" end of the rating scale as in the savings and loan example). These problems negatively affect the reliability and validity of the ratings and resulting data collection costs. Research demonstrates, for example, that (1) self-rated importance weights do not always reflect the weights implicitly given to attributes when making decisions, (2) the information that they do provide decreases as the number of attribute ratings increases, and (3) different methods used to collect importance ratings provide very different results.[17]

In statistical estimation of importances, customers evaluate product or service performance on several attributes and evaluate their overall satisfaction with their consumption experience to date. The variation in rated performance across customers is then used to estimate the impact that an increase or decrease in a satisfaction driver has on customer satisfaction. This approach avoids many of the problems associated with self-rated importances while relying completely on customer input. Moreover, impact scores provide measures of importance that are managerially relevant. They estimate how much satisfaction is likely to improve or decline with changes in the levels of the satisfaction drivers.

Therefore, statistical estimation has emerged as the preferred method for estimating attribute and benefit importance weights. In the context of a CSM, statistical estimation must accommodate two other considerations. The estimation should treat the model as a network of cause-and-effect relationships that extends beyond satisfaction to include customer loyalty, complaint behavior, retention, and profit. The approach should also recognize that customer satisfaction, as well as its immediate antecedents (customer benefits), are inherently abstract and amorphous constructs that cannot be measured directly. As described previously, they can be measured indirectly as abstract or latent variables using multiple concrete proxies.

Just as cumulative satisfaction is reflected in multiple survey items, the customer benefits in figure 8.8 are measured indirectly using several more concrete survey attributes or subdimensions. Notice that the arrows run from the customer benefits to the attributes. This captures the idea that each benefit is not measured directly; rather, each benefit is reflected in multiple attribute ratings and operationalized as an index of these measures.

---

[17]See Anders Gustafsson and Michael D. Johnson (1996).

There are two popular methods for estimating models of this type: covariance structure analysis (using programs such as LISREL) and partial least squares (PLS).[18] Partial least squares is particularly well suited to satisfaction modeling. Whereas covariance structure analysis seeks to explain the strength of empirical relationships, the objective of PLS is to explain variance in the ultimate performance measure in the model (such as loyalty or retention). Like regression analysis, PLS produces effect sizes that indicate the impact that a change in a satisfaction driver has on satisfaction.

These effect sizes are more important to managers who want to understand the likely impact of their decisions to improve quality. Unlike covariance structure analysis (using maximum likelihood estimation), the abstract or latent variables in PLS are easily operationalized as weighted averages of the survey items. This provides managers with performance benchmarks for both satisfaction and its drivers. PLS is also more appropriate for the small samples (as in industrial applications) and skewed distributions that are common in satisfaction modeling.[19]

Finally, a PLS estimation can be approximated using a hybrid of simpler statistical techniques. In either case, the lens of the customer is first constructed using qualitative research. Using the hybrid approach, the customer benefit, satisfaction, and loyalty indices are then constructed using the first principle component of each separate group of construct measures. These principle components are then used as input to a series of regression analyses to provide the impact scores.

Statistical estimation results in importance weights, or "impact scores," at multiple levels. One is the impact of satisfaction on key performance measures. A second is the impact of each of the customer benefits on customer satisfaction. That is, when a particular benefit is improved by 5 points on a 0- to 100-point scale, what is the resulting change in customer satisfaction? Finally, the estimation provides attribute importance weights, or the degree to which each benefit is reflected in a particular attribute and, as a result, which attributes are more important toward improving the benefit.

The estimation also provides important diagnostic information regarding performance levels. Indices are constructed to indicate the overall level of customer satisfaction with a product or service as well as performance levels on desired customer benefits. Performance information at the attribute level is obtained from individual survey items. This enables a firm to observe how its products or services are performing at multiple levels in a CSM. (Examples of statistically estimated impacts and performance levels are provided in the cases at the end of this chapter.)

Keep in mind that labeling performance levels as good or bad is context dependent. Benchmarking performance levels against those of competitors is useful when the competition is direct. When, however, competitors fill different portions of a customer's portfolio or competitors compete in different market segments, benchmarking performance versus competitors can be misleading. Take the example of two

---

[18]Claes Fornell, "A Second Generation of Multivariate Analysis: Classification of Methods and Implications for Marketing Research," in Michael J. Houston (ed.), *Review of Marketing 1987* (Chicago: American Marketing Association, 1987), 407–50.

[19]For a detailed description of the PLS methodology see J.-B. Lohmöller, *Latent Variable Path Modeling with Partial Least Squares* (Heidelberg, Germany: Physica-Verlag, 1989).

data suppliers, one that provides a company with extremely accurate data that takes a long lead time to produce and one that provides a company with quick and dirty market reports. Each data supplier fulfills a different customer need. As a result, it would be a mistake for either supplier to label their performance as poor on accuracy or timeliness just because another supplier rates higher on those attributes.

Priority Setting

Moving from phase II to phase III in the four phases of customer orientation requires a transformation of customer satisfaction data into management decisions and strategy. Two specific questions addressed in phase III are (1) Where should limited resources be allocated to improve quality and satisfaction? and (2) What changes, if any, should be made in target market selection?

The priority-setting and strategy development process utilizes the two types of diagnostic information generated from a CSM: the importance weights or impacts of the various satisfaction drivers and their performance levels. This information is combined by categorizing each of the main customer benefits that drive satisfaction into a strategic satisfaction matrix (also known as "quadrant analysis"), as depicted in figure 8.9. The two cells on the right side of the matrix contain benefits that have a high impact on satisfaction. Low-impact benefits are on the left. In the top two cells of the matrix are benefits on which a product or service provider's performance is strong, and those on which performance is weaker are at the bottom.

Take the example of an automobile dealer whose CSM contains four primary benefits: product quality, service quality, warranty quality, and aesthetic quality. In this example, product and service quality are more important in increasing customer satisfaction (have higher impact) than are warranty and aesthetic quality. The firm's perceived performance is higher on product and warranty quality than on service and aesthetic quality.

From a cost–benefit standpoint, the essential customer benefits to improve are those for which importance or impact is high and performance is low. Customers are

Low Impact Strong Performance	High Impact Strong Performance
Maintain or reduce investment or alter target market	Keep performance up— Competitive advantage
Low Impact Weak Performance	**High Impact Weak Performance**
Inconsequential— Do not waste resources	Focus improvements here— Competitive vulnerability

FIGURE 8.9 Strategic Satisfaction Matrix

looking for higher levels of performance on these benefits than they are currently receiving. Strategically, this cell represents a source of competitive vulnerability in which a competitor that excels in providing these benefits may successfully take customers away. Those benefits in the high impact/strong performance cell represent relative strengths. Although it is not essential to improve performance on these benefits, it is critical to at least maintain the current level of perceived performance. It is essential that the automobile dealer improve service quality, where impact is high and performance is low, and maintain its strong showing on product quality, where impact is high and performance is high.

In those cases in which performance is strong yet impact is low there are at least two possible explanations. A benefit may be categorized in this cell because it is simply not very important to customers. Alternatively, performance may be so strong on the benefit that any increase in performance is not particularly valuable to customers. For example, the dealership may offer either a ten-year, 100,000-mile warranty or a nine-year, 90,000-mile warranty on the vehicles it sells. Although having a high-quality warranty is salient to customers, the variance in warranties provided is not particularly meaningful. An implication is that too many resources may be allocated to these benefits. An alternative strategic option is to target the product or service to a market segment that places greater importance on the benefits in this cell. Finally, benefits in the low-impact and weak performance cell are relatively inconsequential to customers (such as the aesthetics of an automobile dealership). Investing in quality improvements on these benefits would be a relative waste of resources.

BRIDGING INTERNAL AND EXTERNAL QUALITY

Simply knowing that service quality is a priority for overall performance or quality improvement is obviously incomplete. There remains a significant translation process to bridge customers' external perceptions of quality and satisfaction with internal product and service development and maintenance processes. As a starting point, a CSM provides guidelines for how to go about improving quality internally. The attribute weights, which again capture the degree to which improvement on particular product or service attributes enhances performance on key customer benefits, provide a natural starting point. An understanding of how to implement improvements is also generated through the CSM development process, in which qualitative methods help analysts and managers to appreciate customer means–end chains (the very concrete product and service attributes that satisfy more abstract ends).

Improvement in these concrete attributes must still be translated into internal design requirement and parts characteristics, process operations, and production or service requirements. Quality function deployment (QFD) and its "house of quality" has become an increasingly popular method for accomplishing this internal translation process. An important decision logic transcends the priority-setting process in both satisfaction modeling and QFD—resources are deployed to improve those attributes, characteristics, or internal processes that are important in improving customer satisfaction and on which a product's or service's performance is poor. (This translation process is explored in more detail in chapter 11.)

The final sections of this chapter present two CSM case examples from very different types of organizations. The first is from Cathay Pacific, a large service provider in a very competitive and growing Asian air travel market.[20] The second is from DrainCo, a medium-sized industrial manufacturing and sales operation located in the midwestern United States.[21] For illustration purposes, each case focuses on a single CSM for a particular market segment.

Customer Satisfaction at Cathay Pacific

Owned and operated by the Swire Group, Cathay Pacific is the airline of Hong Kong. A traditional market share leader in Asia, Cathay operates both short- and long-haul service over the entire Pacific rim, with some flights to other parts of Asia, Europe, and North America. Customer satisfaction in the Asian airline market is not unlike that in other parts of the globe. Satisfaction is highest for small niche airlines (EVA in Asia, Southwest in North America) whose services are more tailored to a particular market segment's needs. Satisfaction is not as high for larger carriers, including Cathay, that service a wider range of air travel segments.

With the opening of the Chinese market and the building of several new and modern airports in Hong Kong and the mainland, Cathay faces a tremendous growth opportunity. As a result, customer satisfaction became a definite strategic priority at Cathay (phase I of the four-phase framework) and measurement systems were developed to monitor satisfaction (phase II). The challenge facing Cathay is how to model and analyze these data, turn these data into information, set priorities, and implement quality changes (phases III and IV).

Cathay collects tens of thousands of in-flight surveys annually as part of its satisfaction measurement system. Our focus is on a sample of three routes—Hong Kong–Los Angeles, Hong Kong–Singapore, and Hong Kong–Tokyo—for business class customers. The survey itself uses approximately 100 questions and is collected near the end of each flight from a sample of passengers. Most of the survey questions are ratings of various attributes on a scale from 1 (excellent) to 7 (terrible). The questions themselves are organized around several key aspects of Cathay's operations: reservations, check-in, boarding and departure, baggage delivery, cabin crew, food and drink, cabin environment, and in-flight entertainment. Customer satisfaction is measured on a transaction-specific basis, in which customers rate their overall experience with Cathay on the flight using a single 1–7 scale.[22] Customers are also asked categorically whether they would fly Cathay Pacific for their next trip (yes or no).

---

[20]The author thanks Helen Lok and Vivian Chan for providing much of the information and customer satisfaction data used in this case. The CSM presented here was developed by the author using the information provided and is not meant to represent that currently being used at Cathay.

[21]The DrainCo name is fictitious and used to protect anonymity. The CSM model presented here was developed jointly by the author and a supervised student team and is not meant to represent that currently being used at the company.

[22]Cathay also asks a yes/no (Are you satisfied with our service?) question. However, the response rate was relatively low, and there was more information in the overall experience measure.

The CSM presented here focuses on a sample of 1,055 business class survey respondents who traveled the three routes. Of the eight possible benefit drivers, five are salient to the business class segment: check-in, punctuality, cabin crew, food and drink, and cabin environment. The CSM for business class customers based on these benefit drivers and the survey attributes used to measure these drivers are detailed in figure 8.10. With the exception of punctuality, the other four benefits are all measured using multiple survey items, and customer satisfaction and customer loyalty are each measured with a single item.

The model estimation results illustrate several limitations in the methodology.[23] First, the model R^2 or variance explained in customer satisfaction is only 0.21. This means that the model is only able to explain 21 percent of the variation in satisfaction across the business class customers. This relatively poor performance can be traced to several aspects of the measurement system and model. The measurement is

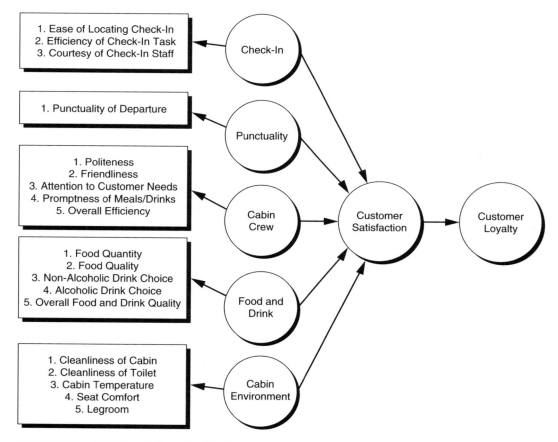

FIGURE 8.10 CSM for Cathay Pacific Business Class Customers

---

[23]Both the Cathay and DrainCo models presented here were estimated using PLS.

based on a particular transaction rather than a customer's experience with Cathay Pacific to date. Naturally there is a host of contextual factors that affect any given flight that cancel out over time.

Another fundamental problem is that the in-flight survey and CSM model are not based on a conceptual model of benefit and attribute drivers from the customers' perspective; there is no lens of the customer. Rather, the survey and model take an internal perspective. The various "benefits" represent various parts of Cathay's internal organization and procedures. The measurement of customer satisfaction is also based on a single 7-point scale, which makes it more difficult to estimate the impact of various benefits or drivers on satisfaction than is the case for a multiple-item index.

The actual level of customer satisfaction is 77.25 for this sample, and customer loyalty is at 93.6 (both on 0- to 100-point indices). The high rating on customer loyalty is misleading. The model R^2 or variance explained in customer loyalty is a dismal 0.01. This means that the model is only able to explain 1 percent of the variation in loyalty across customers. The estimated impact of satisfaction on customer loyalty is only 0.085. This means that a 5-point increase in customer satisfaction increases customer loyalty by only 0.425 points (again on 0- to 100-point indices). It would be a mistake to conclude either that Cathay's customers are particularly loyal or that satisfaction has little to no impact on loyalty. Rather, it illustrates the problem with using relatively insensitive yes/no survey items in a customer satisfaction context. Because there is so little information in the loyalty question (93.6 percent of customers said yes), it provides a poor basis for modeling.

The estimated impact and performance levels for the five drivers are illustrated in figure 8.11. As for satisfaction and loyalty, the performance measures are presented on 0- to 100-point indices and the impact scores represent effect sizes. Where multiple survey attributes are used to measure benefit performance, the level is a weighted index of the attribute values. The cabin environment has by far the largest impact on satisfaction (0.30) followed by cabin crew (0.13), food and drink (0.10), punctuality (0.05), and check-in (0.05). So, for example, a 5-point increase in the cabin environ-

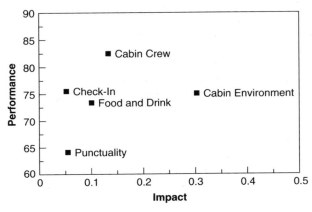

FIGURE 8.11 Performance versus Impact for Cathay Pacific Business Class Customers

ment index results in a 1.5-point increase in the satisfaction index. In contrast, performance is highest on the quality of the cabin crew (82.5) followed by check-in (75.5), cabin environment (75.3), food and drink (73.5), and punctuality (64.1). Therefore, the cabin environment and to a lesser degree the crew's treatment of the customers are the primary drivers of satisfaction. Of these, Cathay performs much better on its cabin crew service than on its cabin environment.

The next step is to classify the various drivers into a strategic satisfaction matrix and set priorities for improvement. This requires managers to make judgments using the information provided. The cabin crew is a relative strength for Cathay (moderate impact, high performance). Disregarding the problems associated with the survey methodology, check-in, food and drink, and punctuality may all be classified as relatively inconsequential. Money used to improve these benefits would not be well spent. Punctuality is more curious in this regard than check-in and food and drink. It may be the case that customers attribute the causes of a punctual or late departure to being beyond Cathay's control.

The cabin environment is more essential to improve. The estimation reveals that, of the five attributes used to measure cabin environment, seat comfort carries the most weight, cleanliness of the toilet received the least weight, and the other three attributes are in the middle. Rated attribute performance is highest for cleanliness of the toilets and lowest for cabin temperature, with the other three attributes in the middle. So, from an implementation standpoint, Cathay has important information on how to go about improving the cabin environment: Improve seat comfort, and keep the cabin temperature at a more comfortable level. Cost considerations are critical here, as managers must then decide which improvements are implementable. Whereas cabin temperature may be easier to monitor and control, improving seat comfort may require costly infrastructure changes.

Cathay Pacific recognized that its customer satisfaction measurement system, while providing important insights and directions for quality improvement, needed to be improved. This prompted a major overhaul of the entire measurement system.

Customer Satisfaction at DrainCo

DrainCo is a medium-sized manufacturer of high-density polyethylene drainage products for use in construction, agricultural, and home building applications. Our focus is on the construction segment, where polyethylene drainage materials have replaced concrete-based materials. An innovator in this market, DrainCo has experienced double-digit growth but is coming under increased pressure as competitors enter the market. It has built a strong reputation for carrying high-quality products and having an excellent sales force. To manage its growth and address the increase in competition, DrainCo has begun to recognize the need to focus more directly on customers and explore the value of a satisfaction measurement system.

In the example presented here, 404 construction segment customers were surveyed by telephone regarding their experience to date with DrainCo as a construction materials supplier. These respondents included construction engineers, contractors, and distributors. Because separate models reveal relatively small differences across the three customer types, a single overall CSM is presented here. In contrast to the Cathay Pacific model, the CSM for DrainCo is based on a conceptual model of the benefits or drivers of satisfaction. Using a series of one-on-one interviews of customers (some involving a laddering-type exercise), an initial model was developed involving eight possible benefit drivers (product choice, product quality, customer inquiries, the quality of printed information, customer assistance, price, shipping quality, and the customer's relationship with DrainCo's sales force) and their attributes. To provide an example that is comparable to the Cathay CSM in figure 8.10, a CSM was developed involving the five most salient benefits: product choice, product quality, price, shipping quality, and sales force. This CSM and the survey attributes used to measure the benefits are detailed in figure 8.12.

There are important differences between DrainCo's survey and measurement system and Cathay's. All the attributes in the telephone survey were rated on 10-point scales. Satisfaction is a weighted average or index of two survey measures: an overall satisfaction rating and a comparison of DrainCo's performance with an ideal sup-

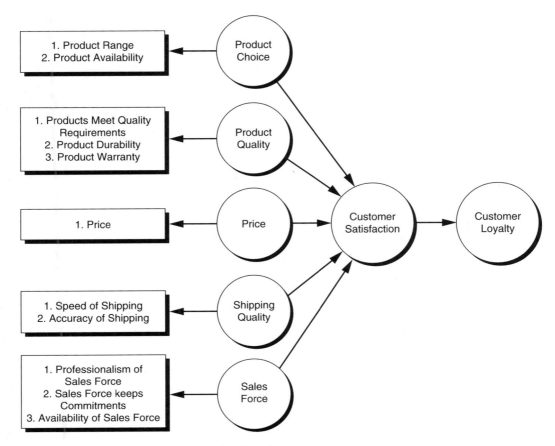

FIGURE 8.12 CSM for DrainCo Construction Customers

plier of drainage products (both on 10-point scales). Customer loyalty is also a weighted average or index of two measures: a repurchase likelihood measure (10-point scale) and a rating of how much DrainCo could increase its prices (as a percentage) before customers would definitely purchase from a competitor.

The estimation results reveal a satisfaction index of 81.2 and a loyalty index of 83.6 (both on 0- to 100-point indices). The model R^2 or variance explained is 0.65 for satisfaction and 0.50 for customer loyalty. Thus, in contrast to the Cathay model, the five drivers explain 65 percent of the variation in the satisfaction index and satisfaction explains 50 percent of the variation in customer loyalty. This illustrates how a measurement system that (1) adopts a cumulative approach to satisfaction, (2) uses a sound qualitative or conceptual model of how customers view performance, and (3) uses sensitive benefit, satisfaction, and loyalty indices is better able to estimate both the drivers and consequences of customer satisfaction. The estimated impact of satisfaction on loyalty is 0.71. Thus a 5 point increase in customer satisfaction results in a 3.5 point increase in customer loyalty. Again, because more sensitive measures are used to tap customer loyalty, this is a better estimate of the impact that satisfaction has on customers' predisposition to repurchase materials from DrainCo.

The estimated impact and performance levels for the five drivers in the DrainCo CSM are illustrated in figure 8.13. As for satisfaction and loyalty, the performance measures are again presented as 0- to 100-point indices. Consistent with its reputation, DrainCo shows strong performance on both sales force (83.9) and product quality (85.1), and to a lesser extent on product choice (81.6) and shipping quality (80.0). Performance is lowest on price (74.4), which is understandable given that the competition is now challenging DrainCo's ability to charge a premium price. Most important to customers is DrainCo's sales force, where an impact of 0.47 compares with 0.24 for product choice, 0.16 for price, 0.11 for product quality, and 0.09 for shipping quality.

Classification of these benefits into strategic priorities again involves some managerial judgment. The relationship between DrainCo's sales force and its customers is obviously a major competitive strength. The impact is so strong relative to the other

FIGURE 8.13 Performance versus Impact for DrainCo Construction Customers

four drivers that the priority setting may effectively focus on these remaining benefits. Among these, product choice is another relative advantage that must be maintained if not improved, especially relative to product quality. At this point, further increases in product quality are not called for. Price may be the top priority for change.

The attribute ratings and weights again provide insight into how these priorities can be implemented. For product choice, having a wide range of products carries more weight than having those products immediately available, although customer ratings on these two attributes are roughly equal. Overall, it appears that the immediate priorities for DrainCo are to provide a wider range of products at more competitive prices.

Summary

Customer satisfaction is a major link in the path from production to profitability. Satisfaction is a lens through which customers evaluate performance and become either predisposed toward or disenchanted with particular product or service providers. To predict customer loyalty, this satisfaction is best viewed as a cumulative evaluation of a customer's purchase and consumption experience to date. Both performance drivers and customer expectations positively affect this cumulative satisfaction. The degree to which performance disconfirms expectations is but one benchmark customers use to evaluate satisfaction, which limits the value of purely disconfirmation-based models.

Cumulative satisfaction provides a solid foundation for building a performance-based customer satisfaction modeling and measurement system. There are several important qualities that enhance the value of such a system. One is to model the translation from attributes to benefits to satisfaction using a conceptual model or "lens" that describes how customers themselves view and evaluate product and service performance. A second is to use sensitive scale ratings and multiple measures to construct benefit, satisfaction, and loyalty indices. A third is to use these indices to statistically estimate the impact the various benefits have on satisfaction as well as the impact that satisfaction has on a firm's own performance measures.

Combining the performance and impact information identifies those benefits whose impact on satisfaction is high and performance is low. This process effectively translates satisfaction data into a set of focused quality improvement priorities. Contrasting the case examples for Cathay Pacific and DrainCo illustrates the advantages of incorporating these qualities into a satisfaction measurement system as well as the analysis required to progress through phases II and III of the four phases of customer orientation.

There are abundant market action implications of a well-developed CSM. A well-developed CSM distinguishes between that which the company controls (attributes) and that which the customer consumes (benefits) in a continuous effort to avoid marketing myopia. Foremost, a CSM effectively identifies quality improvement priorities. In the process, it provides a framework for survey design, construct measurement, and data analysis. The lens of the customer at the core of a CSM also facilitates communication of the voice of the customer throughout an organization as well as communication of quality improvements back to customers themselves. Finally, a well-developed CSM identifies important market segmentation differences that may otherwise be ignored.

Discussion Questions

1. Given the problems associated with the disconfirmation model of customer satisfaction, why does it continue to be so popular in practice?
2. Select a product or service and market segment of interest and build a CSM and satisfaction survey for customers in the segment. The model should include a lens of the customer as well as appropriate organizational performance measures (customer retention, complaints, profit, and so on). The survey should include all the questions you plan to use. Before proceeding, discuss each of the following questions:

   a. Where does the model building process begin and end?
   b. What process steps are involved?
   c. What sources of information will you need?
   d. What is the best way to attain this information?

CHAPTER **Macro Satisfaction and Firm Strategy**

Customer satisfaction models and measurement systems typically monitor satisfaction for particular products, services, and market segments. Chapter 8 details satisfaction measurement systems at this micro level and their use in setting priorities for quality improvement. At the same time, customer satisfaction has taken on national and global significance. The emergence of national satisfaction indices in Sweden, Germany, and the United States has elevated customer satisfaction to a macro level.

This chapter describes the development of these national indices, with special emphasis on the American Customer Satisfaction Index (ACSI). The ACSI is described and used to analyze the nature of competition in the automobile industry. This analysis focuses on the performance of manufacturers from three very different regions of the world—Germany, Asia, and the United States—that compete for customers in the U.S. market.

The Development of National Satisfaction Indices

National satisfaction indices provide a much-needed measure of the competitiveness of companies, industries, and economies. Existing price and productivity measures generally fail to capture the level of product and service quality in an economy, which is critically important when interpreting economic performance. Understanding the overall level of customer satisfaction for particular firms and industries also facilitates the development of firm strategy and public policy.

The first truly national satisfaction index is the Swedish Customer Satisfaction Barometer (SCSB).[1] The SCSB was developed in 1989 as a way for Swedish in-

---

[1] Claes Fornell, "A National Customer Satisfaction Barometer: The Swedish Experience," *Journal of Marketing*, 56 (January 1992), 6–21.

dustries to benchmark and improve their competitiveness and has grown to include thirty-one industries. Germany followed with the Deutsche Kundenbarometer (DK) in 1992, which also includes thirty-one industries.[2] The results of the first American Customer Satisfaction Index (ACSI) were announced in the United States in fall 1994. The ACSI includes more than 200 firms in thirty-five industries representing seven sectors of the U.S. economy.[3]

THE ACSI METHODOLOGY

The ACSI methodology was developed at the University of Michigan Business School's National Quality Research Center.[4] The methodology uses a tested, multi-equation system to construct indices for customer expectations, perceived quality, perceived value, customer satisfaction (ACSI), customer complaints, and customer loyalty. The ACSI model relationships are shown in figure 9.1.

Customer satisfaction has three antecedents in the model. Consistent with the performance model of satisfaction described in chapter 8, overall perceived quality should positively affect satisfaction. Similarly, customers' perception of the value they

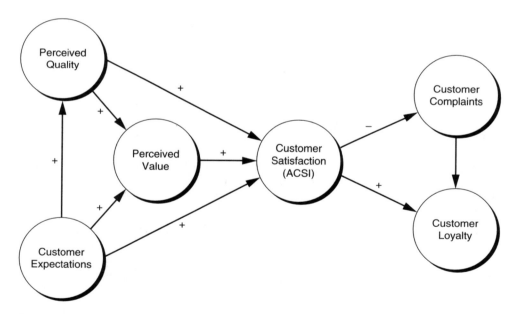

FIGURE 9.1 The ACSI Model

[2]Anton Meyer, *Das Deutsche Kundenbarometer 1994* (München, Germany: Ludwig-Maximilians-Universität München, 1994).

[3]Claes Fornell, Michael D. Johnson, Eugene W. Anderson, Jaesung Cha, and Barbara Everitt Bryant, "The American Customer Satisfaction Index: Nature, Purpose and Findings," *Journal of Marketing*, 60 (October 1996), 7–18.

[4]*American Customer Satisfaction Index: Methodology Report, 1995 Update* (Ann Arbor, MI: University of Michigan Business School, National Quality Research Center/American Society for Quality Control, November 1995).

receive from products and services (quality received relative to price paid) should positively affect satisfaction. The relative influence of value versus quality on satisfaction indicates the importance of price in customers' evaluations of satisfaction. Again following our discussion in chapter 8, customer expectations should have a direct positive effect on satisfaction.

These expectations capture a firm's quality image on the basis of its past history of performance, which anchor customers' evaluations of satisfaction in the vicinity of the expectations. The predicted positive relationships from expectations to both perceived quality and perceived value capture a customer's ability to predict quality and value. The positive relationship from quality to value recognizes that quality is a major component of value and captures the degree to which customers equate or distinguish between the constructs.

On the consequence side of the model, the primary effects of increased satisfaction should be a decrease in customer complaints and an increase in customer loyalty. Loyalty serves as a survey-based proxy for financial returns. As detailed in chapter 4, an increase in customer loyalty and subsequent retention generally increases revenues and decreases costs over time, which increases profits. Although no prediction is made, the estimated effect of customer complaints on customer loyalty provides important diagnostic information. A positive relationship suggests that a firm's or an entire industry's complaint management systems effectively handle customer complaints to increase loyalty. A negative relationship suggests that complaint handling is ineffective and opens the door for customer exit.

The database for the 1994 ACSI includes 45,906 telephone interviews with customers (approximately 250 per firm) from a national probability sample of households in the continental United States with telephones. These customers had significant experience with the products and services involved. Respondents participated in up to three fifteen-minute interviews for individual products and services. The model in figure 9.1 was estimated for each firm and industry sampled. The model produces indices that are themselves weighted composites of multiple survey items.

The survey items and the indices they measure are listed in table 9.1 (page 132). All the survey items were rated on 10-point scales with the exception of price tolerance. Customer satisfaction is, for example, a composite of three of these 10-point scale items: overall satisfaction, a comparison of product or service performance to expected performance (disconfirmation), and a comparison of performance with the customer's ideal product or service provider in the category. Recall that, compared with an individual rating scale, a multiple-item index provides a more sensitive and meaningful satisfaction measure.

Customer loyalty is a composite of two measures, the customers' stated repurchase likelihood (which is also transformed into a customer retention estimate) and a measure of price tolerance. The price tolerance measure is constructed from two survey questions, how much of a percentage price increase the customer would tolerate before switching to a competitor (if retention is likely) and how much of a percentage price decrease would be required to induce retention (if retention is unlikely).

A major emphasis in the methodology is the use of flexible survey items and the construction of indices that are comparable across a wide variety of product, service, and public sector industries. The methodology produces 0- to 100-point indices

TABLE 9.1   Survey Questions used in the ACSI Model

Question	*Index*
1. Overall expectations of quality (prepurchase)	Customer Expectations
2. Expectation regarding customization, or how well the product/service fits the customer's personal requirements (prepurchase)	Customer Expectations
3. Expectation regarding reliability, or how often things would go wrong (prepurchase)	Customer Expectations
4. Overall evaluation of quality experience (postpurchase)	Perceived Quality
5. Evaluation of customization experience, or how well the product/service fits the customer's personal requirements (postpurchase)	Perceived Quality
6. Evaluation of reliability experience, or how often things have gone wrong (postpurchase)	Perceived Quality
7. Rating of quality given price	Perceived Value
8. Rating of price given quality	Perceived Value
9. Overall satisfaction	ACSI
10. Expectancy disconfirmation (performance that falls short of or exceeds expectations)	ACSI
11. Performance versus the customer's ideal product/service in the category	ACSI
12. Whether the customer has complained	Customer Complaints
13. Repurchase likelihood	Customer Loyalty
14. Price tolerance (increase) given repurchase	Customer Loyalty
15. Price tolerance (decrease) to induce repurchase	Customer Loyalty

for all the constructs in figure 9.1. The individual survey items are weighted to maximize the model's ability to explain the ultimate dependent variable in the model: customer loyalty. Aggregate industry sector ACSI scores and an overall ACSI are constructed using averages of the industry-level results, where individual industries are weighted by their dollar sales.

1994 Baseline Index Results and General Comparisons

Figure 9.2 presents the 1994 baseline ACSI results.[5] The overall ACSI for 1994 is 74.5. The industry sector ACSIs ranged from 81.6 for manufacturing nondurables to 79.2 for manufacturing durables (including automobiles) to 75.5 for retailers to 75.4

---

[5]Some industries included in the baseline ACSI report have since been reclassified. For example, the six processed food categories in the baseline are now classified as a single industry.

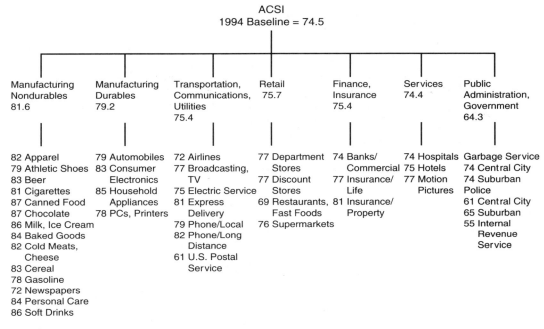

FIGURE 9.2 1994 Baseline ACSI Results

for transportation, communications and utilities to 75.4 for finance and insurance to 74.4 for other services and finally to 64.3 for public administration and government agencies. These findings are largely a result of the ability of different firms and industries to meet the heterogeneous demand of customers in the marketplace.

As introduced in chapter 5, two general factors affect the matching of supply and demand and help to explain the observed differences in aggregate satisfaction: (1) the degree of competition in an industry and (2) the product versus service nature of the industry. In industries with greater competition, customers have a wider range of choice alternatives and satisfaction is generally higher. Satisfaction is also higher for products than for services because it is more difficult to obtain consistently high quality from a service. Whereas products achieve high quality largely through their physical means of production, services rely more on the human resources of the firm and customers themselves, making it more difficult to produce consistently high quality.

Taken together, these factors suggest that satisfaction should be highest in competitive product industries, lower in competitive service industries, and lower still for public or government service agencies (where both competition is lacking and standardization is difficult). The national index results generally support these differences; for example, the ACSI averages 80 for competitive products, 75 for competitive services and retailers, and 64 for public and government agencies (see figure 5.2).

These same factors contribute to observed differences in national index levels across countries. The 1994 baseline ACSI of 74.5 compares with an SCSB of approximately 63.0 and a DK of approximately 61.3.[6] A greater representation of public and government agencies in both the Swedish and German results helps explain this finding. The highly competitive nature of U.S. markets, where customers enjoy a wide range of choice alternatives at very competitive price levels, also contributes to the observed differences.

Overall these comparisons emphasize that the ACSI scores are not simply the result of random variation or culture. The index scores are meaningful and reflect the ability of firms and industries to provide high-quality products and services to a heterogeneous customer population. This suggests that national satisfaction indices such as the ACSI are an important source of information for firms and industries interested in understanding the nature of competition, the strengths and weaknesses of competitors, and the challenges and opportunities they face.

Changes in the ACSI over time also stand to provide interesting insights into firm, industry, and overall economic performance. For example, the U.S. Postal Service has shown the single largest increases in the ACSI from 1994 through 1996 (from 61 in 1994 to 69 in 1995 to 74 in 1996). Not surprisingly, the U.S. Postal Service is reporting record profits. In contrast, the overall ACSI has declined significantly over its first two-plus years of existence (from 74.5 in 1994 to 73.0 by the first quarter of 1996).[7] These declines come from the service sectors of the economy and signal a warning. Downsizing has helped several service firms to reduce their operating costs, but at what price? The decline in service quality suggests that these same firms will suffer from lower profits in the long run due to the economic consequences of customer defection.

Global Competition in the Automobile Industry

The U.S. automobile (and van) market is extremely competitive. Customers choose among a wide variety of manufacturers, models, and price levels. Analysis of the ACSI results for the automobile industry provides an excellent view of the global nature of competition in this industry, where manufacturers from Europe, the United States, and Asia compete head to head for customer satisfaction and repeat sales. The analysis here examines eighteen competitors that were included in the 1994 ACSI results, including three German manufacturers, six Asian manufacturers (Japanese and Korean), and nine divisions of the three large U.S. manufacturers. The survey included customers who had purchased or leased a new automobile (or van) from one of these firms or divisions at least six months ago and up to three years ago.

---

[6]The SCSB and ACSI use the same methodology to produce the 0–100 satisfaction index score. The DK score reported here is based on a simple average of the thirty-one industries for which results are reported. The DK uses a single 5-point scale that ranges from 1 (completely satisfied) to 5 (dissatisfied) to measure customer satisfaction. The 61.3 figure represents a translation of this average 5-point scale rating to a 0–100 satisfaction scale. Thus at least some of the difference observed between the DK and the other two indices is due to the difference in the methodologies and scales used.

[7]Claes Fornell, et al. (1996).

The ACSI provides benchmarks and diagnostics that are central to the development of a competitive global strategy. To keep the identities of the individual firms confidential, results are presented here for the three national groups of manufacturers described previously: German, Asian, and U.S. Table 9.2 presents some of the major results for the auto industry across the three regions of origin. This includes 0–100 point index scores for customer satisfaction (ACSI), customer expectations, perceived quality, and perceived value. The industry averages for these indices are 79 for the ACSI, 84 for customer expectations, 86 for perceived quality, and 82 for perceived value. Given the intense nature of competition in this industry, these figures are all relatively high compared with products and services in other ACSI industries and sectors.

Table 9.2 also includes a ratio of the relative contribution of customization versus reliability toward increasing perceived quality. A ratio greater than one means that improved customization, or having products that are better at meeting customer needs, has a greater effect on perceived quality than does improved reliability, or minimizing things gone wrong. When the ratio is less than one, improving reliability has a greater effect. The table then includes a 0–1 measure of customer retention, which is a transformation of the repurchase likelihood question from table 9.1. Finally, the estimated impact of a 5-point increase in satisfaction on customer retention is reported. This result reflects how much customer retention will increase (as a percentage) when a firm's ACSI increases by five points (e.g., from 75 to 80).

Overall there is relatively little difference among Asian, German, and U.S. manufacturers with respect to their ability to satisfy customers. The relatively equal level of satisfaction across regions is the result of firm- and division-level ACSI scores that vary widely within each of the three regions of origin. These differences are illustrated in figure 9.3 (page 136), which presents the individual ACSI scores for the firms and divisions based in Asia, Germany, and the United States. Each region contains firms or divisions whose scores are both more than and less than the automobile industry average of 79.

The results for expectations, which reflect the level of quality that a customer expects from a manufacturer (i.e., the manufacturer's quality image), show there is a difference across regions. Customers in the United States expect higher average qual-

TABLE 9.2 ACSI Results for Automobile Manufacturers by Region

	Asian	*German*	*U.S.*
Customer Satisfaction (ACSI)	80.0	80.3	79.2
Expectations (Image)	84.0	88.0	84.0
Perceived Quality	87.5	86.3	85.9
Perceived Value	84.3	82.3	81.6
Relative Contribution of Customization versus Reliability	1.47	1.15	1.28
Customer Retention	62%	66%	64%
Impact of ACSI on Retention	5.55	5.17	5.73

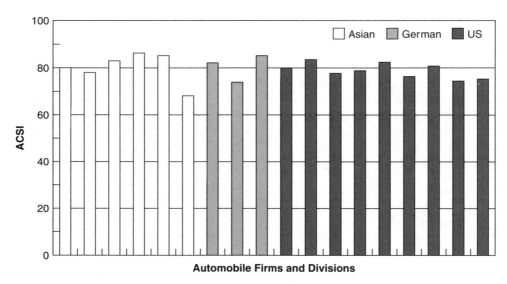

FIGURE 9.3 1994 ACSI Automobile Results by Firms and Divisions

ity from German manufacturers (88) compared with U.S. and Asian manufacturers (both at 84). This may reflect the particular "niche" or position that German cars fill in the U.S. market, where they compete primarily in the more expensive sport and luxury car segments.

Similar to the satisfaction index results, Asian, German, and U.S. manufacturers vary only slightly on perceived quality and perceived value (see table 9.2). The differences are smaller for perceived quality, where the index ranges from 85.9 (U.S.) to 86.3 (German) to 87.5 (Asian), than for perceived value, where the index ranges from 81.6 (U.S.) to 82.3 (German) to 84.3 (Asian). This demonstrates that there are no large differences among the three regions of origin on the key drivers of satisfaction: quality and value. Asian manufacturers do, however, have some advantage over both their U.S. and German counterparts in providing customer value. Although the differences across regions are small, large firm-level differences remain which are valuable in identifying competitive strengths and weaknesses. Comparing individual firms and divisions simultaneously on quality and value helps identify these strengths and weaknesses, as shown in figure 9.4.

The figure shows the perceived quality and perceived value indices by firm or division and includes the regression line across the observations. The regression line shows, for example, the level of value that one would expect from a given level of quality. Firms or divisions that are above the regression line provide higher value than one would expect from their perceived quality. Firms or divisions that are below the regression line provide lower value than one would expect from their perceived quality.

Several observations are interesting. First, there are Asian competitors at both the high-quality/high-value and low-quality/low-value extremes. Consistent with the results in table 9.2, the Asian competitors offer marginally greater value than would

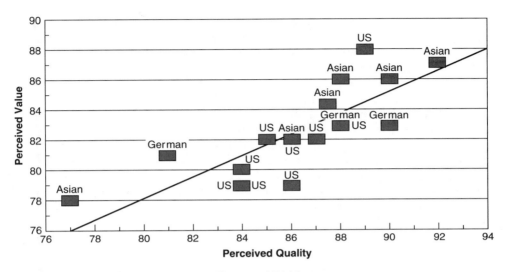

FIGURE 9.4 Quality versus Value by Firms and Divisions

be expected from their perceived quality. With one major and one minor exception, the nine divisions of the major U.S. competitors offer marginally less value than would be expected from their perceived quality. Finally, of the two highest perceived quality German manufacturers, one provides lower value than expected given its level of perceived quality. The third German manufacturer, which is lower on perceived quality, offers a higher level of value than is expected given this quality. Overall, these comparisons illustrate just how the different firms and divisions compete in this market.

Although various philosophies exist on how to improve perceived quality and satisfaction, they all involve two common themes.[8] First, firms must focus on an accurate set of customer specifications or requirements. Second, they must have a production and service or maintenance process that ensures conformance to those specifications. From a customer perspective, these major dimensions of quality translate into whether a product fits the customer's own personal requirements, or how "customized" the product is, and how often things go wrong with that product, or how "reliable" it is.

Questions regarding both customization and reliability are used to operationalize perceived quality in the ACSI methodology (see table 9.1). The ACSI model for each firm or division in the automobile industry provides diagnostic information regarding the contribution of each of these factors toward improving perceived quality. The relative contribution of these factors is presented in table 9.2 as a ratio. The results show that for Asian manufacturers to improve perceived quality, it is 47 percent more important for them to improve customization than it is to improve reliability

[8]Joseph M. Juran and Frank M. Gryna, *Juran's Quality Control Handbook*, 4th Ed. (New York: McGraw-Hill, Inc., 1988). See also W. Edwards Deming, *Management of Statistical Techniques for Quality and Productivity* (New York: New York University, Graduate School of Business, 1981).

(ratio of 1.47). High ratings for Asian versus U.S. and German manufacturers on reliability suggest that this result reflects, in part, diminishing returns to further increases in reliability. U.S. customers may also buy an Asian automobile because of its reliability, despite the fact that it is not exactly the size or type of vehicle the customer wants.

In contrast, it is 28 percent more important for U.S. automobile divisions to improve customization versus reliability (ratio of 1.28), whereas improving customization and reliability are more equally important for buyers of German automobiles (ratio of 1.15). Again, increasing customization may have less impact on perceived quality for German than for U.S. manufacturers because of the well-defined position or niche that German autos have in the U.S. market. Although these regional comparisons are interesting, it is important to note that across all three regions, improving customization has a greater impact on increasing perceived quality than does improving reliability. This suggests that in this industry, it is generally more important to obtain a better understanding of customer requirements than it is to focus on improving conformance to specifications.

The last two results in table 9.2 refer to the customer loyalty component of the ACSI model. The first is customer retention, which is a nonlinear transformation of the repurchase likelihood question. It reflects the likelihood that a customer will purchase or lease his or her next vehicle from that manufacturer. The table shows that customer retention is highest for manufacturers based in Germany (66 percent), followed by those based in the U.S. (64 percent) and Asia (62 percent). The final result in the table is the expected percentage point increase in customer retention that would result from a 5-point increase in ACSI (customer satisfaction). This value is only slightly lower for German manufacturers (5.17) than for either U.S. or Asian manufacturers (5.73 and 5.55 respectively). This suggests that if German manufacturers were, for example, to increase satisfaction by 5 points, their customer retention score would increase from 66% to approximately 71%. These two sets of results are quite consistent when one considers that there are diminishing returns to customer retention from increased satisfaction. While stated repurchase likelihoods are highest for the Germans, they gain somewhat less in retention from increased satisfaction than do their U.S. and Asian competitors.

Time Trends in the SCSB

Although the Swedish automobile market is smaller than the U.S. market, it too represents a very competitive environment that includes many of the world's major manufacturers. Because the SCSB has been in place since 1989, it offers particular insight into the dynamics of customer satisfaction for automobiles. Figure 9.5 presents the SCSB results for the automobile industry over the time period 1989–1994. The average satisfaction index is presented for three groups of competitors: German, Asian, and others (i.e., other European and U.S.).

The most interesting observation is that, whereas customer satisfaction has remained at more or less the same levels for German and other manufacturers, it has steadily declined for Asian manufacturers. The Asian manufacturers have lost the sat-

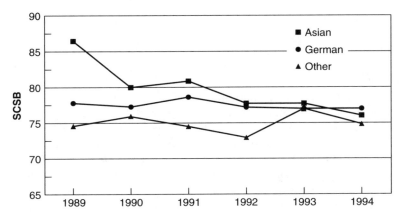

FIGURE 9.5 SCSB Results for Automobiles over Time

isfaction advantage that they enjoyed in the 1980s to a point where, as is the case in the ACSI, customer satisfaction does not vary much by region. An analysis of the individual firm data (not shown) also reveals that year-to-year differences in the SCSB are heavily influenced by new product introductions. The introduction of new automobile models increases firm-level SCSB scores, which then level out and eventually decrease over time.

Summary

The development of national satisfaction indices has turned customer satisfaction into a global measure of performance. It is important that firms use both their own internal satisfaction measurement systems and the information available in macro-level indices to understand the opportunities and challenges they face. An analysis of the U.S. automobile (and van) market illustrates the capability of the ACSI methodology and results to provide important insights into how competitors from Asia, Germany, and the United States compete on customer expectations, perceived quality, perceived value, customer satisfaction, and customer retention. The results of this analysis are summarized here in the form of six challenges currently facing these competitors.

Challenges for the Auto Industry

The ACSI methodology represents a powerful new source of information that firms can use to set strategy. The first challenge to automobile firms is to use this information effectively to understand their strengths and weaknesses. For example, as revealed by our comparison of customization versus reliability, Asian competitors should concentrate more on improving the portfolio of vehicles that they offer for diverse customer needs. Consistent with this, Honda recently introduced sport utility vehicles and minivans into the U.S. market.

It is often assumed that there are differences in quality and customer satisfaction across regions of origin when none, in fact, exist. The ACSI results reveal that there is little difference among German, U.S., and Asian manufacturers on perceived quality and customer satisfaction. The second challenge facing firms in this industry is to avoid country- or culture-based explanations of market performance differences when they are not empirically supported. At the same time, the data supports large differences in firm performance within regions of origin. Asian manufacturers include both Korean and Japanese firms, which differ significantly on quality and satisfaction. Similar differences exist among the various divisions of U.S. manufacturers.

The third challenge relates directly to German manufacturers who enjoy an advantage over their competitors on customer expectations. U.S. customers expect more from German cars than from U.S. or Asian cars. The challenge here is for German firms to take advantage of this opportunity. Their brand equity in the U.S. market is a major asset, but it requires significant and continued investment. This could include investments in advertising that reinforces the market position that German automobiles have in the market as high-quality, high-status products.

The fourth challenge again relates to the observed lack of large differences in perceived quality and value across regions (though not across firms). Specifically, how could strategic advantages on these dimensions be created? Many firms are currently focusing on the development and delivery of high-quality customer service in an attempt to create such an advantage. As the competition to build better products has created relatively small differences in "hardware," differences in "software" have become more important. Firms that can create more effective service delivery and higher service satisfaction stand to differentiate themselves in this highly competitive market.

The fifth challenge relates to the more general observation that customization, or having products and services that fit customer needs, has a greater impact on perceived quality than does reliability, or having products and services that do not break down. The total quality programs of the 1980s were very good at improving reliability. The major challenge now facing automobile firms is how to increase customization.

Improvements in customization will depend on at least three factors. The first is the ability of firms to install effective customer satisfaction measurement systems to focus their quality improvement efforts. A second factor is the use of creative market research to better understand customer needs. Firms must avoid the tendency to let their market research processes become routine and myopic. A third factor, mentioned previously, is the delivery of superior customer service.

Last but not least, the analysis of satisfaction results in both Sweden and the United States shows rather clearly that Asian manufacturers have lost much of the customer satisfaction advantage that they enjoyed in the 1980s. The challenge here is whether any manufacturers can take advantage of this opportunity to create a satisfaction advantage of their own. The time trend results also suggest that firms should not blindly benchmark on particular products or manufacturers. Benchmarking may only be valuable when trying to improve a particular dimension of product or service quality on which a competitor excels.

Discussion Questions

1. What are the key marketing and corporate strategy implications of increases or decreases in a firm's ACSI, overall perceived quality, and/or overall perceived value?

2. What is the value of a national customer satisfaction index vis-à-vis a firm's internal customer satisfaction measurement system? How do they complement and/or compete with each other?

3. As national satisfaction indices grow, what limitations do you foresee in the effectiveness of these indices in identifying differences in the quality of consumption across nations?

10

CHAPTER

Customer Orientation and the Design Function

Implementing a customer orientation requires both communicating customer priorities throughout an organization and developing and delivering improved products and services. This is the essence of goals 2 and 3 of a customer orientation described in chapter 1. Chapters 10 and 11 describe two important processes that directly affect these goals: the development of revolutionary product and service designs and the more evolutionary translation of customer priorities into their means of accomplishment.

Our primary concern in chapter 10 is to gain a better understanding of the design function within a customer orientation. Specifically, how does the design function use customer information as input to develop products and services that better meet customer needs? In previous chapters we explore various types of customer information, from concrete product and service attributes to the abstract consequences and benefits they provide and customer values served. It is important to understand how the design function operates at these different levels of abstraction. We begin by exploring the diverse views of the design function in detail, with a particular focus on industrial or product design. We then examine the more recent and unique phenomena of service design.

Two Schools of Design

Views of the nature and objective of the design function remain deeply divided. Consider the following diversity of opinions:

Corporate management does not know what good design is and would not know what to do with a good designer if it had one. . . . Most people walk in ugliness in terms of

143

architecture and merchandise. American business firms should have a top ranking corporate aesthetician who manages the design concept, standards, policies, and programs of the firm.

—Walter Hoving[1]

The greatest difficulty in the world of design is an extraordinary blindness about its raw material—the consumer. There is no such thing as the right design for all. Designers and design users have failed because of their neglect in studying the needs and wants of the consumer or the market place. The market is the mistress and always has been in design. There is no such thing as universal 'good taste.' Good taste is a function of what it is the audience, purchasers, and public want.

—Edgar Kaufmann, Jr.[2]

The question is just whose opinion is more important, that of the customer and marketplace or the design community itself. At one extreme is a design as aesthetics perspective typified by Hoving's quote. A former chairman of Tiffany & Company, Hoving stresses both the artistic value of design in affecting how products look or appear to the user as well as the failure of the business community to appreciate this perspective. At the other extreme is Kaufmann's emphasis on design as an important function in the customer orientation process, in which the customer is the ultimate judge and jury. These two perspectives are described in the following sections as design as an aesthetic tool and the functionalist school of design.

THE FUNCTIONALIST SCHOOL OF DESIGN

Functionalist design, particularly in an industrial design context, is a decidedly twentieth-century phenomena. Its evolution is the result of a separation of design from other product development functions in which market and customer research are at one extreme and engineering and production are at the other. During the Industrial Revolution, craft production gave way to more modern production methods. Under craft production the same individual was typically responsible for multiple functions, including customer research, design, and production.[3] When craft production gave way to mass production methods early in the twentieth century, these functions were formally separated. The need for a functionalist school evolved from this separation.

In the functionalist school, also known as the pragmatic view, design is defined as the integration of form and function. Many argue that the functionalist school was born in October 1907 in Germany when Peter Behrens, an architect and designer, joined the giant AEG Company in Berlin.[4] It was here that Behrens worked with such famous designers and architects as Gropius and Mies van der Rohe to develop everything from factories to products on a large scale. At this same time Behrens helped to initiate the Deutscher Werkbund as an organization to advance the functionalist

[1]Thomas F. Schutte, *The Art of Design Management* (New York: Tiffany & Co., 1975), p. 1.

[2]Thomas F. Schutte (1975), p. 31.

[3]J. P. Womack, D. T. Jones, and D. Roos, *The Machine that Changed the World* (New York: Macmillan Publishing Company, 1990).

[4]Wally Olins, *Corporate Identity: Making Business Strategy Visible through Design* (Cambridge, MA: Harvard Business School Press, 1989).

doctrine. The main tenet of this doctrine is that an integration of form and function requires designers to work from the inside out. The designer must start with the basic purpose to which a product will be put by its user and work from there to develop a finished form. The entire product is built around its underlying purpose.

In these early years there was no clear split between the artistic and functionalist approaches. Rather, the attitude was that art served more than just an aesthetic function. When combined with a functionalist approach, it added significant value to the user. A good exterior design, from an artistic or aesthetic standpoint, was viewed as a critical cue to a prospective buyer that the functional properties of a product were equally good. However, the seeds of a split were present as a secondary objective of the Deutscher Werkbund was to establish an absolute standard of good design. This effectively moved the evaluation of a good design away from customers and toward the design community.

Lorenz's description of the development of the design dimension provides several examples of functionalist design.[5] These include European automobiles and locomotives of the 1930s, whose shapes were clean, smooth, and heavily influenced by theories of streamlining for speed, stability, and efficiency. About this same time American designer Henry Dreyfuss began an evolution of tractor design at John Deere that drastically improved seating comfort, controls, cab development and insulation, and safety. More recent examples include Sony's successful use of functionalist design in the development of the Walkman and Watchman.

There is a recent trend toward "transgenerational" design within the functionalist school. The basic idea is to design a product that transcends age groups from young to old and, in doing so, develop a design that is universally better for all age groups. One example is kitchen utensils with large, soft-handled grips that are easy for everyone to use, especially the elderly. Another example is large laundry detergent bottle caps that combine a cap with a measuring cup and are easy for elderly people to grasp and open.

DESIGN AS AN AESTHETIC TOOL

The aesthetic approach gained momentum in the United States when manufacturers began to realize the importance of extending advertising into products themselves.[6] Manufacturers began to realize the importance of improving the artistic or aesthetic styling of a product and leveraging those aesthetics through an advertising medium. It was felt that products had to be attractive as well as useful, and that it was up to the art skills of the design community to provide this attraction. This approach had a profound effect on the automobile industry in the United States when, starting in 1926, Alfred Sloan at General Motors began using annual shape and style changes to implement a strategy of planned obsolescence. Harvey Earl's tail fin designs for General Motors cars in the 1950s is a prominent example of a styling change that, from a functionalist view, had no effect on performance.

---

[5]Christopher Lorenz, *The Design Dimension* (New York: Basil Blackwell, Inc., 1986).
[6]*Ibid.*

The long-standing differences in philosophy between the functional and aesthetic approaches has evolved into an open split in the industrial design community. For example, in the 1994 jury deliberations of the Industrial Design Society of America, which recognizes excellence in design through its prestigious bronze, silver, and gold Industrial Design Excellence Awards, "the artsy crowd waged war against what they considered common products for people."[7] The result was that many functionally well-designed products were downgraded in favor of mere appearance. One such controversial product was Rubbermaid's small storage shed. Based on the concept of an outdoor work shed, Rubbermaid's shed is made of low-cost material that will not rust, dry rot, or splinter. Unfortunately, because the product was not aesthetically pleasing, it was downgraded to a bronze medal.

WHICH SCHOOL TO FOLLOW?

On the surface it is obvious which approach is more consistent with a customer orientation. The functionalist doctrine of design as the integration of form and function is clearly compatible with the three goals of a customer orientation in which an organization must understand customer needs (i.e., function), disseminate this information, and follow through to produce high-quality products and services (i.e., design). It is also compatible in the sense that the customer is the ultimate judge of just what high or low quality is and, as a result, what constitutes a high- or low-quality design. As in Kaufmann's earlier quote, "the market is the mistress and always has been in design." The aesthetic approach, with its emphasis on a universal standard of good design, is more incompatible with a customer orientation. The main problem with the aesthetic approach is the need to separate art from design.

The functionalist approach also helps identify the different visions or "functions" in an organization that have the most to contribute to the product development process. Drawing on work done at Philips in the Netherlands, Lorenz describes the "ideal pooling" of cross-functional vision in the product development process.[8] Figure 10.1 is an adaptation of Lorenz's approach, identifying three critical visions in the development of successful products. Market vision is the primary source of customer information or focus. An understanding of the product functions or benefits customers desire is the starting point in the process. Although this information emanates primarily from market and customer research, it can exist elsewhere in an organization. In some highly technical companies, designers, engineers, and technicians have direct contact with customers and provide a valuable source of market vision. Thus the three "visions" in the figure can cross departmental boundaries.

A firm's ability to produce particular product forms is housed primarily in the engineering vision. This is where a firm's technological competence or knowledge of how technologies and materials can be applied to different products resides. The integration of form and function is the home of the design vision, where the different pieces of the puzzle are connected. Put simply, this ideal pooling highlights the im-

---

[7]Noel Zeller of Zelco Industries, as quoted in Bruce Nussbaum, "Winners: The Best Product Designs of the Year," *Business Week* (June 6, 1994), p. 74.
[8]Christopher Lorenz (1986), p. 23.

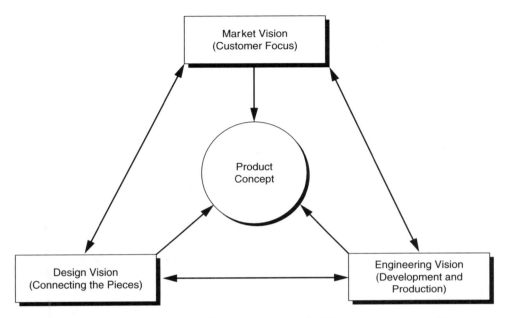

FIGURE 10.1   The Pooling of Cross-Functional Vision and the Product Concept (adapted from Lorenz 1986)

portance of a market vision for understanding what a target market of customers want, an engineering vision for understanding what is possible, and a design vision for linking the two. Notice that each vision contributes to the others. This is similar to the importance placed on the dissemination of information in an overall customer orientation. At the center of these visions is a product concept or a firm's overall vision of just what should be produced.

Although the functional approach to design is more consistent with a customer orientation, the importance of an aesthetic approach may be on the rise. It remains an important source of creativity. The development of radically new products, from notebook computers to videophones, can clearly benefit from the creativity offered by an aesthetic, artistic approach to design. An aesthetic approach is also critically important when aesthetic appeal is itself an important customer benefit that drives satisfaction. Even tail fins on automobiles contribute some aesthetic or status-related customer benefits.

The global increase in competition has also made it increasingly difficult to create functional differences in quality. As development and manufacturing times continue to shorten, competitors can quickly adopt new functional ideas. This increase in competition has created a plethora of available options in many categories. If used with the customer in mind, aesthetic design can help to differentiate otherwise similar products and cut through the clutter to communicate product quality differences. This was, after all, the original intention of the aesthetic approach. Finally, the increasingly small size of electronic components and other technology provides for greater flexibility in the use of aesthetic design, thus increasing its potential to improve product quality and value.[9]

This discussion raises an important distinction in product development between evolutionary and revolutionary design. Evolutionary product design refers to continuous though incremental improvements in existing products and product lines. Revolutionary product design refers to the development of completely new product categories to better satisfy root customer needs. Obviously both are central to a customer orientation.

Evolutionary Product Design

Evolutionary design implies the existence of a basic product form, whether it is an existing microwave oven, computer keyboard, or vehicle. It also presumes that there is a population or segment of customers currently using the product. The key to evolutionary product design is to use the consumption experience of this population as feedback to improve the product continuously. When customer satisfaction is measured through a customer satisfaction model (CSM), this design process is more a matter of implementing quality improvements. Design becomes part of the overall problem of translating the output of a CSM and quality improvement priorities into actual product and service changes. Our analysis of customer satisfaction at Cathay Pacific, for example, revealed a need to improve seat comfort on business class flights.

Evolutionary product design thus falls in large part under the general problem of implementation. Quality function deployment (QFD) is a popular quality improvement method that helps us understand the process of evolutionary design. Product design in QFD is a process of translating desired design requirements, such as reducing the pressure required to open a microwave door to make the door "easier to open," into new parts characteristics for the product. This may involve the installation of a new latch on the oven or reducing the door seal resistance through the installation of a new seal. There is an abundance of design tools available within a QFD framework to help design and develop these new parts. One popular method is Pugh concept selection, in which existing door latch or door seal technologies are evaluated and used to synthesize a new and better latch or seal.[10] (This view of design as part of an overall translation of customer satisfaction into its means of accomplishment is detailed in chapter 11.)

Revolutionary Product Design

The development of totally new or revolutionary product and service designs involves a fundamentally different approach. Surprising and delighting customers requires a process in which the market, design, and engineering visions are free of existing product forms and service processes. Foremost in this process is a focus on the more abstract consequences and benefits that products provide and customer values that are

---

[9]The author thanks Tom Granzow of Herman Miller, Inc. for pointing out these developments.

[10]American Supplier Institute, *Quality Function Deployment: Implementation Manual* (Dearborn, Michigan: ASI, 1989).

served. This abstract customer information can be obtained through various nontraditional research methods such as laddering and value surveys (see chapter 3). A well-developed CSM also provides a starting point for revolutionary design when customer benefits, rather than product attributes, are the primary input to the design process (see figure 8.8).

LADDERING, VALUE PROJECTION, AND REVERSE LADDERING

Several concepts developed thus far help to formalize this creative process into a framework. Any such framework runs the danger of being a contradiction in terms. If designing a revolutionary product were just a matter of following a recipe, surprising and delighting customers would be a relatively easy task. With this limitation in mind, the framework in figure 10.2 integrates existing tools and concepts to identify how customer information serves as a basis for developing future products and services. The framework involves three basic concepts: (1) laddering, (2) value projection, and (3) reverse laddering.

The laddering concept introduced in chapter 3 is a process of understanding how current products and services provide customers with particular consequences and benefits and, in turn, how these consequences and benefits serve customer values. Recall in the mountain bike example that "climbing hills" is a consequence or benefit provided by superior rider training, which in turn provides a "sense of accomplishment." Alternatively, value surveys such as the List of Values can be used to assess customer values directly. It may be important, however, to augment value survey and segmentation information with laddering information. Laddering enables a product development team to understand the connections between desired customer bene-

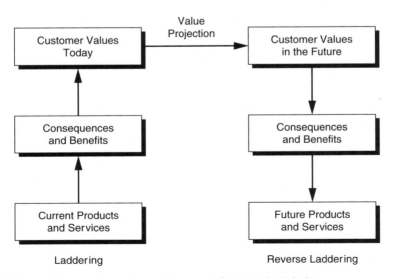

FIGURE 10.2 Laddering, Value Projection, and Reverse Laddering

fits at an intermediate level of abstraction and customer values at a higher level of abstraction.

When captured, a customer segment's current values are projected forward in time. A value segmentation scheme provides insight into the future because these values represent customers' enduring beliefs. This is not to say that customers' values are necessarily stable. Two other sources of information must be integrated into the value projection process. Customer values vary systematically with age; for example, the importance placed on "security" may be lower in high school- and college-aged than in adult customers. Value projection must also take into consideration societal, cultural, or other environmental value changes.

This integration of customers' current values, age changes, and cultural or environmental trends provides a picture of what a customer segment's values are likely to be in the future. This future value segment, in turn, serves as input to a revolutionary design process. This process is labeled "reverse laddering," because it is literally the reverse of the laddering process used to go from current products to current values. In reverse laddering, a cross-functional development team moves from the level of abstract customer values to the consequences and benefits the future products must provide to the actual form the future products will take. In a functionalist approach to product design, the future customer values represent the desired function, the future products and services represent the form, and the reverse laddering process is the integration of form and function.

Consider how to design a completely new exercise alternative for that segment of current mountain bike riders who value "sense of accomplishment." Cross-sectional or time series studies may suggest that, in five years, this segment will continue to place a high value on "sense of accomplishment" and place increased value on "security." The product development team uses this customer information as input. Other sources of input include the technological advances that are likely to be available in the future. At this point the creative juices of the development and design team take over. The same customers who value the best in mountain biking equipment and training today should be a good target market to purchase a combination home exercise machine and virtual reality mountain biking system in the future (which provides the same "sense of accomplishment" while eliminating the potential for serious accidents to enhance "security").

Although reverse laddering is an inherently creative process, there are some tools and methods available to facilitate it. One approach is to use a QFD-type set of matrices, for example, to link customer values to product benefits and consequences in one matrix and then link benefits and consequences to concrete product attributes and design features in a second matrix (QFD is covered in detail in chapter 11). Another approach is to use a strong product concept throughout the development process.

PRODUCT CONCEPTS

The product concept in figure 10.1 represents the common goal that lies at the intersection of the market, design, and engineering visions. Product concepts often use metaphors and analogies to bridge functional boundaries in an attempt to communicate to everyone involved in a product development project just what a product should be.[11] The use of product concepts in the automotive industry illustrates their effectiveness at leveraging the product development process. "A powerful product concept specifies how the new car's basic functions, structures, and messages will attract and satisfy its target customers. In sum, it defines the character of the product from a customer's perspective."[12] The concept of a "muscle car," for example, describes in a very concise fashion the popular domestic coupes with large V-8 engines sold in the United States throughout the 1960s and 1970s. Similarly, the "pocket rocket" provided a useful product concept for the compact sports cars with sport suspensions and peppy engines, known more for their excessive power than their handling, that were popular in the United States in the 1980s.

Honda makes efficient use of product concepts to communicate to all the people in a product team just what it is shooting for in an end product. In the development of the 1990 Accord, Honda used the image of a "rugby player in a business suit" to communicate the qualities of physical durability, sportiness, and professionalism that customers wanted in the car. This helped the product team to make concrete decisions regarding features ranging from the design of the headlights to handling characteristics and power. In a different context, Canada-based Bombardier has used the simple concept of a "thrill seeker" to describe both a particular segment of the personal watercraft market and a Sea Doo watercraft targeted for that segment. Another example is Canon's use of an analogy between an inexpensive aluminum beer can and a disposable photosensitive drum to develop a low-cost manufacturing process for small, self-service copiers for use in homes and small businesses.[13]

The notion of a product concept is far from new. Recall from chapter 7 that product concepts have long played a central role in Howard's model of consumer behavior. Howard uses product concepts to describe that which a customer abstracts away from his or her repeated interaction with a product or service over time and stores in memory. The use of product concepts at the design stage effectively turns the concept on its head. Product concepts enable development teams to envision what they want customers to abstract away with experience and then use that as a goal or target to shoot for. Different members of a team use the same concept to make very different decisions. A "thrill-seeking" personal watercraft communicates desired size and structural characteristics to those working on the body, engine and performance characteristics to those working on the power train, and communication themes to those working on the product launch and promotional strategy.

Service Design

The more recent concept of service design is fundamentally different from product design. Compared with products, services involve more of the human resources of a firm. Services also involve "coproduction," in which the customer and service provider

---

[11]Ikujiro Nonaka and Hirotaka Takeuchi, *The Knowledge-Creating Company* (New York: Oxford University Press, 1995).

[12]Kim B. Clark and Takahiro Fujimoto, "The Power of Product Integrity," *Harvard Business Review* (November–December, 1990), p. 109.

[13]Ikujiro Nonaka and Hirotaka Takeuchi (1995).

are both directly involved in the service delivery. The implication is that many services cannot be designed separately or behind the scenes and simply brought out of inventory when needed. Rather, service design is implicit in the development of a service strategy.[14]

Research in this area suggests that customers judge service quality on five general dimensions: (1) *reliability*, or a firm's ability to deliver a promised service accurately and dependably; (2) *tangibles*, or the physical appearance of a service setting, personnel, and communications; (3) *responsiveness*, or a willingness to help and provide prompt service; (4) *assurance*, or the employees' knowledge, courtesy, and ability to convey confidence and trust; and (5) *empathy*, or the degree of caring and personal attention provided.[15] Naturally, these dimensions do not apply universally to every service. As in the development of a CSM, the primary benefits or drivers of satisfaction are very context specific and vary from service to service. These dimensions do, however, provide a frame of reference for the service design process.

The most important dimension is reliability. A failure to deliver a promised service accurately and dependably is a direct function of the service delivery system and its design. A particularly useful tool for evaluating service designs is a service map. Figure 10.3 provides a visual account of a service map for an automobile dealership, Longo Toyota and Lexus.[16]

Service maps help visualize the service system design by depicting the chronology of service performance, thus making explicit the actions a customer takes when receiving a service. In the dealership example there are eleven separate stages of service delivery, some of which directly involve the customer and some of which occur behind the scenes.

The eleven stages include the following:

1. *Customer arrival:* The customer is greeted on arrival. If there is a line, his or her vehicle is given a numbered "hat" to enter the service queue. The customer is offered coffee and a newspaper.

2. *Repair order:* The service advisor listens to the customer's problem in detail, estimates the amount of time needed to perform the repairs plus the added time to prepare the vehicle for delivery back to the customer. The "promise time" is communicated to the customer. The customer signs the work order and is given a receipt.

3. *Post order service:* If the customer chooses to wait for the service to be performed they enter a queue. A shuttle service is provided to those customers who do not choose to wait.

4. *Service logistics:* The interior of the vehicle is covered for protection. The service advisor determines when the work should commence and finish, leaving one extra hour to wash and vacuum the vehicle after the scheduled work is completed.

5. *Parts delivery:* The technician orders the parts necessary for the work and those parts are delivered when the work is scheduled to commence.

---

[14]Leonard L. Berry, *On Great Service: A Framework for Action* (New York: Free Press, 1995).

[15]Leonard L. Berry and A. Parasuraman, *Marketing Services: Competing Through Quality* (New York: Free Press, 1991).

[16]Leonard L. Berry (1995).

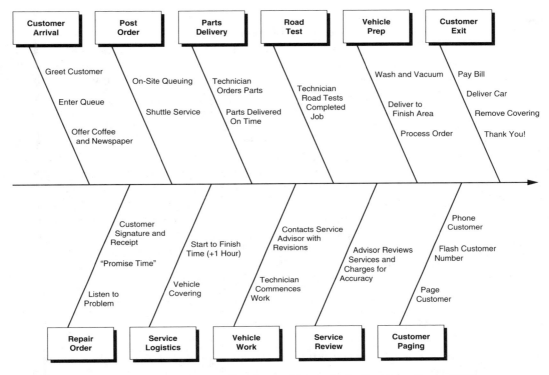

FIGURE 10.3 A Service Map for Longo Toyota and Lexus (adapted from Berry 1995)

6. *Vehicle work:* The technician commences the work at the scheduled time and contacts the service advisor if any problems are encountered that require a revision of the promise time. The service advisor contacts the customer if there is any change in the promise time.

7. *Road test:* The technician who worked on the vehicle performs a road test to make sure that the problem has been rectified.

8. *Service review:* The service advisor performs a complete review of the services performed and the charges to ensure accuracy.

9. *Vehicle preparation:* The vehicle is washed, vacuumed, and delivered to the finished area. The customer's order is processed.

10. *Customer paging/contact:* On-site customers are paged and their queue numbers are flashed on a large board in the waiting area. Off-site customers are contacted by phone.

11. *Customer exit:* The customer pays his or her bill, the car is delivered, the covering is removed, and the customer is thanked.

This well-developed service map addresses many of the problems encountered in the delivery of vehicle service. A good service design anticipates points in the service delivery that are vulnerable, where failures can occur, and prevents them. Service maps offer other advantages. They identify areas where the service delivery could be simplified, where the customer could be helped to better use the service, and the knowledge and skill levels required of service personnel.

Although the reliability of the delivered service is key, at least three other aspects of service design relate directly to the service delivery process. One is service surprise. Simply delivering the promised service should not be a surprise to the customer—that is what they are paying for. A firm must identify opportunities during the service delivery process to impress the customer (such as greeting them by name at every point of contact). A second design dimension is service recovery, or how to deal with problems as they occur in the delivery of a service. Service recovery should be personalized, quick, and performed at the first point of contact. The customer should also be informed as to why there is a problem or delay when it occurs. A third dimension of service delivery is fairness, the service equivalent to customer value (quality received relative to price or cost incurred). Service fairness is often communicated using a service guarantee. On the basis of his research on services and service guarantees, Hart argues that an effective service guarantee should (1) focus on the elements of a service that the company can control, (2) be simple and specific, (3) be easy for the customer to invoke, (4) be worth the customer's time and effort to invoke, and (5) provide a quick payout or benefit.[17]

Summary

There is an ongoing debate in product design as to whether the customer is the ultimate judge of "good design," or products should adhere to some artistic or aesthetic standard. An artistic or aesthetic approach certainly provides an important source of creativity and appears to be growing in importance. Yet the functionalist school of design remains more consistent with an overall customer orientation. The functionalist school views the customer as the ultimate focus of the design process. A superior functionalist design integrates form and function to provide customers with desired functions or benefits.

This integration of form and function varies between evolutionary and revolutionary product development. For evolutionary products, customer feedback is used to incrementally improve the more concrete attributes and features of an existing product. In chapter 11 we view this process as a translation of the "voice of the customer" into its means of accomplishment. For revolutionary products, key consequences and benefits and customers' personal values serve as input to the design process. This more abstract customer input enables the design team to think beyond the boundaries of current products and technologies to design categorically better ways to satisfy customer needs and avoid marketing myopia.

A general framework for this design process is laddering, value projection, and reverse laddering. This approach begins with qualitative research to understand the benefits, consequences, and personal values served by current products and their at-

---

[17]Christopher W. L. Hart, "The Power of Unconditional Guarantees," *Harvard Business Review* (July/August 1988), 54–62.

tributes (laddering). These abstract values and product benefits are then projected in the future to serve as a target or vision for the entire design and development team. Reverse laddering is the process of using this target to design and develop new product categories. Product concepts have become a popular tool at this reverse laddering or design stage. They communicate the intended customer benefits and functions of a product to everyone involved in the development process.

Because services are produced as they are delivered, service design is an integral part of a firm's overall service strategy. The most important dimension of service design is reliability. Service maps are a particularly useful tool for laying out the service strategy and design as a chronology of service performance. Service maps make explicit the actions a customer takes when receiving a service in order to identify areas where service reliability could be improved. Other important dimensions of a firm's service design include the ability to surprise customers with extraordinary service, to recover from service problems quickly, and ensure fairness or value in a service through the provision of an effective service guarantee.

Discussion Questions

1. What are the essential differences and similarities between a functionalist and aesthetic approach to design, and how have they changed over time?

2. How do the differences between functionalist and aesthetic design relate back to the challenges that organizations face in becoming customer oriented, as described in chapter 1?

3. What are the strengths and weaknesses of product concepts as a way to communicate and disseminate customer information?

4. What are the strengths and weaknesses of service maps in the design of new and improved services?

R

From Customer Satisfaction to Quality Improvement

Customer-oriented firms attain customer information, disseminate this information throughout their organizations, and use it to implement change, increase customer satisfaction, retention, and profitability. Implementation in this context refers specifically to the process of following through on improvement priorities to develop, deliver, and maintain new and improved products and services. This requires a translation of quality improvement priorities into their means of accomplishment within an organization. This final chapter describes this translation process.

At a general level, implementation encompasses the development and execution of an entire customer satisfaction measurement and management system covering the four phases of customer orientation. We begin this final chapter, therefore, with a summary of the four phases and their implementation. The discussion then turns specifically to phase IV and the translation of quality improvement priorities into their means of accomplishment using quality function deployment (QFD).

Implementing the Four Phases of Customer Orientation

The four phases is a *process* framework for achieving a customer orientation. In phase I, the importance of customers and customer satisfaction is integrated into an overall corporate strategy. Phase II includes the development of a measuring system for monitoring a firm's most important asset—its customers. Phase III introduces a systematic analysis of these data to provide important diagnostic information and set priorities for quality improvement. Phase IV is the process of implementing these priorities. Whatever is learned throughout the four phases is revisited in a continuous improvement process. The particulars of implementing each phase are summarized in figure 11.1.

PHASE I: CUSTOMER STRATEGY AND FOCUS

Firms have increasingly come to realize that the development of a satisfied and loyal customer base is the key to long-run growth and profitability. Yet a customer orientation can only be as successful as the buy-in and priority it receives at a corporate level. Unless satisfying customers is an important part of a firm's overall mission, efforts spent measuring satisfaction, analyzing data, setting priorities, and implementing those priorities will not have the buy-in required to succeed. The recent development of balanced performance measures, including the Balanced Scorecard[1] and the High Performance Business,[2] has helped a variety of organizations to accomplish this objective through a simultaneous analysis of multiple stakeholder needs.

Two other important parts of the customer strategy and focus phase include the setting of market segmentation and product/service strategies. Although there is much to be learned from customer satisfaction data toward improving a market segmentation scheme, the process must start somewhere. From a product/service strategy standpoint, a firm must strike a proper balance between evolutionary and revolutionary

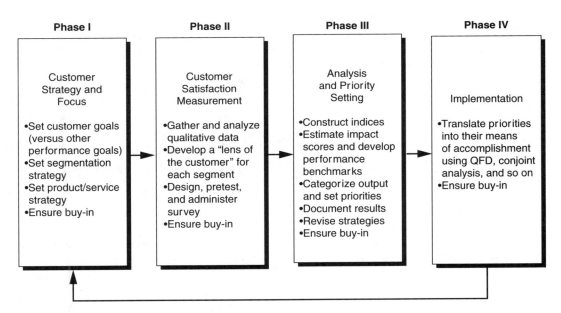

FIGURE 11.1 Implementing the Four Phases of Customer Orientation

[1]Robert S. Kaplan and David P. Norton, "The Balanced Scorecard—Measures that Drive Performance," *Harvard Business Review* (January/February 1992), Reprint No. 92105.

[2]P. Ranganath Nayak, Erica Drazen, and George Kastner, "The High Performance Business: Accelerating Performance Improvement," *Prism* (First Quarter 1992), 5–30.

product and service design and development. For a relatively mature product, for example, the goal should be to use more abstract customer benefit and value information to develop a revolutionary replacement. For a less mature product, the goal may be to continuously and incrementally improve the product. These strategy decisions determine just what customer information is important and how it should be used.

PHASE II: CUSTOMER SATISFACTION MEASUREMENT

Phase II begins as a process of finding out, qualitatively, what is important to customers, how they process information and make decisions, and what perceptual differences they see among competitive offerings. Previous chapters describe approaches for providing this qualitative insight, ranging from the simplicity of focus groups to more complex laddering, verbal protocol, and perceptual mapping techniques. This information is used to develop a "lens of the customer," or customer satisfaction model (CSM), for each market segment of interest. This lens, in turn, provides a template for survey design, measurement, data analysis, and communication. Foremost, the lens is a guide for developing a customer satisfaction measurement instrument in the form of a written or telephone-based survey.

Management buy-in is again crucial during the development of this lens. Those individuals or functions most involved in, or affected by, the quality improvement priorities that emerge from phases II and III of the process must know what changes might be involved and whether they are even possible. The development of a CSM may also require data from a variety of departments (such as segmentation information from product planning, survey information from market research, and cost and profit information from accounting and finance). Without buy-in from these departments, the information needed to leverage the value of a CSM may not be forthcoming.

PHASE III: ANALYSIS AND PRIORITY SETTING

Phase III implementation involves the development of systems for the analysis and interpretation of customer satisfaction survey data collected in phase II. There are five general steps in the process. First is the need to use multiple measures to construct indices for both customer satisfaction and the benefits that drive satisfaction. Because these are abstract or latent constructs, they cannot be measured effectively using individual survey measures. Second is the use of these indices to estimate the relative impact of the various customer benefits and attributes on customer satisfaction.[3] Performance benchmarks are also developed in step 2. Third, the impact and performance information should be categorized into a strategic satisfaction matrix to set priorities for quality improvement, understand a firm's competitive strengths, highlight possible changes in market segmentation, and generally allocate resources more effectively. Fourth, this analysis should be documented to communicate the results and their implications back to other members of an organization. Last but certainly not least, man-

---

[3]In some CSM estimation procedures such as partial least squares (see chapter 8), the indices and impact scores are estimated concurrently.

agement buy-in is again critical. The management of an organization must understand why satisfaction indices are important and necessary in this process and become comfortable using them to track performance and initiate change.

PHASE IV: IMPLEMENTATION

The quality improvement priorities that emerge from phase III must then be translated into their means of accomplishment. This involves a bridging of the quality–satisfaction gap, where improvements identified using the external perceptions of customers must be transformed into action implications within a firm. Although there are a variety of methods available to accomplish this translation, QFD is an increasingly popular method described here to illustrate the importance and complexity of the translation and implementation process.

Quality Function Deployment[4]

Much has been published about QFD since the concept was first initiated in the mid 1960s in Japan.[5] QFD uses a series of matrices to help companies focus on customer-driven product and service improvement priorities and certify that these desired abilities exist in the final product or service. It also helps companies to improve internal processes through reduced design costs and shorter product development times. Other benefits include improved communication and cohesion within a product development or improvement team and solidifying design decisions early in the development cycle.[6] Although originally developed in a product context, the method has been adapted and gainfully applied to services as well.

The traditional QFD methodology uses the four-phase system presented in figure 11.2 (page 160). In this approach, QFD starts with an input list of desired customer attributes. These attributes are often ordered hierarchically to handle the large number required to describe a complex product (e.g., an automobile door system). At the highest level are primary attributes (e.g., a door system that operates well), followed by secondary attributes (e.g., a door system that is easy to open and close), followed by tertiary attributes (e.g., a door system that is easy to close from the outside).[7] All these attributes are relatively concrete compared with the customer benefits in a CSM. It is at the level of tertiary attributes that the QFD translation process begins.

---

[4]The next two sections of the chapter draw on Anders Gustafsson and Michael D. Johnson, "Bridging the Quality-Satisfaction Gap," in Anders Gustafsson, *Customer Focused Product Development by Conjoint Analysis and QFD* (Dissertation No. 418: Paper A, Division of Quality Technology, Linköping University, Linköping, Sweden, 1996), pp. 55–88.

[5]S. Mizuno and Y. Akao, *QFD: The Customer-Driven Approach to Quality Planning and Deployment* (Tokyo, Japan: Asian Productivity Center, 1994).

[6]Abbie Griffin, "Evaluating QFD's Use in US Firms as a Process for Developing Products," *Journal of Product Innovation Management*, 9 (2, 1992), 171–87.

[7]American Supplier Institute, *Quality Function Deployment: Implementation Manual* (Dearborn, MI: ASI, Inc., 1989).

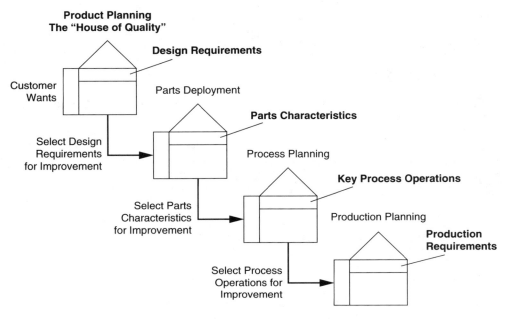

FIGURE 11.2 The Four Phases of Quality Function Deployment

In the first phase, called the "House of Quality," these attribute objectives are translated into design requirements. In subsequent "houses," design requirements are translated into parts characteristics, targeted parts characteristics are translated into key process operations, and key process operations are translated into production requirements or work instructions. This system is altered slightly when applied to services. The main difference is that, because services are coproduced with the customer at the point of consumption, it is difficult to distinguish between key parts characteristics and key process operations. Thus the parts and process houses are often combined. (In this sense QFD shares some of the features of service maps described in chapter 10.)

The four phases of QFD fulfill only a small portion of the planning needed for a new product or service. It does not focus explicitly on matters such as new technology, reliability, and cost. Recent variations on QFD use a more flexible system of matrices, in which separate matrix systems are used for product quality deployment, technology deployment, cost deployment, and reliability deployment throughout the planning, design, trial, manufacturing, and service phases of product development and launch.[8] Because, however, the two variants are essentially similar in their approach and purpose and the four-phase system in figure 11.2 is better known and easier to grasp, it is used here to illustrate the QFD approach.

---

[8]S. Mizuno and Y. Akao (1994).

The QFD process begins with the voice of the customer. Without solid information regarding the attributes that are most important to customers, QFD is based on a shaky foundation. The methods commonly used to collect this information include personal interviews, focus groups, and surveys.[9] The output of these methods is analyzed to determine the meaning customers attribute to particular statements or attributes. When these "customer needs" are structured into primary, secondary, and tertiary attributes, they become input to the House of Quality.

THE HOUSE OF QUALITY

The House of Quality, illustrated in figure 11.3, is used to understand the voice of the customer and translate it into the voice of the engineer. Similar to the priority-setting phase in customer satisfaction modeling, QFD is a focusing tool that strives to make efficient use of a company's limited resources. This requires assigning importance weights at the level of product or service attributes. These importance weights are typically obtained using different types of direct customer ratings or measures. The most popular is to use a questionnaire in which customers rate each stated attribute need using a 1–5 importance scale. The analytic hierarchy process (AHP) is another method for obtaining the weights that is well accepted among QFD users.[10] In AHP, researchers use paired comparisons of attributes and ask customers how important one attribute is relative to another, producing a set of relative importance weights for the attributes.

Customer input is also used to provide competitive performance assessments in the House of Quality. Here customer perceptions are used to evaluate how the prod-

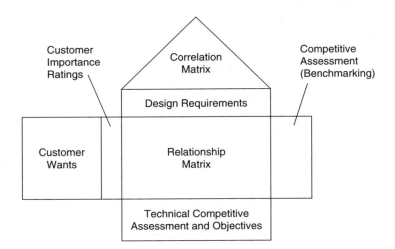

FIGURE 11.3 The House of Quality

[9]Abbie Griffin and John R. Hauser, "The Voice of the Customer," *Marketing Science*, 12 (1, 1993), 1–27.

[10]T. L. Saaty, *The Analytic Hierarchy Process* (New York: McGraw-Hill, 1980).

uct or service of interest performs on the attributes in question, often relative to immediate competitors. This performance information is obtained through different kinds of surveys of customers, again using self-explicated measures.

The customer wants are often called the "whats," or what QFD is ultimately supposed to improve. The next task is to determine the "hows," or design requirements (also called engineering characteristics) that will determine how the whats are to be fulfilled. These design requirements should be expressed in measurable terms (such as the amount of pressure required to close a door system from the outside). It is also important to point out that these design requirements are not design solutions, which come in the second house (parts deployment). There are two types of relationships specified in the House of Quality. The first is that between the design requirements and the customer attributes. A cross-functional product development team determines whether there is a strong, medium, weak or nonexistent relationship between the whats and the hows. When determined, these relationships dictate which design requirements are targeted for improvement.

The other type of relationship described in the House of Quality is that among the design requirements themselves in the "roof" of the house. Essentially a correlation matrix, these relationships capture any conflicts that exist among the requirements such that the improvement of one leads to the deterioration of another. Making a door easier to close may, for example, increase the noise level in a vehicle.

The same priority-setting logic used previously in the analysis of customer satisfaction information is used here to choose attributes in need of improvement. Both attribute importance and performance levels are examined and quality resources are deployed to improve those attributes that are important to customers *and* on which the product or service is performing poorly relative to competitors. Design requirements are then selected for improvement on the basis of their relationships to the chosen attributes. Technical benchmarking is then used to evaluate how the competition performs on the design requirements, which in turn helps the development team determine specific targets for improvement.

Figure 11.4 contains a simplified House of Quality example for a toaster.[11] Although the example highlights the main components of the first house, the reader should keep in mind that QFD matrices are generally more complex and detailed in practice. The whats that serve as inputs to the first house include attributes such as serving multiple people, being fast, being easily adjustable, and being fireproof. Relative importance measures are included to the right of the attributes. The hows used to improve the toaster's performance in this case include the amount of material that can be toasted at a time (toasting capacity) and the amount of heat produced for toasting (thermal capacity).

Notice that the design requirements should not contain design solutions or actual parts of the toaster; if they did, the product development team's ability to improve the toaster would be limited. The relationships between the hows and the whats

---

[11]This example is adapted from *What Everyone Should Know about Quality* (Linköping University, Sweden: Division of Quality Technology, 1994).

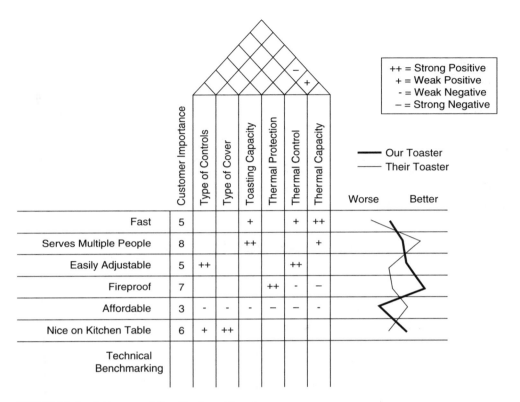

FIGURE 11.4   A House of Quality for a Toaster

are captured in the center of the matrix, where, for example, increasing the thermal capacity of the toaster has a strong positive effect on the toaster's ability to be "fast," whereas increasing the toasting capacity has a strong positive effect on ability to "serve multiple people." The roof of the house shows how increasing thermal capacity has a negative effect on thermal protection.

To the right is the competitive assessment of relative performance, where "our" toaster is compared with "their" toaster. This performance information is combined with the importance ratings to identify attributes and subsequent design requirements in need of improvement. In the example, "serves multiple people" is relatively important to our customers and is an attribute on which our toaster is rated lower than the competitor's, making it a good candidate for improvement. The matrix also shows that the main design requirements that require improvement to increase the toaster's performance on this attribute are toasting capacity and thermal capacity, particularly toasting capacity. In subsequent technical benchmarking (not shown), competitive benchmarking on these design requirements informs the team as to how much improvement is needed and where design targets should be set (e.g., increase toasting capacity by 25 percent).

PHASES 2, 3, AND 4

Subsequent houses or phases in the QFD process ensure that areas with high impact on customer satisfaction are controlled throughout the production or service delivery process. They enable people in an organization to have a better understanding of their role in satisfying customers. An evolutionary design process occurs between phases 1 and 2.[12] In phase 2, the targeted engineering or design requirements from phase 1 are transformed into different parts of the product or service. The hows from the first matrix become the whats in the second matrix. In phase 3, process planning, decisions are made as to how the new parts will be manufactured. In phase 4, production planning, instructions on how to manufacture the improved product are developed. In the case of a service, flow charts or service maps could be used to describe the redesigned service to those responsible for service delivery.

Bridging the Quality–Satisfaction Gap

In previous chapters we explore the details of customer satisfaction measurement, analysis, and priority setting. As we encounter the complexity of QFD, one thing becomes clear: Bridging the gap between a firm's internal quality improvements and external measures of customer satisfaction is a complex translation process. The translation runs from satisfaction to customer benefits to product and service attributes through design and eventually to production and service or maintenance processes. This process has traditionally been studied in two different domains: An external focus on customers has been the domain of marketers and market researchers, and manufacturing and engineering-based approaches to quality management and improvement have traditionally taken a more internal, process improvement focus.

Both areas have recognized the need to broaden their focus and bridge the gap between internal quality and external customer satisfaction. Both engineers and marketers are learning to wear multiple hats in a cooperative effort to increase business performance. Yet there are several hidden problems that plague the bridging of internal and external perspectives when moving from phase III through phase IV of the four phases of customer orientation. It seems appropriate, therefore, to end this text with a discussion of the challenges that these hidden problems present and their possible solutions. The complexity of the problem is illustrated using a framework that links the external perspective of customers with internal quality improvement methods.[13]

The framework (figure 11.5) integrates the two leading approaches to improving quality and customer satisfaction described thus far: QFD and CSM. When considered together, the approaches illustrate the qualitatively different steps in the translation process. CSM translates customer satisfaction into desired customer benefits and subsequent product or service attributes. QFD translates these attributes into their means of production. CSM identifies three distinct translation phases: customer sat-

---

[12]Recall from chapter 10 that a more revolutionary QFD-based design process might use customer values or desired customer benefits as input to the first house rather than existing product or service attributes.

[13]Anders Gustafsson and Michael D. Johnson (1996).

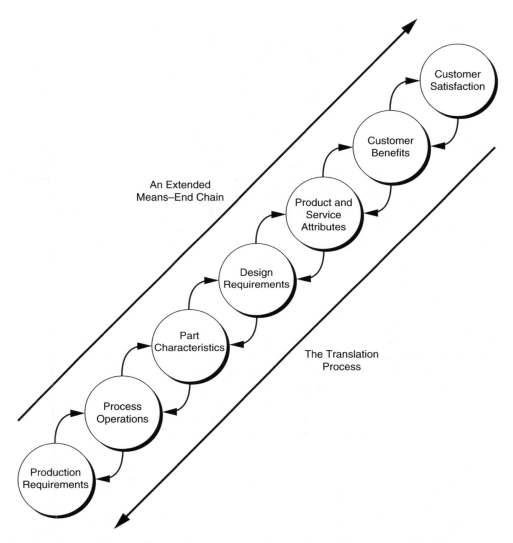

FIGURE 11.5 Bridging the Quality–Satisfaction Gap (from Gustafsson and Johnson 1996)

isfaction, desired customer benefits, and desired product and service attributes. As these attributes represent the input to traditional QFD applications, the four houses of this process can be used to represent phases 4–7 of an overall translation process.

The framework illustrates that the translation is a long, sequential process that moves from the most abstract information of interest to the most concrete. We have defined customer satisfaction as a customer's overall evaluation of his or her purchase and consumption experience with a product or service to date. This abstract, overall evaluation is the ultimate customer-defined measure of a firm's performance. Moving downstream from satisfaction to production is, therefore, a process of translating abstract, subjective evaluations into concrete, objective means of accomplishment.

Meanwhile, the process of moving upstream in the framework from concrete processes and attributes to abstract benefits and overall satisfaction is an extension of the laddering process introduced in chapter 3. Accordingly, a product or service is a concrete means to an abstract end. Making links from concrete product attributes to consequences or benefits and eventually to root customers' needs or values determines which concrete product or service attributes best meet customer needs and drive customer choice. It is straightforward to extend this process of laddering from concrete means to abstract ends into the four phases of QFD. Superior production processes, for example, are a means to accomplish superior parts characteristics, and superior parts characteristics are a means to accomplish superior product and service designs.

The framework also underscores how CSM and QFD are complementary rather than competing. Whereas CSM is aimed externally at understanding the product and service attributes and abstract customer benefits that drive customer satisfaction, QFD uses this external information as a starting point for translation into production processes. Nevertheless, there are hidden problems in this translation. Finding solutions to these problems is the key to a successful phase IV implementation strategy.

CUSTOMER NEEDS AS BENEFITS VERSUS ATTRIBUTES

The first hidden problem is the distinction between customer benefits and product or service attributes and their translation. This distinction is often blurred in focusing tools such as QFD, in which applications categorically refer to the voice of the customer as "customer needs." Although distinctions are made among primary, secondary, and tertiary customer attributes, they are all relatively concrete product or service *attributes* in many QFD applications. Disconfirmation or gap models of customer satisfaction similarly fail to distinguish between attributes and benefits.

As argued throughout the text, attributes are not synonymous with customer benefits. Customer needs and personal values are more abstract still. The solution is to clearly distinguish among these different levels of abstraction in the customer information pyramid (see figure 3.2). Customers do not value product and service attributes per se, but rather the consequences and benefits they provide and ultimately the personal needs and values they serve. Quality improvement initiatives must be explicit as to what information constitutes the voice of the customer and what information goes beyond the voice of the customer to examine more underlying or latent customer needs and values.

BENEFIT AND ATTRIBUTE IMPORTANCE

A second hidden problem in the translation from satisfaction through to production is how we evaluate "importance." There are a variety of methods currently used. Although statistical estimations of benefit and attribute importance are becoming the norm in CSM, customers' direct ratings of importance (as obtained using the AHP method) are common in QFD. The problem is that using more than one method confounds the overall priority setting process; a benefit, attribute, or internal process may become more or less important only because different methods were employed at different stages in the overall translation. An obvious solution is to use the same method for obtaining importance information in both CSM and QFD.

Wherever possible, this method should be a statistical estimation of importance. Recall that there are several problems with asking directly for importance ratings. First, it involves assuming that customers understand what you mean by "important." Second, it involves assuming that customers know what attributes are important to them. Customers do not always understand how benefits are actually produced. Third, it involves assuming that even if customers know what is important to them, they are willing to tell us. Because of these problems, asking directly for importance information may result in socially acceptable or status quo answers and poor discrimination, which negatively affects data collection costs and the reliability and validity of the responses.

In contrast, statistical estimation of importance as the impact that one variable has on another has emerged as superior to direct customer ratings of importance. Statistically determined importance weights help researchers avoid many of the problems encountered when using direct importance ratings. Statistical estimation provides measures of attribute importance that are based on customer input yet show where a firm can increase quality to improve satisfaction. From a quality improvement standpoint, importance and impact are synonymous.

Another hidden problem in determining attribute importance weights occurs in the interface between the output of a CSM and the input to QFD. Using CSM estimation provides statistical estimates of the impact that each customer benefit, or quality driver, has on customer satisfaction. It also provides measures of the degree to which each of these benefits is reflected in salient product or service attributes. These attributes are used to operationalize latent customer benefits as indices of multiple concrete measures. If, in an ideal situation, all the measurement loadings or weights placed on the attributes are equal, they provide no diagnostic information for the next phase of the translation. The size of the loadings or weights also varies with the number of attributes (measurement variables) used to measure each benefit (latent variable). If more attributes are used to measure a particular benefit, the loadings or weights for these attributes may be artificially low compared with other attributes.

There are several possible solutions to this problem. One is to keep the number of attributes per benefit relatively constant and take advantage of what information there is in the measurement weights and loadings. Another solution is to run a series of statistical models in which, for example, the impact of individual product or service attributes on either a customer benefit or overall satisfaction is estimated. A third solution is to calculate, and rely upon, mean performance levels for each attribute, recognizing that low performance and impact are not the same. Finally, market research methods such as conjoint measurement (described subsequently) could be used to disentangle attribute importance information.

BENCHMARKING AND PRIORITY SETTING

Priority setting, in both CSM and QFD, involves a combination of importance and performance information. As suggested, this priority-setting process is flawed if the basis for determining benefit, attribute, or process importance changes as one progresses through the translation process. The process is likewise flawed if the performance benchmarks change. Therefore, a third hidden problem within the overall translation process is the potential for performance benchmarks to change and evolve through the translation.

Performance benchmarks in both CSM and the first phase of QFD are typically based on market segmentation considerations. If, for example, the product or service of interest competes directly with two other competitors in a well-defined market segment, then these competitors are appropriate benchmarks (e.g., a Ford Escort, a Dodge Neon, and a Toyota Corolla). However, the nature of benchmarking practices often changes to include a broader range of products and services as one moves to internal process improvements. This internal or process benchmarking involves visiting firms with high-quality reputations to gauge their practices or reverse engineering their products to learn what these firms are doing, see how they are doing it, and understand what is possible.[14]

This broad-based internal benchmarking is a double-edged sword. On the one hand, it is important to look at how firms both inside and outside one's market segment or industry do things. It keeps firms from becoming myopic. On the other hand, it can result in benchmarking targets that are inconsistent with those used earlier in the translation process. This increases the likelihood that the priorities set in the QFD phases are inconsistent with those set in the CSM phases. A recent empirical study of QFD users supports this argument. Although firms that actively benchmark on the internal processes of admired peers increase their ability to improve their own internal processes when using QFD, they lose customer focus.[15]

The solution is to have a more focused benchmarking strategy, in which market segmentation considerations guide benchmarking practices and targets throughout the translation process. Consider the example of a full-service airline that accommodates both business and leisure travelers on short, long, and international hauls. From an output benchmarking standpoint, it makes sense to target other full-service carriers. When it comes to improving its reservation system, it would be inappropriate to benchmark on a highly niched competitor who excels on this aspect of its operations. The competitor's operations may be unrealistic and inappropriate in a mass market context. Southwest Airlines helps keep its costs low through a relatively simple, unsophisticated reservation system that works extremely well in its market niche (short haul, business travelers) but is unrealistic in other markets (in which longer hauls, advanced seating, and connecting flights are necessary).

METHOD MYOPIA

A fourth hidden problem is more general and has a relatively straightforward solution but may be the most difficult to overcome. Perhaps the most important lesson in our discussion of implementation is that a combination of existing tools or methods is needed to bridge the quality–satisfaction gap. Although engineers and marketers

---

[14]R. C. Camp, *Benchmarking* (Milwaukee, WI: ASQC Quality Press, 1989).

[15]John E. Ettlie and Michael D. Johnson, "Product Development Benchmarking versus Customer Focus in Applications of Quality Function Deployment," *Marketing Letters*, 5 (2, 1994), 107–16.

attempt to adapt to one another's methods and not "reinvent the wheel," there is a natural tendency to focus on a preferred method or tool.

The focus should be on the translation, not the method or tool employed. This problem is easier to recognize than to solve. Just as people in an organization become tied to a particular functional expertise and view of the world, particular methods and tools become the solution to every translation problem. A good example is the controversy over purported failures of total quality management (TQM), as well as CSM and QFD. Proponents of these approaches argue categorically that TQM cannot fail, CSM cannot fail, or QFD cannot fail. The problems, they argue, are problems of implementation and not with the methods themselves. Many of the failures of these methods can be traced to implementation; yet to view the methods as inherently infallible is unproductive and tautological.

To avoid this myopia it is important to consider a variety of methods that can be gainfully employed to bridge the quality–satisfaction gap. Conjoint analysis is one such method that can provide statistical estimates of attribute importance downstream. Conjoint analysis has respondents *consider joint*ly bundles of two or more attributes and rate their attractiveness.[16] Respondents are asked to evaluate product or service concepts or attribute combinations on their likelihood of purchase or some other preference measure (e.g., "How would you rate an IBM personal computer with 4 MB of RAM, a 420 MB hard drive, and a 17 in. color monitor for $1,999?"). Statistical analysis is then used to provide both an overall attribute weight (such as for size of monitor versus price) as well as "partworth" utilities for individual attributes (such as importance differences among 15, 17, and 21 in. monitors).

Conjoint analysis can be particularly helpful in identifying attribute importance weights when moving from a CSM to QFD. Alternatively, it can be used to help set design targets (as when finishing phase 1 of QFD before going into phase 2). The number of comparisons required in a conjoint study, whether using full-profile or trade-off matrices, remains a problem. Still, conjoint analysis uses customer input to derive importance weights that reflect attribute impact on customer utility. Therefore, although conjoint analysis shares the methodological rigor of CSM estimation, it is applicable at a lower level of abstraction in the translation process.

Summary

At a general level, the implementation of a customer orientation encompasses all four phases of customer orientation. At a more concrete level, the quality improvement priorities that emerge from an analysis of customer data must be translated into their means of accomplishment within an organization. Overall, this involves a complex translation process that runs from customer satisfaction to customer benefits to product and service attributes to design requirements, parts characteristics, process plan-

[16]Paul Green and V. Srinivasan, "Conjoint Analysis in Marketing: New Developments with Implications for Research and Practice," *Journal of Marketing*, 54 (October 1990), 3–19.

ning, and production requirements. Quality function deployment illustrates the complexity of the latter stages of this translation.

Our analysis reveals that CSM and QFD-type methods are clearly compatible. Their integration bridges the gap between external customer perceptions and internal quality and process change. Nevertheless, there are several hidden problems that pose a challenge to this integration. Customer preferences for existing products, services, and their attributes must be recognized as distinct from a deeper understanding of desired customer benefits and personal values. The approach to determining important performance criteria should also be consistent, whether focusing on customer benefits, product/service attributes, design requirements, or production processes. Likewise, unless performance benchmarks are consistent throughout the translation, the changes made may be an artifact of the process. Finally, an overall translation process requires the use of multiple methods and techniques along the way.

Going Forward

A customer-oriented firm attains customer information for the purpose of taking market action. This simple goal requires a variety of skills and capabilities. To go forward, it is important for the reader to explore in detail the approaches to strategy, research, and implementation introduced throughout the text. They are the building blocks of a customer orientation.

A customer orientation highlights those areas in need of further study and understanding. Clearly, a customer orientation requires having people in an organization who can work together to implement the process, learn from it, and keep it going. Given the importance of organizational buy-in to the customer orientation process, the challenges associated with developing appropriate organizational structures and change processes is a natural area for the reader to explore. There are obvious links between a customer orientation and corporate strategy development as well. Why, for example, does a customer orientation come so naturally to some corporate executives yet remain so foreign to others? A customer orientation also provides marketers and market researchers with directions for future research. These disciplines should further their integration with design and engineering to bridge the gap between internal quality improvement and external customer satisfaction. Equally critical is the need for market researchers to enhance our understanding of the complex links from customer satisfaction to financial performance.

Some readers may ask, "What comes after customer satisfaction?" Our own experience suggests that customer satisfaction is not a passing fad. More firms are discovering that creating a satisfied and loyal customer base is the key to creating a valuable business organization. As a result, the number of firms taking a customer orientation continues to grow. Customer satisfaction is even being measured on a national level around the world to capture the quality of consumption. The idea that customers and customer satisfaction are important is far from new. Rather, it appears that customers are finally receiving the attention they deserve.

Discussion Questions

1. Now that the four phases of customer orientation have been described in detail, reevaluate where your firm, division, or organization stands in the four-phase process. What specific challenges do you face in moving the customer orientation process forward?

2. What are the strengths and weaknesses of QFD as a translation tool? What factors make QFD better suited for some organizations and/or applications than for others?

3. You have "successfully" implemented the four phases of customer orientation to the point where your customers are both satisfied and profitable. What factors may keep you from revisiting phase I? What factors will facilitate your revisiting phase I in a continuous process of customer orientation?

Index

A

Abstraction, 74
Abstraction process, in information pyramid, 31
Accounting profits, 45–46
Acquisition
  of customers, 41–46
  of information, 79–83
Acquisition costs, 43
ACSI. *See* American Customer Satisfaction Index (ACSI)
ACSI model, 130–32. *See also* American Customer Satisfaction Index (ACSI)
  survey questions used in, 132
Adaptation, 60–61
Adaptive expectations model, 58, 59–60
Adaptive rationality (AR) model, 80–81
Additive difference strategy, 87, 88
Aesthetic (artistic) approach, to design, 145–46
  functionalist school versus, 146–48
Aggregate consumer confidence information, 14
Aggregate-level behavior, 53
Aggregate satisfaction, 133. *See also* Customer satisfaction
Aggregation, and expectation models, 60–61
Akao, Y., 159n, 160n
Alden, Scott D., 74n
Alderson, Wroe, 2n, 62
Alloy, Lauren B., 111n
Alternative expectations models, 58–60
American Customer Satisfaction Index (ACSI), 45–46, 129. *See also* Customer satisfaction index (CSI); Swedish Customer Satisfaction Barometer
  auto industry by firms and divisions (1994), 135–36
  and auto industry global competition, 134–38
  and automobile manufacturers by region, 135
  baseline index results (1994), 132–34
  general comparisons in, 134
  methodology of, 130–32
  model, 130–32
  and product-oriented industries, 64, 65
  quality versus value by firms and divisions, 136–37

Analysis and priority setting phase, of customer orientation, 16–17, 158–59
Analytic hierarchy process (AHP), 161
Anderson, Eugene W., 15n, 45n, 61n, 104n, 111n, 130n
Anderson, John R., 73n
Antil, John H., 73n
Apple, 98
Archival data, 33
AR model. *See* Adaptive rationality (AR) model
Artistic approach, to design. *See* Aesthetic (artistic) approach, to design
Asia, auto manufacturers and global competition, 134–38
Asset value, of customer satisfaction, 43
Associative memory network, 82–83
Attention and involvement process, in information processing, 73–74
Attitudinal studies, 14
Attribute/benefit importance estimation
  in CSM, 116
  and quality–satisfaction gap, 166–67
Attributes
  in CSM, 114–15
  in Kano model, 28–29
  in QFD, 159
  versus customers needs as benefits, 166
Automobile industry
  aesthetic design approach and, 145
  challenges for, 139–40
  competition, ACSI, and, 129
  global competition in, 134–38
  product concepts in, 151
Automotive sales. *See* Vehicle purchase process
Availability heuristic, 93

B

Bagozzi, Richard P., 108n
Balanced performance measures, 157
Balanced scorecard, 7, 13, 157
Banking industry, managers in, 8
Bantel, Karen A., 8n
Barriers, organizational and structural, 6–7

Barsalou, Lawrence W., 83n
Base revenues, 43
Basic attributes
  in information pyramid, 31
  in Kano model, 28
Bateson, J. E. G., 110n
Beach, Lee Roy, 79n
Beatty, Sharon E., 35n
Becker, Gary S., 53
Behrens, Peter, 144–45
Benchmarking process, 5–6
  and ACSI, 135
  and quality–satisfaction gap, 167–68
  and satisfaction evaluation, 113
Benefit and attribute importance estimation. *See* Attribute/benefit importance estimation
Benefits, and customer satisfaction, 119–20
Bergman, Bo, 10n
Berry, Leonard L., 152n
Blomqvist, Marie, 18n
Bombardier, 151
Boyes-Braem, Penny, 84n
Brand concept, 96
Brand-level choice strategies, 86–90
Brand-level evaluation process, 87
Brands, in multidimensional scaling solutions, 75, 76
Brown, Junius, 39n
Bryant, Barbara Everitt, 45n, 111n, 130n
Buzas, Thomas, 113n

C

Cacioppo, John T., 73
Cadotte, Ernest R., 113n
Camp, Robert C., 5n, 168n
Campbell, Donald T., 33n
Canon, 99, 151
Carmone, Frank J., 78n
Cascading strategy, 98–100
Categories, in multidimensional scaling solutions, 75, 76
Categorization, in learning process, 83–84
Category-level alternatives, 90–91
Cathay Pacific airline, 18
  CSM case example of, 121–24
Caveat emptor philosophy, 56
Central processing unit, in information processing system, 71, 72
Cha, Jaesung, 45n, 111n, 130n
Chan, Vivian, 121n
Chatterjee, Subimal, 95n
Choice process. *See also* Choice strategies; Howard model
  Howard model and, 95–100
  mapping price and quality into value model in, 91–92
  risk in, 92–95

Choice strategies, 86–91
  brand-level choice, 86–90
  category-level choices, 90
  noncomparable choice, 90–91
Churchill, Gilbert A., 108n
Clark, Kim B., 28n, 151n
Clausing, Don, 17n
Clinics, 27, 29
Clinton, William J., 64n
Clustering technique, 14
Cobweb expectations model, 58–59, 60
Cognitive representation, in information processing, 79–83
Collins, A. M., 81n
Comparative advertising, 82–83
Comparing noncomparables method, in proactive research, 38
Competition. *See also* Global competition
  measuring in auto industry, 129
Complaints, in ACSI model, 131
Compounding effect, of customer retention, 44–45
Concreteness–abstractness attributes, 74–75
Conformance, to customer specifications, 3
Conjoint analysis, 169
Conjunctive strategy, 87, 88
Consumer, 1. *See also* Customer(s)
Consumer behavior. *See* Howard model, of consumer behavior
Consumer Reports, 57
Consumer research. *See* Research
Consumption process, 102
  and customer experience model, 46–48
Consumption/satisfaction component, in customer experience model, 46
Consumption utility, 1
Contrived observation, 33
Coproduction, and services, 151–52
Cost–benefit trade-off, 79
Covariance structure analysis, 118
Craft production, 144
Credence information, 57
Crosby, Philip B., 5
Cross-functional teams, 6–7
Cross-sectional studies, 150
CSI. *See* Customer satisfaction index (CSI)
CSM. *See* Customer satisfaction model (CSM)
Cultural factors, in proactive research, 32–33
Cumulative satisfaction, 104, 105. *See also* Performance model
  modeling, 109–10
Customer(s)
  acquiring and retaining, 41–46
  expectations in marketplace, 58–61
  and marketplace, 52–67
  service quality and, 152

types of, 41, 49–51
use of term, 1
Customer acquisition and learning models, 79–83
Customer behavior. *See also* Howard model
  and economic models, 52–55
Customer choice. *See* Choice strategies
Customer costs, 43
Customer dissatisfaction, 65–66
Customer exit, 65–66
Customer experience model, 41–51, 46–49. *See also*
  Acquisition; Customers; Retention
  and customer types, 49–51
  Disney purchase–consumption–repurchase cycle,
    48–49
Customer information process, 68–85. *See also* De-
  sign function
  information processing paradigm, 71–84
  models for, 71–72
  vehicle purchase process and, 69–71
Customer input, in House of Quality, 161–62
Customer learning process, 63
Customer life-cycle profits, in credit card industry,
  44
Customer loyalty, 1
Customer needs. *See also* Needs
  as benefits versus attributes, 166
Customer "orbit," at Walt Disney World, 48–49
Customer orientation, 2, 103
  analysis and priority setting phase, 16–17, 158–59
  challenges to, 47
  customer satisfaction measurement phase, 16, 158
  customer strategy and focus phase, 15–16, 157–58
  design function in, 143–55
  goals of, 2–4
  implementation phase of, 17–18, 143, 156–71
  perspectives in, 7–9
  phases of, 15–18
  Sweden Post example of, 18–24
  versus market orientation and TQM, 9–10
Customer oriented firms, 2
Customer referrals, 43
Customer research. *See also* Research
  reactive, 26–27, 27–30
Customer satisfaction, 1, 2. *See also* American
  Customer Satisfaction Index (ACSI); Customer
  satisfaction model (CSM); National satisfaction
  indices
  asset value of, 43
  customer responses to, 65–66
  disconfirmation model of, 105–107
  downsizing and, 134
  effect of expectations on, 110–12
  framework for, 103–104
  improving, 137
  in Kano model, 28

macro, 129–41
market matching process and, 62–64
micro, 102–28
national/global significance of, 129
performance model of, 107–109
perspectives of, 42, 104–105
predicting through performance model, 109–10
priority setting and, 119–21
psychology of, 103, 104–12
and repurchase behavior, 49–51
Customer satisfaction index (CSI), 112–13. *See also*
  American Customer Satisfaction Index (ACSI);
  Swedish Customer Satisfaction Barometer (SCSB)
  of Sweden Post, 20–21
Customer satisfaction measurement phase, of customer orientation, 16, 158
Customer satisfaction measurement system, 21–22
  components of, 112–14
Customer satisfaction model (CSM), 103. *See also*
  Customer satisfaction
  Cathay Pacific example, 121–24
  customer expectations and, 110–12
  and customer orientation implementation, 158
  disconfirmation model, 105–107
  disconfirmation vs. performance model usage,
    108, 109–10
  DrainCo example, 124–27
  elements of, 114–19
  evolutionary product design and, 148
  and importance weight estimation, 116–19
  performance model and, 107–109
  and price as satisfaction driver, 115–16
  and quality function deployment (QFD), 164–66
  revolutionary product design and, 149
  and satisfaction consequences, 115
  service design and, 152
Customer specifications, 2–3
Customer strategy and focus phase, of customer orientation, 15–16, 157–58
Customer voice
  and customer dissatisfaction, 65–66
  and QFD process, 161
Customization, and auto industry, 137–138, 139

D

Dahlsten, Ulf, 19
Darby, Michael R., 57n
Decision framing, in risk perception, 93–95
Decision making, and economic models, 53–55
Decisions
  market strategy, 12–13
  monitoring-based market action, 13–14
  problem-driven market action, 14–15

Deere, John, 145
Defensive marketing, 42, 46
Dell, 98
Deming, W. Edwards, 2n
Design, concept in functionalist school, 144
Design function
  evolutionary product design in, 148
  revolutionary product design in, 148–51
  schools of, 143–48
  service design in, 151–54
Design requirements, and House of Quality, 162
Design tools, for evolutionary product design, 148
Design vision, in functionalist design approach,
  146–47
Deutsche Kundenbarometer (DK), 130
Deutscher Werkbund, 144, 145
Diagnostics, of ACSI, 135
Differentiation, in marketplace, 63
Dimension attributes, 75
Direct importance ratings, 117
Disconfirmation model, of customer satisfaction, 15,
  105–107
Disjunctive strategy, 87, 88
Dissatisfaction, customer responses to, 65–66
Dissatisfied repeaters, 50
Dissatisfied switchers, 50
DK. *See* Deutsche Kundenbarometer (DK)
Downsizing, and customer satisfaction, 134
Doyle, Arthur Conan, 33, 34n
DrainCo, CSM case example of, 124–27
Drazen, Erica, 157n
Dreyfuss, Henry, 145

E

Earl, Harvey, 145
Economic impact, of customer retention, 43–46
Economics of information (EOI) model (Stigler),
  79–80
Economic theory. *See also* Expectation models
  and customer behavior, 52–53
Economist's perspective, 7, 8–9
Edwards, Ward, 53n
Eiglier, P., 110n
Elaboration Likelihood Model of persuasion (Petty
  and Cacioppo), 73
Elimination by aspects (EBA) strategy, 87, 88
Emery, Fred, 91
  mapping of price and quality into value model of,
  91–92
Engineering characteristics, 162
Engineering vision, in functionalist design approach,
  146–47
Estimation
  of importance, in QFD, 166–67
  of importance weights in CSM, 116–19

Ettlie, John E., 5n, 168n
Evaluation process, brand-level, 87
Evolutionary product design, 148
Exit, and customer dissatisfaction, 65–66
Expectation models. *See also* Expectations
  adaptation and aggregation in, 60–61
  customer, 58–61
Expectations
  in ACSI model, 130–31
  in disconfirmation model, 105–107
  effects on customer satisfaction, 110–12
  in performance model, 107–109
Experience information, 57
Extensive problem solving (EPS), 95–96
External perspectives, 5
Extrapolative expectations model, 58, 59, 60

F

Faris, Charles W., 96n
Feature-dimensionality attributes, 75
Federal Trade Commission (FTC), 56
Feigenbaum, A. V., 2n
Focus, 1. *See also* Customer orientation
  customer, 6
  organizational, 5
Focus groups, 27, 29, 115
Ford Motor Company, 5, 28
Forecasts, in proactive research, 39
Fornell, Claes, 15n, 18n, 19n, 42n, 45n, 61n, 63n,
  75n, 79n, 104n, 111n, 113n, 118n, 129n, 130n,
  134n
Framing effect. *See also* Decision framing
  in risk perception, 93–95
France, Karen Russo, 95n
Franklin, Benjamin, on decision making, 54, 55
Frantz, James Paul, 81n
Friedman, Milton, 53n
Friedman, Monroe, 72n
Fujimoto, Takahiro, 28n, 151n
Functionalist school, of design, 144–45
  aesthetic approach versus, 146–48

G

Gap model. *See* Disconfirmation model
Gateway, 98
General Electric, 30
General Motors, 145
Germany
  auto manufacturers and global competition,
  134–38
  and national satisfaction indices development, 130
Global competition, 46
  in automobile industry, 134–38
  product design and, 147–48

Goal, of customer research, 26–27
Graded structure, in categorization, 83–84
Granzow, Tom, 148n
Gray, Wayne D., 84n
Green, Paul, 78n, 169n
Griffin, Abbie, 30n, 159n, 161n
Gropius, Walter A., 144
Grönroos, Christian, 63n
Grove, Janet Belew, 33n
Gryna, Frank M., 2n, 137n
Guarantee, of service, 154
Gustafsson, Anders, 116n, 159n, 164n
Gutman, Jonathan, 36n, 74n

H

Habitual choice, 87
Haire, Mason, projective techniques study of, 38–39
Hamel, Gary, 27n
Hart, Christopher W. L., 154
Hauser, John R., 17n, 30n, 90n, 161n
Heath, Timothy B., 95n
Herrmann, Andreas, 79n
Heterogeneity, 62
Heuristics, in risk perception, 92–93
Hideo, Tsuda, 32n
Hierarchical clustering schemes, of cognitive representations, 76, 77
High Performance Business, 157
Hirsch, Albert, 61n
Hirschman, Albert O., 65n
History factors, in proactive research, 32–33
Hogarth, Robin M., 54n
Hoglund, Dean, 39n
Holmes, Sherlock, and unobtrusive observations, 33, 34
Homer, Pamela, 35n
Honda, 28, 139, 151
Horizontal corporate structures, 6–7
Horne, Daniel R., 75n, 79n
Horne, David A., 78n, 83n
House of Quality phase, in QFD, 17, 160, 161–63
Houston, Michael J., 84n, 87n, 118n
Hoving, Walter, 143–44
Howard, John, 90n, 95n, 97n
Howard model, of consumer behavior, 48
  and cascading strategy, 98–100
  of customer behavior over product life cycle, 95–100
    extensive problem solving (EPS) stage, 95–96
    limited problem solving (LPS) stage, 96
    management over the life cycle model, 97–98
    product concepts approach and, 151
    routinized response behavior (RRB) stage, 96–97
Hoyer, Wayne, 80n

I

Implementation phase, in customer orientation, 17–18, 159
Implementation process, of customer orientation, 4, 156–71
  and analysis and priority setting phase, 158–59
  and customer satisfaction measurement phase, 158
  and customer strategy and focus phase, 157–58
  evolutionary product design and, 148
  and implementation phase, 159
  and quality function deployment (QFD), 159–64
  quality–satisfaction gap and, 164–69
Importance
  estimating in CSM, 116–19
  estimating in QFD, 166–67
Incidental learning, 80–81
Index of Consumer Sentiment, 14
Individual-level assumptions, in economic theory, 53
Industrial design community, 146
Industrial Design Society of America, 146
Industries. See also Automobile industry
  factors affecting aggregate satisfaction in, 133
Information. See also Customer information process; Information processing paradigm
  customer, 3–4
  types of market, 57–58
"Information acceleration" projection, 39
Information processing component, in customer experience model, 46
Information processing paradigm, 71–84
  categorization in, 83–84
  information acquisition and memory in, 79–83
  involvement and attention allocation in, 73–74
  limited processing resources in, 72–73
  models in, 71–72
  perception and cognitive representations in, 74–79
Information pyramid, 31–32
Information search costs, 53
Interface system, in information processing system, 71, 72
Internal knowledge component, in customer experience model, 47
Internal perspectives, 5
Internal process improvement methods, 17
International comparisons, 32–33
Interviews
  one-on-one, 27, 30
  small group, 30
Ishamaya, Junya, 32n

J

Jacoby, J., 74n
Janssens, Glen, 39n

Japan, national fundamental factors comparison with U.S., 32–33
Jaworski, Bernard J., 2n
Jenkins, Roger L., 113n
Johnson, David M., 84n
Johnson, Michael D., 5n, 8n, 15n, 38n, 45n, 59n, 61n, 63n, 64n, 74n, 75n, 78n, 79n, 80n, 83n, 87n, 89n, 90n, 91n, 104n, 111n, 113n, 116n, 130n, 159n, 164n, 168n
Jones, Daniel T., 37n, 144n
Juran, Joseph M., 2n, 137n

K

Kahle, Lynn R., 35n
Kahneman, Daniel, 59n, 92n, 93n
   Prospect Theory of, 93–95
Kano model, 28–29
Kano, Noriaki, 29n
Kaplan, Robert S., 7n, 13n, 157n
Karni, Edi, 57n
Kastner, George, 157n
Katona, George, 14, 61
Kaufmann, Edgar, 144, 146
Kerwin, Kathleen, 70n
Klefsjö, Bengt, 10n
Kohli, Ajay K., 2n
Kotler, Philip, 5
Krueger, Richard A., 29n
Kubovy, M., 78n
Kujala, Jouni T., 79n, 80n

L

Laddering, 30, 149
   in proactive research, 36–38
   value projection, and reverse laddering framework, 149
Laissez-faire economic approach, 56
Langeard, E., 110n
Law of supply and demand, 54
Leadership perspective, 6
Learning models, 79–83
Lehmann, Donald R., 45n, 75n, 79n
"Lens of the customer," CSM as, 158
Levitt, Theodore, 2n
Levy, Alan S., 81n
Lexicographic strategy, 87, 88
Limited problem solving (LPS), 96
Limited processing resources, in information processing, 72–73
Linear compensatory (additive) strategy, 87
List of values (LOV) survey, 35–36, 149
Loftus, E. F., 81n
Lohmöller, J.-B., 118n
Lok, Helen, 121n

Loken, Barbara, 84n
Long-term memory, 72
Lorenz, Christopher, 30n, 98n, 145, 146
   and pooling of cross-functional vision/product concept adaptation, 146, 147
LOV. *See* List of values (LOV) survey
Lovell, Michael, 61n
Lovelock, C. H., 110n
Low uncertainty (LU) model, 80
Loyalty
   in ACSI model, 131
   customer, 1–2, 41–42, 104
Lutz, Richard J., 83n

M

Macro-level models, of customer satisfaction, 16
Macro satisfaction, 129–41
Management buy-in, in customer orientation implementation, 157, 158, 159
Management over the life cycle model (Howard), 97–98
Manager
   and balancing perspectives, 7
   and economic models, 53–54
   information needs of, 12–15
   use of term, 8
Manager's perspective, 7, 8
Mansfield, Edwin, 54n
March, James G., 80n
Market behavior, and economic models, 53–54
Market economy, 52
Market information
   expansion of, 56
   types of, 57–58
Market information component, in customer experience model, 47
Marketing
   and customer orientation, 2
   defensive, 42, 46
   Kotler's definition of, 5
   offensive, 42, 46
   as specialist function, 6–7
Marketing myopia, 30
Marketing strategy, 1–2
Market/market segment behavior, 8–9
Market matching process, and customer satisfaction, 62–64
Market orientation, and customer orientation, 9–10
Marketplace
   customer dissatisfaction in, 65–66
   customer expectations in, 58–61
   customer satisfaction in, 62–64
   defined, 52
   government regulation in, 64
   historic view of, 56

Market research. *See also* Research
  proactive, 27, 30–39
Markets, maturing of, 46
Market segmentation, 14–15, 16, 157–58
Market strategy decisions, 12–13
Market vision, in functionalist design approach, 146,
  147
Maslow's need hierarchy, 35
Mass production methods, 144
Mathews, Odonna, 81n
Mazumdar, Tridib, 81n
McGill, Andrew R., 8n
Means–end chains, 36, 37, 165
Measurement system, for customer satisfaction, 16,
  112–14
Memory
  and information acquisition, 79–83
  models of, 81–83
Memory unit, in information processing model, 71, 72
Mervis, Carolyn B., 84n
Metcalf, Barbara L., 81n
Meyer, Anton, 130n
Micro level, of satisfaction, 102–28
Micro-level models, of customer satisfaction, 16
Mies van der Rohe, Ludwig, 144
Miller, George, 72
Mitchell, Terence R., 79n
Mizuno, S., 159n, 160n
Models, 1. *See also* models by type
Modified rebuy, 96
Monitoring-based market action decisions, 13–14
Monroe, Kent B., 81n
Morgenstern, Oskar, 53
Multidimensional scaling solutions, of cognitive rep-
  resentations, 75, 76
Muth, John F., 60

N

Nader, Georg, 111n
National Quality Research Center, University of
  Michigan Business School, 130
National satisfaction indices, 16, 129–34
  ACSI methodology and, 130–32
Nayak, P. Ranganath, 157n
Needs, of customers, 26–40
Nelson, Philip, 57n
Netscape, 98
New buy situation, 96
Newell, Albert, 71
Nolan, Catherine A., 81n
Nonaka, Ikujiro, 151n
Noncomparable choice alternatives, 90–91
Nonreactive measures, in proactive research, 33
Normative models, and customer/market behavior,
  53–54

Norton, David P., 7n, 13n, 157n
Nussbaum, Bruce, 146n

O

Oberle, Valerie, 48n
Observations, in market research, 33
Offensive marketing, 42, 46
Olins, Wally, 144n
Oliver, Richard L., 109n
  model of customer satisfaction, 110
Olson, J., 74n
One-on-one interviews, 27, 30
Operating costs, 43
Organization (firm). *See also* Manager
  and customer orientation barriers, 6–7
  process benchmarking and, 5–6
  role in customer orientation, 3–4
  shared vision and perspectives of, 5
Organizational barriers, to customer orientation, 6–7
Orientation, customer. *See* Customer orientation
O'Shaughnessy, John, 78n
Outline, of CSM, 114–15

P

Parasuraman, A., 152n
Partial least squares (PLS) estimation, 118, 158n
Perceived performance, in performance model, 108
Perception, in information processing, 79–83
Perceptual mapping technique, 14
Perceptual scaling methods, of cognitive representa-
  tions, 76–78
Per-customer profit stream, 44
Percy, Larry, 73n
Performance, and customer satisfaction, 119–20
Performance attributes, 29
  in information pyramid, 31
  in Kano model, 28
Performance benchmarks, 158, 168
Performance information, 57
Performance model, of customer satisfaction,
  107–109
Personal interviews, 115
Perspectives. *See also* Balanced scorecard
  economist's, 7, 8–9
  manager's, 7, 8
  psychologist's, 7, 9
Persuasion, routes to, 73–74
Petty, Richard E., 73
Phased or hybrid strategies, 87, 88
Philips, 146
Pirsig, Robert M., 102
Plott, Charles R., 54n, 59n, 61n
Pomerantz, J., 78n

Pooling of cross-functional vision, and product concept adaptation, 146, 147
Post-purchase evaluations, customers', 14
Pragmatic view. *See* Functionalist school, of design
Prahalad, C. K., 27n
Predictive models, and customer/market behavior, 53–54
Preferences, in customer attitudinal studies, 14
Prepurchase monitoring research, 13–14
Price
    in CSM modeling, 115–16
    in customer choice process, 91–92
Price and quality into value model, mapping of, 91–92
Price information, 57
Price/performance expectations, in expectation models, 58–60
Price premiums, 43
Priority-setting process, 16–17
    bridging internal and external quality, 120
    customer satisfaction and, 119–21
    and quality–satisfaction gap, 167–68
Proactive market research, 27, 30–39
    comparing noncomparables methods, 38
    history and cultural factors in, 32–33
    laddering techniques, 30, 36–38
    projective techniques in, 38–39
    versus reactive research, 31
    unobstrusive/nonreactive measures in, 33
    value segmentation in, 33–36
Problem-driven market action decisions, 14–15
Problem solving, in Howard model
    EPS stage, 95–96
    LPS stage, 96
    RRB stage, 96–97
Process benchmarking, 5–6
Process framework, for customer orientation, 156
Product attributes, in Kano model, 28
Product concepts approach
    and Howard's model of consumer behavior, 151
    in product development process, 147, 150–51
Product design. *See* Design function
Product development process, 146–47
Product hierarchy, in categorization, 84
Production and service/maintenance process, 3
Production memory, 73
Product life cycle, and customer behavior in Howard model, 95–100
Product-oriented firms/industries, 2, 63–64
Product reliability, 3
Products and services, market information about, 57–58
Product/service design tools, 17
Product/service strategies, 157–58
Profitability, of customer retention, 44, 45–46

Projective techniques, in proactive research, 38–39
Prospect Theory (Kahneman and Tversky), 93–95
Psychologist's perspective, 7, 9
Psychology, of customer satisfaction, 103, 104–12
Public sector agencies, 64
Pugh concept selection, 148
Purchase–consumption–repurchase cycle, at Walt Disney World, 48–49
Purchase environment, changing nature of, 56–58
Purchase process, and customer experience model, 46–48
Puto, Christopher P., 87n, 89n
    framing effect business application of, 94–95

Q

Quadrant analysis, 22, 119
Quality
    in customer choice process, 91–92
    improving perceived, 137–38
    perceived, 130–31
    in priority setting process, 120
Quality function deployment (QFD), 17, 120, 148, 159–61
    and CSM, 164–66
    final phases of, 164
    House of Quality phase, 160, 161–63
Quality information, 57
Quality–satisfaction gap, 164–69
    benchmarking and priority setting in, 167–68
    benefit and attribute importance in, 166–67
    bridging, 164–66
    customer needs as benefits versus attributes, 166
    method myopia and, 168–69
Qualls, William J., 94n
Questionnaires, 161

R

Ramaswamy, Venkatram, 113n
Ranking, value, 35
Rational expectations model, 58, 60, 61
Reactive research, 27–30
    Kano model, 28–29
    limitations of, 29
    versus proactive research, 31
Reder, Melvin W., 54n
Regression line, in ACSI, 136
Regulation, in marketplace, 64
Reichheld, Frederick F., 7n
    on economic impact of customer retention, 43–44
Reilly, Michael D., 108n
Reliability
    and auto industry, 137–38, 139
    of product, 3
    in service design process, 152

Representativeness heuristic, 92–93
Repurchase behavior, 49–50
Repurchase cycle, 13
  in customer experience model, 46, 47
Repurchase decision, 42
Research, 1
  attitudinal studies, 14
  on customer retention profitability, 45–46
  customers' post-purchase evaluations, 14
  goal of customer, 26–27
  methods, 6
  prepurchase monitoring, 13–14
  proactive market, 27, 30–39
  proactive vs. reactive, 31
  reactive customer, 27–30
  tools, in proactive research, 32–39
Retention, of customers, 41–46
  compounding effect of, 44–45
  economic impact of, 43–46
  and repurchase behavior, 49–51
Rethans, Arno, 83n
Return on investment (ROI), 45, 46
Revenue growth, 43
Reverse laddering process, 149, 150
  product concepts approach and, 150–51
  QFD-type set of matrices approach, 150
Revolutionary product design, 148–51
  laddering, value projection, reverse laddering and, 149–50
  product concepts approach and, 150–51
Reynolds, Thomas J., 36n
Risk, in customer choice process, 92–95
Robinson, Patrick J., 96n
Rokeach's instrumental and terminal values, 35
Roos, Daniel, 37n, 144n
Root needs, of customers, 26
Root values, 26. See also Values, customers'
Rosch, Eleanor, 83n, 84n
Routh, Guy, 56n
Routinized response behavior, 96–97
Rubbermaid, 146
Russell, Gary J., 81n
Russo, J. Edward, 2n, 54n, 81n
Ryan, Michael J., 113n

S

Saaty, T. L., 161n
Satisfaction. See Customer satisfaction
Satisfaction drivers, 108
Satisfaction index. See Customer satisfaction index
Satisfaction measurement systems. See Customer satisfaction model
Satisfaction scale, 112–13
Satisfied repeaters, 49–50

Satisfied switchers, 50
Schlumberger, 2, 12
Schoemaker, Paul J. H., 2n, 54n
Schucker, Raymond E., 81n
Schutte, Thomas F., 144n
Schwartz, Richard D., 33n
SCSB. See Swedish Customer Satisfaction Barometer (SCSB)
Search information, 57
Sechrest, Lee, 33n
Semantic memory, 81–82, 83
Seraku, Nobuhiku, 29n
Service delivery system, 152–54
Service design process, 151–54
Service fairness, 154
Service map, 152–53
Service-oriented industries, 63
Service recovery, 154
Services, market information about, 57–58
Service surprise, 154
Shared vision, customer orientation as, 5–6
Shareholder value, 45–46
Shepard, Roger N., 78n
Simon, Herbert, 52n, 71
Simple observation, 33
Slavery, of customer, 27
Sloan, Alfred, 145
Small group interviews, 30
Smart, Tim, 2n
Smith, S. M., 78n
Sony, 30, 145
Southwest Airlines, 168
SP. See Sweden Post
Spatial scaling, 78, 79
Specifications, customer, 5
Srinivasan, V., 169n
Stable market, 60
Staelin, Richard, 81n
Standardization, in marketplace, 63
Statistical estimation, of importances, 117, 118, 167
Status quo, and customer orientation, 6
Stephenson, Marilyn, 81n
Stigler, George J.
  on economics of information, 52–53
  economics of information (EOI) model of, 79–80
Straight rebuy, 97
Strategic market planning, and customer orientation, 2
Strategic satisfaction matrix, 22–23, 119
Structural barriers, to customer orientation, 6–7
Strumpel, Burkhard, 61n
Supply and demand, in market matching process, 62–64
Suprenant, Carol, 108n
Surprise and delight attributes
  in information pyramid, 31
  in Kano model, 29

Survey Research Center, University of Michigan, 14
    list of values (LOV) survey, 35–36
Surveys, 27, 29, 30
Swasy, John L., 83n
Sweden
    and national satisfaction indices development,
        129–30
    public sector agencies in, 64
    SCSB and auto industry in, 138–39
Sweden Post (SP), 7, 18
    case study in customer orientation approach,
        18–24
    customer satisfaction index, 20–21
    measurement process in, 20–23
    transformation process in, 19–20
Swedish Customer Satisfaction Barometer (SCSB),
        19, 45, 129–30, 134n
    and product-oriented industries, 64
    time trends in, 138–39
Swire Group, 121

T

Tabachnik, Naomi, 111n
Takahashi, Fumio, 29n
Takeuchi, Hirotaka, 151n
Target market segments, 2
Technology, and product design, 147–48
Tenney, Janet E., 81n
Thaler, Richard, 95n
Time series studies, 150
Time trends, in SCSB, 138–39
Total quality management (TQM)
    and customer orientation, 9–10
    and customer satisfaction index, 21
Toyota, 99
TQM. *See* Total quality management (TQM)
Transaction-specific satisfaction, 104–105. *See also*
        Disconfirmation model
    modeling, 110
Transgenerational design, 145
Translation process
    in information pyramid, 31
    in quality–satisfaction gap, 164–66
Treelike (hierarchical) scaling method, 78, 79
Tse, David K., 108n
Tsuji, Shinchi, 29n
Tversky, Amos, 59n, 90n, 92n, 93n
    Prospect Theory of, 93–95
Tybout, Alice M., 108n

U

"Understanding the whole" concept, 13. *See also*
        Balanced scorecard

United States
    auto manufacturers, global competition, and, 134–38
    national fundamental factors comparison with
        Japan, 32–33
United States Postal Service, 134
University of Michigan
    Business School, National Quality Research Center of, 130
    Survey Research Center, 14, 35–36
Unobtrusive measures, in proactive research, 33
Urban, Glen L., 39n
Urbany, Joel E., 80n

V

Value
    in customer choice process, 91–92
    perceived, 130–31
Value function, of Prospect Theory, 93–94
Value ladders, 36–38
Value projection process, 149–50
Value ranking, 35
Values, customers', 27, 33–35
Value segmentation, 150
    advantages of, 36
    in proactive research, 33–36
Value survey, 149
Van Raaij, W. Fred, 68n, 72n
Van Veldhoven, Gery M., 68n, 72n
Vaughn, Patrick, 39n
Vehicle purchase process, 69–71
Voice. *See* Customer voice
Von Neumann, John, 53
Von Winterfeldt, Detlof, 53n

W

Walker, Beth A., 83n
Walt Disney World, purchase–consumption–
        repurchase cycle at, 48–49
Ward, James, 84n
Wärneryd, Karl-Erik, 68n, 72n
Webb, Eugene J., 33n
Westbrook, Robert A., 108n
Wick, Terry, 48n
Wilton, Peter C., 108n
Wind, Yoram, 96n
Womack, James P., 37n, 144n
Woodruff, Robert B., 113n
Woodside, Arch, 73n
World Wide Web, and market information, 57

X

Xerox, 2, 12, 99

Y

Yi, Youjae, 109n
Young, Brian, 39n
Young, R. F., 110n

Z

Zeithaml, Valarie, 109n
Zeller, Noel, 146n
"Zero defects," as goal, 14